D11724O1

a memoir

MICHAEL SLEDGE

SIMON & SCHUSTER
New York London Toronto Sydney Tokyo Singapore

SIMON & SCHUSTER
Rockefeller Center
1230 Avenue of the Americas
New York, NY 10020

Throughout this book the names have been changed to protect the identities of those involved.

Designed by Hyun Joo Kim

Manufactured in the United States of America

10 9 8 7 6 5 4 3 2 1

Library of Congress Cataloging-in-Publication Data

Sledge, Michael.
Mother and son : a memoir / Michael Sledge.
p. cm.
1. Mothers and sons. 2. Sledge, Michael. I. Title.
HQ755.85.S549 1995
306.874'3—dc20 95-12741 CIP

ISBN 0-684-81064-6

"Archaic Torso of Apollo" by Rainier Maria Rilke: *New Poems*. Copyright © 1964 by The Hogarth Press. Reprinted by permission of New Directions Publishing Corp.

Excerpt from "Some Trees" by John Ashbery from *Some Trees* (New York: The Ecco Press, 1977). Reprinted by permission of Georges Borchardt, Inc. for the author. Copyright © 1956 by John Ashbery.

ACKNOWLEDGMENTS

I'd like to thank Richard Locke and Elaine Markson, who were crucial at this book's genesis; and Celia Bolam and Francisco Gonzalez, who were crucial during the trip it took me on. I also wish to express gratitude, in advance, for the forbearance of those who appear in these pages.

for T. C. S. W. S. H., of course

Though we've not known his unimagined head
and what divinity his eyes were showing,
his torso like a branching street-lamp's glowing,
wherein his gaze, only turned down, can shed

light still. Or else the breast's insurgency
could not be dazzling you, or you discerning
in that slight twist of loins a smile returning
to where was centred his virility.

Or else this stone would not stand so intact
beneath the shoulders' through-seen cataract
and would not glisten like a wild beast's skin;

and would not keep from all its contours giving
light like a star: for there's no place therein
that does not see you. You must change your living.

—*Rainer Maria Rilke,*
"Archaic Torso of Apollo"

MANHUNT

I

My father disappeared; otherwise, the summer continued on as normal. I didn't know where he'd gone, and I didn't really care. The news had broken in the car on our way home from camp, my two older brothers in the backseat reading comic books and I in the furthest reaches of the station wagon keeping company with our trunks. Alone in the front seat, my mother spoke to the windshield as we glided beneath a canopy of East Texas woods. I was too happy in our reunion to perceive any hint or warning in her voice, which floated back through the car as soft and shimmery as the filaments of spider's silk I'd seen blowing across the fields at camp. The front doors of the house had been removed, she said, because she was having panels cut out of the wood and replaced with glass. At the ranch she'd stocked both ponds with translucent fingerling bass; by next summer they'd be big enough to eat. My brothers ignored her, but I hung on every word. I loved her plans, the more extravagant the better: she wanted to dig a goldfish pond in the backyard; build a floor-to-ceiling birdcage in the kitchen and fill it with singing finches; plant fruit trees around the house, from which we would pick peaches, pomegranates, bananas, and mangoes. I was her partner in this vision of a lush and perfect Eden.

My mother caught my eye in the rearview mirror and said, "I meant to write and tell you Blackie died."

"He did?" This information caught me off guard, and

she was so cavalier with it that I lay back into the bed of pillows I'd made for the drive.

"I thought you didn't even like him," she said.

"I didn't."

Blackie was a mouse, one of my pets. He hated captivity and repeatedly escaped from the confines of his cage, roaming the house for weeks until my mother and I devised a strategy for his recapture, which usually occurred in the middle of the night, using a cookie as bait. He bit me whenever I tried to pet him, and yet now I felt I might begin to cry. If that happened, my brothers would pounce.

We drove for an hour or so in silence while I privately nursed my hurt. The trees outside had given way to coastal plains by the time my mother spoke again. "Before we get home, there's something I have to tell you boys." Suspicious, my brothers looked up from their comic books. "While you were gone, your father moved out of the house. He and I are going to have a separation. I don't think it's permanent." Her words had become so fragile they seemed to pop and disappear before they reached me; I could barely hear them. The separation had to do with problems the two of them were having, she said. It was not our fault; our father loved us just as much as ever. In spite of her reassurances, it was clear she was telling us that the world had just come crashing down on our heads, but mulling it over I found the news didn't surprise me. A week earlier my name had been blasted over the loudspeakers during swimming class and, pulled from the water, I was hurried with my brothers to the camp's administrative office, where we discovered our father, who waited frowning in his dark suit. The four of us ambled down a dirt road lined with the fallen orange needles of pine trees, a towel still draped over my shoulders like a superhero's cape, while my father remarked on the fragrance of the pines and professed a great love for life outside the city. I watched his black shoes become covered with fine red dust, the same dust that hung in the air after he drove off in his Cadillac, never having explained why he'd made the surprise visit.

For the rest of the drive home, my mother tried to speak soothing words. My brothers hid their tears with the comic books they still held in their fists. I knew that I was supposed to be sad also, but I wasn't. What had changed? My father was never home anyway. When we finally pulled into our driveway, the four of us remained in the station wagon for several moments, then my mother hefted open her door and we followed. My brothers dejectedly pulled their trunks from the car, but my attention was drawn to the house. As my mother had warned, the front doors were missing. Where they had once been now hung a dark green bedspread, billowing in the breeze, beckoning, like the entrance to a bazaar in a foreign city.

Then, Houston was a patchwork of farms and housing developments, thickets and bayous and office buildings. We lived in a secretive, rural pocket of town that had once been a cemetery; our street wound through forested lots and patches of pristine woods where you could still find gravestones etched with dates from the previous century. One family owned a chestnut horse they rode daily around the block; another had sheep. Some of the houses were stately, while others had slipped into the kind of shoddiness that suggested old spinster inhabitants. Ours was one of the newer ones, full of bedrooms for the children my mother kept producing at regular intervals, and full of glass and light, built to my father's specifications on a large piece of land recently hacked out of the woods. Behind it lay a trickling bayou populated with alligators, which I had never personally seen, and with water moccasins and snapping turtles, both of which I'd bagged with my own hands and a stick. The size of my family was average for the street; five or six kids lived in nearly every house, and this was a rich, green world, a wonderland, for children. We roamed the neighborhood in packs, using anyone's yard as our own, playing kickball on their lawns and swinging on their swing sets with lordly proprietorship. We played hours-long games of kick-the-can, Marco Polo, and TV tag; engaged in tournaments of daredevil bicycling; or just two of us played softball with several invisible teammates. On twilit evenings, one of the older boys revved up his family's powerful riding lawn mower and dragged us around the yard, hanging from ropes tied to the back.

My father's absence didn't change a thing. Through July and August my oldest brother Nick, called Little Hitler by neighborhood mothers, led their sons in daily calisthenics and organized them into warring armies. John, a year younger, camped out alone in the copse of woods beside our house, emulating mountain men he'd seen on television. Though there were five children in my family, I was something of an island, separated by four years from Nick and John, who were old enough to begin straying from our domestic world, and by five years from Celeste and Scotty, who were babies, hardly companions of any interest. I whiled away my days playing neighborhood games, poring over animal encyclopedias, and inventing combinations of my two hobbies, Hot Wheels cars and pet mice. Alone, I explored the woods and bayou, fully expecting all animals, the dogs and cats I encountered, even the wild birds in the trees, to recognize the love I bore for them and to reward me with their fervent devotions. This never happened. Still, I felt open to mystery and sensation and surprise. I was eight. It was high summer, and I was free.

But I never wandered too far from home. Spending as much time as possible with my mother had always been a high priority, so I helped her prepare meals, keep watch over Celeste and Scotty, weed and water the garden. During her marriage she'd never held a job, and this didn't change after my father left; all of her energy and creative force was directed like a beam of light upon her home. Together we still frequented dusty, dimly lighted antique shops, where we wandered through labyrinths of rickety chairs and tables. From these she had filled our house with treasures: a chest of golden inlaid wood from seventeenth-century Italy, Persian carpets in whose rich designs I found tales of Oriental kingdoms, a chair with a blue velvet cushion too ancient to sit upon. All were purchased with the allowance my father gave her. She took me along to nurseries, where I pulled a red wagon full of plants she'd chosen, and when I became tired I climbed in with the seedlings and flowers; then she took up the handle to tote me. Hibiscus, frangipani, and other tropical plants filled our house, and the gardens that surrounded it she cared for with nearly obsessional devotion. I too loved these things, but it was a love indistinguishable from the love I felt for her. To be in her presence was to feel the sun dazzling in my veins. I existed in a pre-Copernican universe; my mother was the center around which all else orbited.

Each afternoon, in the celebratory mood following our forays, we had tea at the kitchen table. Her father had been gone a lot too, she told me, when she was a girl. He was away for the entire war, first on the European front and then in the Pacific, and she never knew exactly where he was. When he did visit, it was always a surprise, and he didn't stay long. "I remember one Christmas he just appeared on the doorstep and told us we were moving. Moving on Christmas day! But we didn't mind. We were always excited to be moving to a new place. We opened our presents and packed them straight into our trunks."

Like me, she was a middle child, the second of three daughters. Her father was a submarine commander from New Orleans. Her mother was from Memphis, but, also born to a navy family, she'd lived in Guam, in China, and in Panama during the jazz age, where she had broken the hearts of countless suitors when she accepted my grandfather's proposal of marriage. My mother had grown up all over the country and even in Central America, changing schools as frequently as the seasons changed, before her family eventually settled in Alabama. It was different then, she told me sadly. People used to respect the military, not like now, with Vietnam. She painted a picture of military life that was as aristocratic and genteel, if unmonied, as that of her antebellum heritage, and I saw myself easily assuming a role in that decorous, globe-trotting style of existence.

One afternoon after school had begun in the fall, my mother sipped her tea and told me shyly, "I got a ticket this morning. I was writing a letter in my head to my parents, about your father, and I didn't even notice I was speeding. The policeman was thoughtful, though. When he saw that I was crying, he wanted to escort me home."

"But he gave you the ticket anyway?" I was outraged, though perhaps my anger sprung from the mention of my father. He could intrude in a flash upon the domestic life my mother and I shared, so vividly conjured with a word that he destroyed our momentary peace. Here was a fact I did not want to recognize: though he'd left, my father was to her, still, as she was to me, the center of her life.

I knew this because so many of her stories included him. Newly married, my parents had moved to Houston from Alabama so that my father could free himself from the rigid social hierarchy of the South, where he, the son of a country lawyer, would always have been considered a bumpkin. In those days—the 1950s and '60s—there was something raw and reckless about Houston; it was a frontier, a gold rush town. Anything could happen, and did. My mother's sister moved there and went dancing with a young millionaire; my father's sister arrived in town and married him. And though my mother was a housewife, she was of a Texas mint; she could host her bridge club in the morning, brandish a shotgun on the hunting fields in the afternoon, and that night attend a cocktail party where women with bouffant hairdos wore psychedelic minidresses and men talked of money. But the heightened importance of appearances, of wealth and its attendant hypocrisy, my mother grew to abhor. During her childhood in the Depression, manners had formed the mainstay of her social and family life; in Houston, she found wealth but few manners. Soon after making Houston their home, my father began work at a stock brokerage firm in one of the new, sleek skyscrapers downtown, and among the young couples that courted them he sought out the established, monied ones with the precision of a heat-seeking missile. My father didn't just want to become rich, though money was essential to his plans; he wanted to be recognized as what he already knew himself to be: better than other people, made of finer stuff. By the time he was thirty-five, when he paid his visit to me and my brothers at camp, he owned a ranch, a bank, and had built an impressive house of his own design. His friends were socially prominent. A tailor made his suits. He was envied for his beautiful wife.

Out of my mother's stories I was able to construct a rudimentary idea of their fifteen years together. I knew that it was at the Mobile Mardi Gras, where she was a princess waving to the crowd from a float and he, her knight, rode behind on a horse, so drunk he kept falling from the saddle, that he asked her to marry him. Early in their marriage they took a trip to Mexico, and after she had run from dinner crying, my mother was prevented from entering her room by a parrot that hissed and paced before her door. My father bought a Jaguar sports car, then drove it into a ditch at high speed. He often came home drunk or late or not at all. One night, at the symphony, he had pulled my mother running up three flights of stairs; she was seven months pregnant, and several hours later she gave birth to my brother Scotty. Not once did she tell me directly that her marriage was unhappy, but no matter; by the time my father moved out this equation was clear to me: if he was unwilling to appreciate her, then he made himself negligible.

2

One afternoon I was playing Catapult, using a technique I'd developed to propel mice across my bedroom. A couple of neighborhood friends, Dwight and Robert, waited against the far wall with outstretched hands. The game ended badly. Dwight begged to be the catapulter, and against my better judgment I explained to him how to place a mouse in the center of a pillow and pull gently on the ends. All the while I suspected that he didn't understand. "You have to pull very, very, very softly," I urged, but when Dwight snapped the pillow, the mouse shot upward with a rocket's velocity, smacking into the ceiling and dropping to the floor, where it writhed in awful contortions. I scooped it up and, wailing, rushed to find my mother. At the foot of the stairs I encountered my father instead, and I stood immobilized before him with the spastic mouse in my hands. I knew he wouldn't understand the complicated nature of my grief; it was not simply that I felt certain the mouse would die, but that through my own carelessness I had caused pain to a creature I loved. "To be crying over a mouse," my father said and turned his back.

Under my mother's ministrations, the mouse had fully recovered by dinnertime. Its survival was more of a surprise to me than the appearance of my father, who showed up out of the blue every so often and in September stole back into the house for good. Or so my mother told me. As before their separation, I rarely saw him, though every room smoldered as if he'd just left it. From my bed I occasionally heard the boom of his voice when he arrived home late from work, but in the morning he was always gone before I woke up.

I was glad not to see him. I feared my father, with an elemental fear. On the instances he did walk through the door before I'd gone up to bed, I was seized by violent, rushing panic. I feared how his face gathered up in anger, I feared the storm of his voice. And I feared most what I saw reflected in his eyes: a boy who cried over a mouse.

Again and again I found myself drawn to the carved wooden chest in the front hall, brought back by my grandmother from Guam. Opening it, I inhaled a spicy aroma I believed to be the very essence of the Orient. Inside were the seashells my mother had collected from the beaches of Panama when she was my age. Pressing a conch's smooth, pink mouth to my ear, I listened to the surf of her childhood shores. Then there were the photographs of military men, my great-grandfather in uniform, my grandfather on the deck of his submarine, even my father during his short stint in the air force. In these men I saw the masculine virtues my mother extolled: valor and athleticism, courage verging on the foolhardy, a stoic mien.

For hours I pored over the pictures of my father. He held my brother Nick, a newborn baby, with his arms stuck straight out from his torso. In group photographs he was consistently the only person scowling, but he looked handsome and proud beside the admiral's daughter in their wedding pictures. On that day, they'd both been twenty years old, in my opinion an inconceivably mature age. I did not wonder as I looked at these pictures what had brought my parents together; I accepted their marriage as a historical fact. But the questions that emerged later, after I had reached the age of my parents on their wedding day, seemed always to have lain in my mind, torpid and hibernating until I had the words to articulate them. Why was my mother willing for so many years to endure a marriage in which she received virtually nothing for herself? Had she been taught by her parents, or the times, or the Bible that a woman could find fulfillment only by living under a tyrant? Did she find my father's ambition and arrogance sexy? Why on the night of Scotty's birth did she allow him to pull her up the stairs?

At school we studied the human body. Mrs. Hendrix flipped transparencies of the skeleton, musculature, and circulatory system onto the overhead projector. My third grade class plucked organs from the Invisible Man, arguing over which was the most grotesque. Our final project was to illustrate the insides of a life-size body, and for this, Mrs. Hendrix requested a volunteer we could trace onto a large sheet of paper. A boy, she said, preferably a small one.

Eyes began turning toward me. Over the last three years I'd become increasingly grateful for the presence of Jonathan, a raspy-voiced boy of excessive politeness who was actually smaller than I, saving me from the humiliation of being chosen last for teams in P.E. But he did not save me from the acute embarrassment I felt about my own body. This was the same embarrassment that had recently made me shy of my mother's touch. Each night as she put me to bed, I snuggled beneath my blankets away from her. "You were always the most loving child," she sighed, and though she spoke lightly, I understood that I'd wounded her.

Not all of the other kids in the class were finely attuned to the important distinction between me and Jonathan. Only half volunteered him to be drawn, and half pointed to me. To get to the truth of the matter, Mrs. Hendrix had us stand on adjacent desks. As she appraised and compared our heights, Jonathan's face intensified to the color of beets, and he asked in a statesmanlike manner if he could please be excused from the exercise, then stepped down.

I stood alone in the center of the room engaged in invisible battle: pride against fear. It was pride that finally swept me along in the wake of Mrs. Hendrix to the sheet of paper she'd unfurled on the floor. As I lay upon it, my classmates quickly congregated around me, some sitting, others huddling behind them, until a cloud of faces gazed down in an excruciating collective stare.

I closed my eyes to calm myself. A mild squabble ensued over who would trace me, and then a hush as two or three pencils began outlining me at once. Fanned out on the paper, my hands felt the delicate sliding touch of the pencils' painted surface drop between my fingers and glide over each tip. A hand brushed my cheek as it traced the curve of my neck. I heard the scratch of the pencil's lead and felt the warmth of the child, boy or girl, I didn't know, who knelt at my head. My embarrassment was interrupted by a wholly unexpected sensation: pleasure at these glancing touches, the closeness of other bodies. But a pencil was moving upward from my ankle along the inside of my calf and thigh, and the pleasure broke. The pencil reached my crotch, and shame catapulted through me.

Then it was over. I scrambled away from the paper, and as my heart galloped in my chest I looked down at the outline of an unremarkable boy.

3

On the way home from school I looked over at my mother to find that her face was wet with tears. "Why are you crying?" I asked, and strangely, she answered, "I'm not crying, honey." Several nights later, I was alone in the kitchen watching television when my father came in with an uncharacteristically sad look on his face. "Look who it is," he said. "It's Mickey Mouse." He sat beside me and then drew me roughly into his lap. "I was looking for you, Mickey Mouse." I resisted at first, but it was so seductive—the warmth of his body, the soft rumble of his voice, his arms cradling me with my head against his chest—that I curled up as snugly as an infant. Still, I knew what was coming; I had to harden against him.

"Sweet pea," he said and ran his hand across my forehead. "Your mother has asked me to leave again. I don't want to go, but I have to do what she says." I wanted to blame him, but instead, as he held me, my buried love began to burst from its confinement. I willed myself not to cry, and still tears stung my eyes. It was not my father, I realized, but myself that I was guarded against. I couldn't bear what this meant: that in spite of everything I didn't want him to go away. It wasn't my father's fault he had to leave us; people were subject to the same unstoppable forces that cracked continents, that could flood or incinerate the earth.

The following day I watched the movers wheel away his furniture. Afterward, it wasn't his absence I noted, since that was nothing new. The missing desk, gun cabinet, and leather chair were the proof of my father's permanent departure.

"I sincerely believed when I married your father that a marriage was to last forever." We were driving around Houston, and as she sometimes did, my mother was thinking things through with me, trying to convince herself she'd made the right decision. I gazed at her profile. In the weeks since my father had left she was often muted like this, unavailable to me, and rather than clamor for her attention, I too drifted into my own quiet recess. As we entered the freeway, a strand of her hair was tugged out the open window, where it danced wildly in the wind. "According to the Bible," she continued, "there's only one reason for a woman to divorce a man." She didn't specify what the reason was, but I figured that it had to do with sex. Marriages on TV were always breaking up because of an affair, but of course that wasn't why I suspected. I knew. Television only substantiated the knowledge. "But maybe there's not even one reason."

As if by magic, my father would materialize every now and again only moments after my mother left the house on an errand. His green convertible came sweeping into the driveway, and he barged through the front doors as if into a saloon. On his heels, I silently recorded every transgression: he poked his head into her closets, rifled through her personal papers, cursed any disorderliness. One day, as he stood gazing through the plate glass windows of the living room into the backyard, he said absently, "I love this old house," not really speaking to me at all. It was a beautiful house: two stories with big, high-ceilinged rooms, a sloping shingled roof, and a porch of light brick, fronted by Ionic columns reminiscent of his Southern plantation ancestry. There was a pool in the backyard, a sweeping lawn, and flowering gardens my mother had poured her whole heart into. My father had reason to be proud of it. He had travelled such a great distance, from the Alabama town of red clay streets where he was born to the big, glittering city, in order to build this house, and at the time of its construction he'd been only thirty-two years old, at the height of his power, a shooting star.

Prince, our German shepherd, dropped a tennis ball at my feet, and perhaps to get my father's attention I kicked it. "Goddamn it, son," he said, but without much conviction, "don't kick the ball in the house." He went outside and circled the pool, appraising my mother's upkeep. He must have felt rage at her for exiling him from his kingdom, for destroying his plans, and as I watched him, I too became angry. He no longer had jurisdiction here; he couldn't tell me what to do. I waited for him to turn, and when I was sure that he could see me through the plate glass, I kicked the tennis ball with all my strength. Prince raced across the room, upsetting chairs, and onto my father's face leapt absolute disbelief. He charged inside, his eyes wild, and grabbed me by the shoulder, the only time he'd ever laid a hand on me except in affection. His aim was off as he spanked me, hitting my legs and back. "Don't you *ever* disobey me," he bellowed over and over, until he flung me away from him and left the house.

Several months passed before he accepted an invitation from my mother to dinner. By that time, he had installed himself in a bachelor apartment that smelled of leather and alcohol, its walls ornamented with exotic animal heads. Next door lived his best friend Jimbo, who struck me as a more extreme version of my father: bigger, broader, more boisterous, his face betraying even more suspicion and disappointment in the world. Jimbo had recently been booted out of marriage by my mother's friend and sister in Christ, Susan, who, like my mother, was a red-haired woman of gentle, sad-eyed beauty.

My mother fed the kids early and then set to work preparing the meal she'd planned. She hadn't seen my father in a while, and her anticipation communicated a buzz of excitement to me and my sister. After our older brothers went to their rooms, she and I kept our mother company in the kitchen until my father arrived. We lingered in the adjoining living room as they ate, listening to them talk and laugh, until Celeste fell into a groggy stupor and finally tiptoed back to her room. I must have fallen asleep as well, because I was jolted awake by the sound of a chair screeching across the kitchen floor.

"Let go of me." My mother said this firmly, but I could hear the fearful bluff in it.

"Don't you dare stand up when I'm talking to you."

"You're hurting my arm."

"Sit down."

I raced from the room and past the kitchen door, where I saw them frozen: my mother holding the dinner plates, my father sitting at the table with his hand clamped upon her forearm. From my bedroom I listened to the escalation of their fight, he shouting drunken nonsense while she tried to talk him out of his rage. Then I heard a sound that seemed to shake the world, what could only have been a slap, and I pressed a pillow to my face to silence my own shouts. My mother rushed back under the stairs to her room, her sobs convincing me that he'd harmed her. The front door slammed, and the house fell quiet.

By the time I crept tentatively to my mother's room in the morning, I was already beginning to doubt what I'd heard the previous night. I sought proof. My mother was trying to read the newspaper in bed, but Celeste and Scotty romped among the covers. As the three of them played, I knelt at the end of the bed, eyeing her. Could she actually laugh freely if he had hit her? I searched for a mark on her face or a private communication of knowledge, but she showed not the faintest trace of either.

I never asked. To hide from painful truth was a rule I learned early. Perhaps that is why I recollect so little unhappiness, neither hers nor mine, during that period in our lives. Despite the erratic comings and goings of my father, what I remember is the joy and constancy of my mother's companionship. I was more creature than sentient being, not yet divorced from the natural world; simple existence—feeling the sun's warmth, exploring my elysian neighborhood, being near my mother—was enough to saturate me. At the same time, I possessed a primitive knowledge that prevented me from being surprised when my father first left or when, the next summer, he married the formal and sharply beautiful Mrs. Lollar, a friend of my parents I'd known all my life.

After my father remarried, the matriarch of my mouse dynasty, Charlotte, developed a lump under her right front leg. My mother fingered the tumor and made a call to the veterinarian. "He's never done this procedure before," she told me. "He's not sure she'll make it." We took her in a shoe box to the vet, and while he performed the surgery, I sat in the waiting room gnawing on my lip. At last the vet appeared, smiling.

Charlotte was returned to me, reelingly drunk on ether, with black sutures where the tumor had been. My mother settled the bill, then drove us home, while I watched Charlotte tottering across the floor of the shoe box, alive. Years later I would recall this episode to her. I asked my mother why, given that millions of mice each year were given tumors purposefully, she had spent a hundred dollars to save one of them. "Because you loved her," she said.

4

Shortly after my father left for good, my mother plunged into a dating frenzy. The year was 1971; in my parents' circle, divorce had recently become a popular solution to ailing marriages, with a tendency toward a reshuffling of spouses. My father married Mrs. Lollar, Mr. Baker married Mrs. Winston, and so on until most of the loose parts were paired up again. Word of my mother's single status spread quickly among these loose parts, and it wasn't long before she had one or two dates a week. Often I kept her company as she prepared for their arrival. During the day, her style of dress was rich in ethnic and hippie influences. She wore hip-hugging suede pants with flared legs, a skirt stitched with tiny mirrors, Mexican blouses embroidered with flowers and birds, and long beaded necklaces or clunky ones of carved wood and seashells. Her hair hung straight to her waist. Before her dates, she changed out of these casually bright and exotic styles and rolled up her long hair in heated curlers. She carefully brushed on makeup and performed lipstick kisses on sheets of kleenex. Finally, she put on a formal, monotone dress, emerging from these operations transformed into a Houston lady suitable for dating. Only one hint of her true self remained: on her hand, a monogram ring with three letters of white gold—MOM—a Christmas present I had ordered out of the Sears catalogue.

When the doorbell rang, my mother let the man inside, and while he waited in the front hallway shuffling his feet, she gave the baby-sitter last-minute instructions. Having dinner at the kitchen table with my brothers and sister, I would sneak a look over my shoulder. Invariably, her date was tall, with dark, slicked-back hair, and was dressed in a suit, more like an advertisement for a man than a real human being. He kept his hands in his pockets. He smiled when my mother approached, then helped her slip on her coat. She snatched up her purse from the hall table and gave one last wave to us, almost a plea, as they walked out; then the slam of the door cut off her nervously energetic conversation. I resumed my dinner.

Though none of these dates appeared more than two or three times, there was a relentless source of them out there in Houston's maw, and each Friday night brought another man much like the last. This didn't surprise me. If my father were no longer in the picture, it made sense that there would be plenty of other men eager to take his place at my mother's side, though my judgment of these men in person was far from generous. On the occasions that she introduced me, I would mumble something unintelligible to her date's shoes, my shyness masking a deep disdain. I suspected that he was a roughneck, loutish and ill-mannered, though I assumed that he must at least be solvent. Each night she went out on a date we were swimming in the richness of possibility. I was a gold digger.

After she left, I settled in for a night of television. Up close, the screen electrified the hairs on my arm as I played over the channels, zeroing in. Every day, I watched hours and hours of TV, rushing home after school to catch *Dark Shadows* and an afternoon of reruns, and then planting myself in front of the television after dinner with my homework in my lap. I flipped past any images of the real world—Vietnam coverage, student protests—out of lack of interest, but beyond the news there was hardly a show I didn't like, and I often faced the dilemma of having to choose between two of my favorites in the same time slot. I wrote out schedules for particularly busy nights so that I didn't have to waste time deciding which channel I had to turn to next. I loved TV. It was how I learned about other families, about how people were supposed to treat one another. Friday nights, after my mother had gone out on a date, were the best. The evening began with *The Partridge Family*, then *The Brady Bunch*, and culminated hours later in *Love American Style*, which documented the misadventures of newlyweds and the wacky ways in which people fell in love. The theme song still plays in my mind: *Love American style, truer than the red, white, and blue.*

My mother gave me a syringe and a navel orange so that I could practice giving injections. This was because, even though I didn't feel particularly unwell, it had been decided that I suffered from allergies severely enough to warrant daily allergy shots. I hated the idea. I was no fan of hypodermics. While my mother cooked dinner, I sat at the kitchen table, Mr. Rogers speaking to me from the television, and filled the syringe from a cup of water. At first I treated the orange gingerly, but soon enough I was plunging the needle deep into its crenellated surface. This exercise dulled my fear, but as I walked home from school the day I was to go for my first allergy shot, it did not prevent my arm from feeling an anticipatory ache. In the station wagon, my mother and I traveled the familiar route across town. Either for my own or for my siblings' ailments, I had visited the pediatrician's office nearly every week of my life, its architecture becoming as familiar to me as that of my own home. Against one wall stood a bubbling goldfish tank with a treasure chest on its blue gravel floor that rhythmically opened to reveal plastic doubloons. *Humpty Dumpty* and *Jack & Jill* magazines, full of jokes, cutouts, and suggested games, fell from their ordered stacks and lay splayed on the stained beige carpet. A tabletop was illustrated with an intricate map whose pathways led you through a fairy-tale kingdom. Large squares of cork glued with multicolored felt clowns hung on the walls. This buoyant atmosphere was calculated to allay the fears of waiting children, but for me, each of these over the years had become laced with sinister meaning. As the children were called one by one behind the door to the examination rooms, I was certain I wasn't the only one who looked up at the clowns and felt the sharp talons of fear clawing his stomach.

At last my name was called, and the supportive pressure of my mother's hand on my back guided me toward the doctor's assistant, a woman, I noticed, who looked a little like a blond That Girl wearing a nurse's cap. Rolling up my sleeve, the assistant set her mouth in what could only have been an entirely false smile, since the needle lay in full view on a stand beside the examination table. She dabbed alcohol on my skin and told me to look away. I turned toward my mother and closed my eyes for extra measure, though this proved to be a mistake. In my mind I saw a long needle jabbing into an orange. "You'll feel a little pinch," the assistant said, and then a trajectory of fire shot through my arm. As my mother kissed the top of my head, I heard a familiar gravelly voice greeting her. It was Dr. Curtis.

He asked me how everything had gone, and I told him that the shot had felt like a pinch. He rested his big, warm hand on my back and said, "It will hurt less as you get used to it." He had a pleasant, cheery face with dark eyes, a dark three o'clock shadow of a beard, and dark hair graying at the sideburns. His smile was genuine. In these rooms, I had experienced countless invasions of my body—inoculations, throat cultures, abdominal proddings—but Dr. Curtis had made them bearable. His touch was without exception gentle, he treated me with kindness and humor, and I felt for him a sure and trusting love. From that day on, he appeared immediately after his assistant had administered the allergy shot in order to offer his support, and over time, just as he'd promised, the shots ceased being painful altogether. One afternoon, as I was rolling down my sleeve, Dr. Curtis and my mother stood talking by the door. I listened to the comfortable, informal rhythm of their speech rather than to the words. He said something that made her laugh, and I thought: she should marry him.

It was a breakthrough moment. As often as I had watched her prepare for dates, I had never envisioned any of those men as her potential husband; the idea of one of them living in my house struck ludicrous, frightening ground. Keeping her company while she'd dressed was like helping her suit up for a deep sea dive in search of buried treasure, a risky, even dangerous venture that would probably only turn up sand. Marriage struck me as entirely different; it was as cozy and safe as watching television.

Once the idea of marriage entered my head, however, it spilled out to ensnare every man in sight. By this time, my mother had incorporated the visits to Dr. Curtis into her afternoon schedule of errands, and so I accompanied her almost every day for several hours after school. I suppose I loved going on errands—the word itself thrilled me—because driving around town released me from the boring routine of school and home into the great, wide world, but it was also on those errands that I began developing the habit of searching for men for my mother. She drove along Houston streets, past strip malls and the occasional corral of ponies or sheep, beneath spaghetti bowls of freeway overpasses toward her destinations—the cleaner's, the hardware store, the grocery—while I kept my eye to the window looking for possibilities. Often I didn't leave the car when she parked; she left the engine running, conducted her business, and returned. We listened to songs on the radio until we knew all the popular ones by heart, singing softly to ourselves the choruses of "Those Were the Days," "Gypsies, Tramps and Thieves," and "The Night They Drove Old Dixie Down."

I was guided by a single criterion: kindness. Though she frequently worried about money, I didn't concern myself too much with the wealth of potential suitors. I believed that men were financially stable by their very nature, a piece of knowledge parallel to my belief that adult men did not possess the biological ability to cry. Among the men I knew, I certainly had my favorites. Ranking nearly as high as Dr. Curtis was Mr. Baker, a lawyer friend of my parents whose wife had died of cancer, leaving him with four motherless children, but he married my mother's friend Susan instead and not long after moved to Washington. Given such capricious change of circumstance, I was unwilling to discount anyone, and cashiers, pharmacists, and policemen all came under my scrutiny. The butcher gave me a slice of cheese at every visit, and it was no small point in his favor.

Beneath my newly appraising eye, these men transformed from mere landmarks by which we navigated our errand-laden day to objects of covert study. I began to pay attention to how their faces brightened as my mother approached, how their conversation took on spirited, energetic, and mildly deferential inflections. They were not simply acting under the influence of her beauty, I believed, but recognized in her a true rarity, a generous and guileless spirit whose presence lingered after her departure like a balm.

Inevitably, back in the car she confided to me things these men would never know, the fears that hounded her. Scotty didn't seem to be catching up from his premature birth. Nick was running wild with a band of older teenage boys; he needed a father. And of course, there wasn't enough money. There was never enough money.

"Why not?" I asked.

"Your father gives me next to nothing in child support."

She had told me once how much it was, and I said now that it seemed like a lot to me.

"The house payment alone is five hundred dollars a month. Everything is so expensive. I'm not even sure I can buy groceries this week."

Though the subject of our poverty never lost its preeminent position, its effects were confusingly invisible to me. She always did manage to buy groceries, to clothe us, even to hire a maid who helped with Celeste and Scotty in the afternoons. Our house, by any account, was big. Still, I felt our situation to be extremely precarious; at any moment, without warning, we were liable to lose everything.

"I'm going to have to sell the house." She had worked herself up into a quiet panic. "I just don't have the money to keep it."

"When?"

"I don't know, honey. Maybe I should take your father back to court to get more child support. But that judge was so hideous to me." Anger tinged her voice. "Your father is forcing me to do things I never wanted to do. All I wanted was to be a mother, and his wife. I never wanted to have to make decisions. I never wanted to live on my own."

As a child, she had ceded responsibility for her life to her totalitarian father, and as an adult, to her husband, and now, at thirty-six, she was for the first time forced upon her own resources. She had dropped out of college to marry, but it wasn't lack of a degree that prevented her now from getting a job; it was lack of desire. She expected to be taken care of. Instead of seizing the reins of her life, she wanted someone else to take them from her hands, and without father or husband she threw this responsibility onto an even more distant authority, one she called upon daily: "But God is watching out for us," she said, and smoothed my hair.

Breathing in this promise always revived her, and I took comfort in my mother's relief. The rest of her life might erode from beneath her—her husband gone, her financial security stripped away—but her faith in God never wavered; since childhood it had served as her bedrock. Like the long line of Southern stock that produced her, she'd been steeped in a combination of Christianity and militarism, and from it she drew her deepest beliefs. The Lord she imagined seemed to me much like her own father, an unremittingly strict but ultimately benevolent man whom she adored. Certainly God put you through trials, but it was for a very good reason that we couldn't yet understand, and He never gave you more than you could bear. Just when you felt the waters pulling you under, He threw you a life raft.

She rarely went to church. Her faith was profound but extremely private; she never made more than glancing reference to it, though she read nightly from the Bible on her bedside table, and she exerted little force in passing on her beliefs to her children. Early on she'd attempted to enroll Nick and John in Bible study, but a policeman busted Nick smoking pot in the field beside the church. In me my mother found a more willing audience, but only because I received my Bible tutoring directly from her. During our drives she ran through the Old Testament standards. I loved hearing them. In Adam and Eve, I saw that we were all part of a great, interconnected family of man; in Abraham, that the terrible violence committed by fathers on sons could be forgiven; and in Noah, a bestiary beyond my wildest imaginings.

"Noah was lucky," I said.

"But it wasn't fun on the ark," my mother corrected. "The world had become corrupt, and God was destroying it. According to the Bible, He will destroy it again, but the next time it will be with fire."

I pictured the world in flames, my house burning, my family, my pets, and frankly it was a terrifying portrait. If the God she sensed was similar to her father, then perhaps I felt Him to be like my own: violent, mercurial, impatient. I eased my mind with a theory; in school, we had recently studied the stages of a star, from birth to white dwarf. "Maybe that will happen when our sun becomes a red giant," I said. "In five billion years it's going to expand all the way out to earth's orbit."

"I don't know if God will wait that long. But we'll have warning," she reassured me. "First He will send His son. Christ will be reborn."

"When will that happen?" I'd forgotten about the flames.

"I'm not sure, honey."

"Will he be born as a regular boy?"

"I suppose so."

My mind was spinning. "Would he know that he was Christ?"

"Maybe not at first."

I was not so immodest as to believe that I might be Christ, but it was a possibility I felt curious to explore. I searched my memories for any indication that I might be chosen—an astounding recovery from sickness or nearly fatal accident—but came up blank. So I asked my mother, the keeper of my history. "Did I ever almost die?"

"Not that I know of."

"How about that time I cut my head open?"

"There was a lot of blood," she said. "But the cut wasn't too serious."

The memory of that accident took Christ's place for the moment; my father had held me in the emergency room, telling me over and over how good I was being, how proud he was of me. But my mother must have continued to consider my question, because she said, "I will tell you something, though. Before you were born I was pregnant, but I lost the baby. It was a boy. I prayed to God to return that child to me, and a year later you were born. So I got you after all, but you're just a little younger than you would have been."

She touched my head, and I smiled back at her. But it was a strange, rather startling piece of information, and I couldn't quite get my mind around it. At first, I felt gypped; to a child, older is always better. I would have been one grade higher at school and closer in age to Nick and John, so they wouldn't have pushed me around so much. Then a different, deeper significance unfolded, and I understood that by the very ferocity of her love she had snatched me back from death. I *was* chosen, but chosen by her. Slowly, even this interpretation struck me as wrongheaded. The child who had never taken breath was not me at all. He deserved to be alive, sitting here now with his mother, and I should never have been born.

5

My best friends at school were two towering twins, and lately I'd been romanticizing the possibilities of twinship: the tricks you could play on people, especially teachers, and the constant companion you'd have. For a while I used my dead brother, who was only about six months older than I was, as a kind of ghost twin. I included him in my games, we spoke telepathically, and he shared my bedroom. Then I forgot about him.

My surviving brothers were rarely home, but they were more vivid than the ghost. Nick had become addicted to motorcycles. He worked in a motorcycle shop and owned three motocross racers, returning every weekend bearing trophies and occasional stitches from his latest race. He was almost fifteen and had adopted an adolescent disdain for anything familial or establishment, though neither his long hair nor his grease-stained clothes could obscure his resemblance to our father. He had the same deep dimple in his chin, the same scowl. John looked like our mother, with a round face, a gentle, soft smile always on his lips, and long limbs. He was a dutiful, genial boy. He had a job at the James Coney Island hot dog restaurant up the street, where I would sometimes visit him after school. I had not always worshiped him, but I entered a period when, in my eyes, John was absolute. I followed him ceaselessly around the house, and when he broke his arm in a football game, I felt his sufferings to be my own. I always took his side in his ages-old battle with Nick. The two of them were like natural enemies; they each bore a hideous scar the full length of one arm acquired after crashing through the panes of a window during a fight. No betrayal was as cruel as the rare occasion when John allied with Nick to direct their combative energies upon me.

Often I was exported to the Houston suburbs to keep my strong-willed cousin Hayley, an only child, company. Hayley was two years older than I, and just as her mother had spent her childhood exercising her will over my mother, so Hayley dominated me. With crayons, she illustrated the titillating parts of the human body and had me copy variations of them repeatedly. Then she wrote out in large yellow block letters, FUCK, instructing me not in its meaning but in the fact that it was a transgressive, even dangerous word to know. On bicycling forays, she struck up conversations with unfamiliar kids, taking drags from their cigarettes and cussing impressively. We terrorized by telephone a man we'd found in the phone book with the unfortunate name of Harry Butz.

Her father, a surgeon, had grown up in poverty, and so he granted Hayley's every material wish. She had a ham radio, and later her own CB, right in her room, on which she struck up communications with the faceless voices of men all over the country. Late at night she made calls to crisis hot lines and reeled out spontaneous tales of trauma, then thrust the telephone receiver into my hands, forcing me to continue her fabrications of parental abuse. The voices on the other end were so sympathetic, so warmly encouraging, that I found myself believing my own lies. Hayley threw out tethers to an unknown, outside world, and I allowed her to drag me after. We shared a love of supernatural mysteries, H. P. Lovecraft, and frogs.

Nearly every weekend I drove with Hayley and her parents to the farm they owned outside of Houston, where we stayed up until two in the morning watching movies about Japanese monsters, space exploration, shrunken people, and giant insects. During the day we collected bullfrogs and, much to her mother's disgust, played with them in the shower. Often on my weekend visits with Hayley I felt like the poor relation; she had everything I did not have, not just material riches but a complete family: a mother and father who lived together, ate meals together, played board games with her. Secretly I faced down moments of deep envy.

One Friday night, after I had come to Hayley's house in preparation to leave for the farm in the morning, we were particularly excited about a double feature on television: first *Frogs*, the plot of which the TV guide failed to synopsize but which we knew we'd love anyway; and then *Night of the Lepus*, in which giant, vicious rabbits promised to overrun a small Western town. We pushed aside the clothes, games, and magazines that were always strewn about Hayley's room as though distributed by natural disaster, and sat in front of the TV with our dinners in our laps. My enjoyment was short lived. As the movie began, queasiness replaced my appetite. Halfway into *Frogs* a splitting headache robbed me of the pleasure of witnessing the triumph in a Southern mansion of amphibian over man. I began to tremble with feverish chills. My aunt gave me some aspirin, but what I really wanted was to go home. I called my mother.

She was going out to dinner with someone, she told me, and was waiting for him to pick her up any minute. "But I'll come out to get you as soon as he does," she promised.

I was satisfied, but it was a long wait. By the time my mother arrived, I was so ill she virtually had to carry me out to the car, a shiny new Cadillac driven by a man she introduced as Walter. I lay upon the backseat, where the weight of my sickness pressed my face into the cushiony, strong-smelling leather. Walter drove stonily back to my mother's house while she, in her nicest dress of blue cashmere, cast worried looks back and forth between us. The car banked a curve. My nausea intensified. Perhaps it was the combination of the powerful leather smell and Walter's speedy driving that provoked my stomach to revolt at last. A vise gripped my guts, and I tried to give warning. "I'm going to throw up," I said weakly. My mother cried, "Oh, no," just as my prophesy was borne out. As paroxysms wracked me, she leaned over the seat, and I imagined that somehow by her very touch she would end my misery. She put her hands to my head and gripped it tightly. It was a slow dawning before I understood that she was directing me to throw up upon myself rather than on Walter's car seat. Disgusted, I fought her, but she held on, whispering, "I'm sorry, honey, I'm sorry." Walter looked grimly forward. Home at last, she carried me to bed, cleaned me up, and sat with me until I slept, then went out to Walter's car with a can of Ajax. An apron protected her cashmere dress as she scrubbed. Later, at dinner, my mother tried to joke about the episode, but her date refused to crack a smile. Walter wasn't heard from again.

In fact, around that time my mother stopped dating altogether. The frenzy had lasted less than a year. She told me that she'd hated the dates because the men "were all creeps," and I was ready, in the words of one of my favorite television commercials, to knock their blocks off for whatever they'd done to displease her. Later, I interpreted her comment to mean not that they were simply boors but that they had pressed her to have sex, which she did not believe in outside of marriage; or perhaps they'd been both boorish and sexually aggressive, and the combination of the two she found particularly distasteful. After her decision, no more men rang the doorbell to take her away, and in the evening she did not change out of her mirrored skirts or embroidered blouses. She stayed home every night. Often, she sat with me to watch *The Carol Burnett Show* and *Sonny and Cher*, and because I was glad to have her to myself again, I assumed that my relief and the relief I sensed in her flowed from the same source. The possibility of her loneliness, or fear, did not enter my mind. She was thirty-six years old, with five children and no money of her own. All of her life she had been given to understand that a woman alone was worth nothing. When I think now of the urgency she must have felt to find a man, a husband for herself, but, perhaps even more, a father for her children, her decision to stop the dating strikes me as an act of courage.

6

I fingered the belt of braided leather, handsome but not my mother's style, that had arrived that morning in the mail. "It's pretty, isn't it?" my mother said with forced cheer. "Marie made it."

"Is she still in the hospital?"

"Yes."

"How long will she be there?"

My mother came close and hugged me. "I don't know, honey. I hope not much longer."

Marie had had a nervous breakdown. I understood murkily that it had something to do with the breakup of her marriage. My mother and I went every week to Marie's empty house to water the garden and pick up mail, a task she performed with a weary, faraway look. I wandered through Marie's house poking at odds and ends, finding on the dresser a picture of her boring-looking businessman husband with his arm around Marie, whose long mournful face was drawn up like that of a skittish horse. She was my godmother, and I was given to believe that we shared a special relationship. For my birthday she sent me the collected poems of D. H. Lawrence, inscribing the book to a fellow tragic romantic. When she finished recovering at the hospital, Marie came straight to our house, where she lay sobbing in my mother's arms, loudly proclaiming that it was her love affair with my father that had sent her there.

My mother didn't bat a lash. She was used to this kind of treatment. Marie was typical of the women my mother chose as friends, who commanded her devotion and support but returned little of either, as though she needed to replace the bullying she no longer received from my father. Another friend, Marsha, full of the cynical exuberance that came from a bitter marriage, marched into our house like a one-woman band, her jewelry jingling and jangling, her voice like crashing cymbals, whenever she'd hatched yet another scheme. Repeatedly, Marsha borrowed money to begin entrepreneurial ventures, then filed bankruptcy and borrowed more. She owed my mother, who never refused her, seven thousand dollars.

But these women friends were greatly outnumbered by the group of men who frequented our house, not dates or romantic partners but, rather, die-hard bachelors who had each developed a unique symbiotic relationship with my mother. With five children, she was so far from being marriageable that she didn't threaten their independence, and in such a safe setting they felt free to lavish upon her their faithful friendship and admiration. She might carry Marie's emotional woes and Marsha's financial ones around her neck as though they were her own, but with her men friends she simply sat back and enjoyed their attentions. These men were allowed to roam freely throughout the house, and when I came home from school in the afternoon, I never knew which one of them I might encounter. There was Harry the inventor, who might be up on a ladder in the living room, wiring a new stereo system; Bill, who took my mother on a camping trip to Colorado, where at midnight he played a recording of the screams of a dying rabbit in order to attract howling coyotes; Robert, an Austin journalist, who'd been shot in the shoulder by a sniper aiming from the University of Texas tower, which gave him, in my eyes, the golden, unimpeachable aura of heroism; and Richard, another journalist from Austin, who when he breezed into town, swung me up and stood me on his shoes, then danced with me around the room.

"Marry Richard," I told her.

"But he's younger than I am."

"What difference does that make?"

One of the men who roamed the house was a Christian singer named Kirby, whose albums I sometimes listened to after dinner. He was handsome in the way of glowering, dimple-chinned movie stars, and in fact he aspired to be a movie star himself. To my disappointment he moved away to Hollywood, and several months later he sent a letter announcing that he'd just been cast in his first television role. We finally saw him flying a helicopter in an ABC Afternoon Special, but after he'd spoken his lines my mother turned to me and said, "He's not very good, is he?" I had to agree. We didn't see Kirby on television again.

It was clear to me even then that these men were each slightly in love with my mother, and though she obviously enjoyed their company, I was also certain none of them had captured her heart. "We're just friends," she finally said as her reason for not marrying Richard. Unlike the dates, and unlike my father, they treated me kindly, without condescension, conquering the shyness that normally made me anxious around adults, and because of that I welcomed their constant presence in the house. My mother gathered eccentrics around her the way other moms collected Big Bonus stamps, as though the group of them were equivalent to something of less quantity but greater value. Twenty-seven books of stamps could get you a new 19″ color TV; two journalists and a dying rabbit might have equaled a new dad.

One evening Richard appeared at the door with a fish in a bag, a live one. An old terrarium of my mother's was immediately cleaned of its loamy contents and filled with water. Set free, the fish suspended itself motionlessly in the center of the tank as though frozen in an ice cube. "What kind is it?" I asked, but Richard said he didn't know. The fish was about two inches long, icy blue with fine, dark striations, and it had big lips that it stretched out in a gaping yawn. All evening I sat watching it. The fish hadn't been a gift specifically to me, but my fascination granted me ownership. During the next day's errands, my mother and I stopped at a pet store, where we learned the identity of our fish, a gourami, and also purchased a filter, air compressor, gravel, food, heater, a book on tropical fish, and a couple of companions, two black and tan tiger barbs.

Adjacent to Dr. Curtis's office was Neptune's, a tropical fish store that now became a required stopping place after every doctor's appointment. There, my mother and I looked into each of the aquariums that ringed the store in tiers, pointing out the fish we particularly liked and together deciding which we should buy to add to our collection. "It's funny the things you remember," she told me at home. We were floating two plastic bags containing our new fish in the aquarium to allow the temperatures to equalize. "When I was six, I went to get ice cream with my mother. I wanted vanilla, but my mother said, 'No you don't, you want chocolate; vanilla is vile.' " We opened up the bags, and the fish swam out into the aquarium. "This isn't just for you," my mother said. "It's for me too."

So our roles were set. She became the financial backer and I the laborer. I made certain the pH and calcium levels were kept in the proper ranges, that no incompatible species were placed in the same tank, and that the tanks were clean and not overcrowded. By that time, Charlotte the mouse had succumbed to a second tumor, and the rest of my mouse population, to which I had less strong emotional attachments, I traded at the pet store for aquarium supplies. Afternoons I spent parked before my aquariums meditating on the aqua gourami, the deep red and purple sail-like fins of the fighting beta, the darting, electric neon tetras, and the sinuous black and red koolie loach that couldn't help but listen to genes commanding it to leap from its aquatic home. Every few weeks we'd find a koolie loach dried and flat on the kitchen floor, and we'd have to replace it.

At Neptune's, my mother and I gazed into the saltwater tanks at fish of otherworldly beauty, both of us desiring to possess them as though they embodied the most sensual delights. "Maybe we should try a saltwater tank," I hazarded. My mother eyed the prices. "This fish costs twenty-five dollars!" she cried. "I don't have that kind of money." But the idea hung in the air between us.

Scotty dumped a glass of milk and a peanut butter sandwich into the kitchen aquarium. The fish went into a feeding frenzy over the bread and didn't seem to mind the organic brew whipped up by the filter. Just then, my father arrived. He did this not infrequently, showing up unannounced to sweep me, Nick, and John away for the evening, much to my mother's frustration. She begged him to call first to make plans, but he never did. He barged in through the front door without knocking and towered over me. "Go tell your brothers we're going out."

"I've already started cooking," my mother said, a particular kind of exhaustion settling upon her as she prepared once again for capitulation. Her protest was made not out of belief in its effectiveness, but out of necessity; it was like an animal cry.

My father didn't respond, and I was caught between them. In these situations, my fear of him always proved to be the dominant motivating factor, and so I went upstairs to alert my brothers. My mother watched from the door as we all piled into my father's car. Quietly she said, "Is it really so hard to do as I ask?"

I gave her a look of sympathy, and then we were off. We were on our way to the Astrodome for a football game, where, my father said, we'd probably see the Oilers get their asses kicked, but I relished the opportunity to spend time as a near equal to my brothers. Though I was youngest, I sat up front. In our father's presence, the three of us entered a rare, pacific realm; Nick and John forgot their bitter quarrels, and both treated me with sympathetic interest. Also, going to a football game meant that I would get to eat fried shrimp, my favorite food. Anything public my father performed in high style, and at the Astrodome we always sat in box seats. Each box had its own small lounge with a bar and big, deep pans of fried shrimp, kept warm by the purple flames of Sterno.

For the first half of the game, I sat beside Nick and John with a plate of fried shrimp in my lap. On the field far below, players underwent maneuvers made mysterious by their resemblance to ants. John hogged the one pair of binoculars. I returned often to the bar in order to pile my plate with shrimp, and there I glimpsed my father watching the game on television with a gin and tonic in his hand. The atmosphere of the bar was faintly lurid. Its walls and furniture were a plush blue, and a smiling black man poured drinks for the white patrons. In this bar during a previous football game, my father had punched another man in the face for, as he described it, acting ungentlemanly in the presence of ladies. At halftime, when my brothers and I joined him there, he turned to a couple of his cronies and said proudly, "Here come my boys."

One of the men placed a paw on my head. "Are you in school yet?"

I found this question to be of such idiocy it was difficult to answer politely. I gave a weak smile and nodded.

"That's Mickey Mouse," my father told him, "the inscrutable Sphinx." Eyeing me, he had a big grin on his face, as though I'd done something that pleased him. "Are you having a good time, sweet pea?"

I said that I was. Because the truth was this: in spite of everything, I loved him. I wanted my father to think well of me and to love me back, but I couldn't bear to have his attention on me. Being older, my brothers had grown up with him in a way that I had not; he wasn't a stranger to them, and so they did not fear him as I did. I was grateful for their presence now because they deflected my father's attention, allowing me to be near him without being seen by him.

What I saw in his eyes when he looked at me was an unspoken and terrible expectation; I knew I could not be the kind of boy he wanted. Recently, Nick had run away from home after my mother chased him through the house brandishing scissors in an attempt to shear his straggly hair, and this had earned him a lot of respect in my father's eyes. John had begun developing a careful ministry of finance that delighted my father. But I was no hell-raiser, nor did I possess John's economy, and worst of all, I was a mama's boy. I knew this to be true. Early in my life I had been forced to choose between my parents, and my loyalties were so unalterably aligned with my mother that for my father simply to look at me was to witness blatant, blazing betrayal. I was the kind of mama's boy he could never forgive.

As predicted, the Oilers lost the game by an embarrassing margin. While the Astrodome emptied, John and I visited every bar along the box seats to collect aluminum cans from the trash, getting smeared in the process with various liquid refreshments. Recycling had become our latest venture, though where I saw pristine forests and clear streams free of pollution, John saw profit. My father encouraged this entrepreneurial spirit and didn't mind driving us home, John and I smelling of garbage, with three large Hefty bags full of crushed cans in the backseat of his convertible. We sat on top of the seat, exhilarated by the roar of the wind. I held out my arms to feel the full force of our speed. "Faster," I screamed, and my father hit ninety on the last stretch of freeway before home.

Traveling by bicycle on weekly bottle-collecting forays, John and I traversed the vast suburban territory of Houston, through apartment complexes, the alleys behind supermarkets, and fenced pastures holding various breeds of livestock. John played the elder in a diplomatic way; though he was certainly in command, he was not averse to hearing my suggestions and encouraged my faithful sidekick status. On one such trip, we discovered that the large field beside the bayou, a landmark of significance in both our childhoods, had been bulldozed, and a placard announced the construction of the first office building to go up in our neighborhood. The skeleton of the building was erected with lightning speed. One evening, John entered my room wearing black jeans, a black turtleneck, and a black knit cap. His face was smeared with burnt cork. I dressed in similarly dark clothes, and he brushed the cork against my forehead and cheeks, then we slipped out the backdoor. As night fell, we approached the construction site through the woods beside our house. The concrete floors of the building had recently been poured, but it still had not acquired walls, either interior or exterior. Flanked by empty elevator shafts, two red steel staircases zigzagged upward. Catlike, we ascended to the roof.

We lay on our stomachs at the roof's edge overlooking a residential street, and John opened the carton of eggs he'd been carrying. From our Olympian perch, we let them fly at passing cars until the drivers screeched to a halt, jumped out, and gazed up at the unpredictable heavens.

During dinner, John and I laughed every time we glanced at each other, and the old saying that a criminal could be caught returning to the scene of the crime began to resonate deeply within me. We couldn't stay away from a good thing. The following Sunday, three other neighborhood kids joined us, primed for guerrilla action. From the roof of the building we could see out over the changing face of Houston. The Galleria had recently been built upon the field where we had traditionally gone berry picking in the spring, and the cattle and sheep were being replaced with herds of identical town houses. None of us could look upon that scene without feeling impotent anger at the destruction of our homeland.

In the daylight we found treasure in abundance; each floor was full of construction materials. Pretending a pipe he'd found was a javelin, John hurled it into space out the back of the building, and inspired by this act, we went on a rampage. Huge rectangles of Sheetrock, spools of electric wire, bags of cement, lumber, buckets, and anything else we could get our hands on all flew through the air to land several stories below in the mud. I felt alive and powerful in my destruction. Descending to a lower floor in search of new materials, I caught sight of two blue-clothed figures, each rushing up a stairwell to prevent our escape. "It's the cops," I shouted, but not quickly enough to prevent Dwight, who had once narrowly missed catapulting my mouse to death, from almost assassinating a policeman. Down one of the empty elevator shafts he dropped a wheelbarrow, which plummeted past the policeman, seemingly close enough to shave his afternoon beard.

We'd emptied the floor of construction materials; there was nowhere left to hide. The policemen rounded us up and asked if we understood that we were trespassing. "We're just exploring," John said.

"Someone across the street reported that you were throwing rocks at cars."

"We weren't," I said strenuously.

"You could really hurt someone that way."

"But we weren't throwing rocks."

Fortunately we were grouped near the side of the building facing the street, where our vandalism remained invisible. The policemen were young, not so far from kids themselves, and they didn't attempt to hide their amusement. When they said they were taking us downtown to the police station to file a report, I wasn't too frightened. Only as we were herded down the stairs did I become nervous, but by some miracle they never thought to look out the back of the building, where they would have been eyewitness to thousands of dollars' worth of damage. I closed my eyes in gratitude. My mother was right. The Lord was watching over me.

As they locked us into the caged backseat of the police car, one of them chuckled. "Which one of you yelled that it was the cops? Was it you?" When he looked at me, I smiled with a rare, budding pride, as though I'd displayed the kind of spunk that he, and my father, might admire.

That was the end of the excitement. We spent the rest of the day in what looked like a school classroom, which was punishment enough, while a detective repeatedly tried to call our parents, none of whom were home. In the belief that they were using this as an interrogation technique, Dwight began to cry. John got us all to agree on a story, but we were never questioned. Finally, one of the captains, who had a tired and kindly, rumpled sort of face, drove us home. We asked him if being a policeman was at all similar to how it was portrayed on TV, and he said softly that sometimes it was. It was rather exotic to have a police captain pull into my very own driveway, but once he'd gone, John and I went inside to find the same old scene. My mother was cooking dinner. We sidled in with mock innocence, and nonchalantly John let drop, "Guess where we were all day."

She sliced a tomato and asked us where we'd been.

"At the police station," I said.

"That's nice," she said, stirring the spaghetti sauce.

Her response disappointed both of us, so we proceeded to dole out a lavish description of our adventure, skimping only on the part about the vandalism, but she was not easily alarmed. My mother's style of parenting had always been somewhat laissez-faire. Her own father had been a strict disciplinarian who'd never admitted wrong, her mother a religious martinet criticizing grammar and moral comportment without cease. My mother was a different kind of Christian and had promised herself she'd be a different kind of parent. She lived by rules of kindness and decency, fully expecting her children to be decent people as well. In our house we breathed a sustaining atmosphere of absolute trust, and my wish to live up to that trust guided most of my actions in the larger world. As if she knew this, our occasional lapses into trouble didn't seem to worry her, and not even Nick's antics, which were after all only the fits of a teenager in a period of rebellion, resulted in punishment.

Though my mother remained unimpressed, I knew I'd pulled a stunt that would make Hayley proud. The next Saturday on the way to her farm I decided not to spill the news right away; I'd wait to place it for maximum impact. On the last stretch of dirt road, however, my plan was interrupted. We rounded a corner and my aunt gasped. Their neighbor's house had disappeared entirely, and it wasn't until we neared the site that we could see the perfect rectangle of white ash where it had once stood. The toolshed and surrounding trees were undisturbed, and an eerie calm suspended us in a warplike stupor as we stumbled to the perimeter of the ash.

Rattled, we continued up the road, recovering a little when we saw that my aunt and uncle's house was still standing. After we unloaded the car, Hayley and I caught the horses and tore off bareback up the road to spend a while longer at the scene of the fire. I spied an ember still red-hot and smoking, and when I showed it to Hayley she nodded sagely, as though I'd done good work. Then we went on with our ride, past small farms, herds of cows, trickling creeks. Hayley led. Her hair hung long and wild over the buckskin jacket she wore, like a frontier girl kidnapped at birth by Indians.

As our horses progressed at a slow gait, Hayley dropped back beside me. "I've got a plan for tonight," she said. "Have you ever gotten drunk before?"

"No."

"We're going to take a six-pack of beer after Mom and Dad go to bed."

"Sounds good." I was only ten, but it seemed to me high time to start drinking beer. The effect of this plan was to heighten all our activities for the rest of the day. We executed the preparation of a secret campfire with particular finesse. Playing the board game Masterpiece after dinner, I displayed a zeal in competing against the others that was uncharacteristic. Hayley and I laughed uproariously at jokes on *Carol Burnett* that were not by any standard very funny.

Hayley's parents finally bid us good night, and after waiting tensely for what seemed an appropriate amount of time, she slipped the six-pack from the refrigerator and we stole out of the house. I'd felt guilty during the day that I was going to steal the beer, but you had to live life when you could; your house might burn down tomorrow. As our campfire crackled, we sat back and popped open the beer, taking voluminous gulps. I found it delicious. We lit cigarettes and stared into the night sky. We'd been scouring it for weeks for signs of comet Kahoutek, which had proven disappointingly not to be the glittery spectacle promised us by scientists. I thought the time was right to tell her about my adventure. "Guess what," I said.

"My mom's going to have a baby."

I laughed out of surprise, but I didn't believe for a moment she was joking. She'd been holding on to her own news. "When?" I asked.

"In seven months. It's a boy. She already knows."

She would be thirteen by then, the end of a long reign as an only child. Unlike her, I had spent most of my childhood with babies. It was difficult to explain that though they were a demanding, destructive presence in a household—they destroyed your homework, they poured milk into your aquarium—I loved them. Babies didn't obscure their feelings. They threw dishes to the floor when they were angry, cried when they were hurt or sad, and kissed and hugged you when they were happy. "There are lots of kids in my family," I said, trying to cheer her up, "but Mom always made me feel like I was the only one."

"Really?"

"Babies are great."

Hayley was not convinced.

"Hey," I said. "I got hauled down to the police station last weekend."

She gave me a long look. "Liar."

I was extremely offended, and for a while I held my tongue. "I did too. Swear to God."

"Put out the fire," Hayley finally said. By that point we'd each had three beers, and I was reelingly drunk. I threw a handful of dirt on it. "No," she said sharply. "You have to put it out the way a man would."

She was right, of course; we couldn't allow any more fires to get out of control. But out of stubbornness I asked, "How do you mean?"

"You have to pee on it."

I refused to answer.

"Because that's what men do."

I remained where I was, frozen.

"I won't look." She stood and walked a few steps away.

"Turn around," I told her.

"Men put out campfires by peeing on them."

"Okay, okay."

If there was a model to describe our relationship, it was that of master and slave, perhaps the first relationship in which I sought the comfort and security of following another person's will. The thought of imposing my will upon someone weaker felt to me like a form of evil, but I was more than willing to be imposed upon. Something in me longed to be contained and ordered. So I did what Hayley requested. Turning my head to keep an eye on her, I unzipped my pants. The fire sizzled, and I left it thoroughly extinguished. We staggered back home, leaning over a barbwire fence on the way to throw the empty beer cans into a neighbor's field. As each can left my hand, I felt increasingly buoyant, strong and capable like a man. Hayley and I entered the house in the firm belief we were being as quiet as mice, and then climbed into our beds, where I swirled happily into sleep. I felt proud of myself.

7

When school ended, I breathed in the redolence of summer's promise, but my mother was somber as she gathered us together. She hated to leave this house, she said, but she had so little money it was becoming unavoidable. She offered us her plan: for a year she'd rent out our house in Houston while we rented a less expensive one in Austin. If we liked it after the year was up, we'd stay there.

We stood like a tribunal before my mother, her hands pressed to the kitchen counter as she waited for our response. We gave her silence. Nick maintained the usual sullen expression of his teenagehood. John looked expectant and good natured. A pellet of anticipation had burst in my chest. I thought that this could be a very good thing.

I'd never been to Austin, which lay 150 miles to the west, but every adult spoke its name with the longing and glazed look that a city of gold might inspire. It was smaller than Houston and closer to the frontier; it maintained an edge of wildness. Also, people were friendlier there. They weren't as caught up in getting ahead as they were in Houston, but led more casual, bohemian lives. In that conducive climate, I thought my mother might just marry a journalist after all.

"Well, think about it," she said, and then left us.

A couple of weeks later we drove to Austin for the day to look at houses, and since we were doing this as a family my mother took along all five kids. During the three-hour drive, there was more than a little complaining, from Nick, who would have preferred any activity not related to the family, and from Celeste and Scotty, unused to the constraints of the car. They kept attempting to crawl into my mother's lap, claiming her constant attention. Though no longer babies, they were still hardly more than extensions of her; unlike me and my older brothers, they shared her redheadedness, as though she'd created them alone by acts of parthenogenesis. Separate from the melee, I lay in the back of the station wagon with my nose in a book. Hayley had tipped me off to C. S. Lewis's Narnia series, and I was in the grip of *The Lion, the Witch, and the Wardrobe,* a tale of unhappy boys and girls who escaped their oppressive lives through a secret doorway, finding themselves in an alternate world rich with magic and the emergence of their own latent majesty. I was drunk on its implications.

In Austin, Robert met us at the rosy granite dome of the capitol building and took us to lunch at a restaurant overlooking the fecund, green river winding through town, where he related in detail the story of how he'd been shot by the sniper. Covering the event for the newspaper, he was crouched behind a car when he saw another man get shot in the street. Instinctively, Robert had run from his cover to pull the man to safety, and that's when the sniper hit him in the shoulder. Doctors said that he'd never use his arm again, but after several years of hard work he'd gotten it back in functioning order. After lunch, we walked past the university, and he pointed out the tower that had served as the sniper's roost. Throughout the story, Robert had spoken with gentle modesty, as though he'd simply been a very fortunate fellow to have survived, but in him I saw a compassion, courage, and iron resolve that surpassed my furthest hopes for my mother's future husband. I knew that Austin would be a lucky place for us. Later, in a hilly neighborhood thick with beautiful gnarled oaks, we inspected a three-story house with a wood-burning stove in one of the bedrooms. John and I fought over who would get it. Among the rooms and counters of another house set on the bank of Lake Austin, I sought out the ideal positioning for my aquariums.

My shift of mind on the matter of moving did not occur suddenly. Over the next few weeks, we made several more house-hunting trips to Austin, where our steps echoed through empty rental houses with growing disappointment; none of them suited us. During the long drives, I immersed myself in Narnia. I flew through *The Voyage of the Dawn Treader, The Silver Chair,* and finally, dreading to come to its end, *The Last Battle.* Halfway home from a trip to Austin, after we'd stopped at a Dairy Queen, I read the closing pages, then threw the book away from me. Hoping I'd made a mistake, I reread them only to learn again of the deaths in a train crash of every one of the characters I'd grown to love. Then they entered Narnia forever, as though it were heaven, but this seemed to me a bitter reward.

I burned too much from the betrayal to begin another book right away. During the next few trips, I stared out the window watching the flatness of the plains take on the gentle undulations of Central Texas. It began to sink in just how far we were traveling from what I considered my home, Houston's familiar terrain, the house I'd grown up in, the fragile web of friends I'd managed to spin. On the surface, my mother's nomadic childhood appeared exotic: so many new cities, including foreign ones, so many new friends. But the fragmentation of it had always made me a little sad. She'd left many people she loved, gone through the hardship of changing schools countless times, four times in ninth grade alone. I did not want that kind of life.

This unrest fermented in me until one June morning when I lay on my mother's bed while she dressed, feeling sorry for myself. Perhaps I even convinced myself to cry, partly out of anticipated loss and partly out of strategic manipulation, and waited for her to notice. When I finally caught her attention, she rushed over to sit beside me, so quickly, I noticed, she had not even taken time to fasten her skirt. "I don't want to move," I told her.

"Oh, honey, I don't want to go either. But I have to." Again she catalogued her woes, those unyielding external forces, speaking with a resignation that was by now familiar to me. Had she possessed an ear attuned to her own unadulterated internal voice, I believe she would have told me something quite different, that the reason we were moving was that she had to get the hell out of Dodge. My father had recently remarried; all the men she'd dated were losers. Houston must have felt worse than claustrophobic to her; it was suffocating, dead. She wanted to pass through that magic gate herself, to begin over in a new, more hopeful world. But she preferred to believe that powers greater than her own directed her there. Even if she had heard any internal voice through that static, she would not have trusted it.

"Sometimes it's so hard for me to go on," she said, and with that admission, everything snapped back into focus for me. She was even sadder than I, so it would be selfish of me to give in to my own sadness. The certainty that it was my job to offer unflinching support made me feel strong. We had found our places again.

Near the end of the summer, my mother hit a lucky streak. Only days after a man of respectable profession, a judge, decided to rent our house, she came across one in Austin that she liked. When I saw the house, I agreed that it was a true find; the door to what would become my bedroom was plastered with stickers of Cancer the crab, which happened to be my sign of the zodiac. A date was set to sign the contracts. The judge would come to our house in the morning to finalize the deal, and then my mother would drive lickety-split to Austin to sign another set of contracts that afternoon. We would move immediately. The judge never showed up. My mother lost the house in Austin and fell into despair, until one morning several weeks later when she came running inside with the newspaper. On the front page, headlines proclaimed the arrest of our felonious judge. He was later convicted and imprisoned for accepting bribes. "The Lord is watching over us," my mother declared, holding the newspaper with reverence as though it had been delivered to our doorstep directly from above. "Whenever I begin to doubt, He gives me a sign." The plan to move to Austin was shelved in concordance with His wishes, though her complaints of poverty continued.

8

For my eleventh birthday in June, not long after I'd made the brief fuss about moving to Austin, my mother had given me a book on saltwater fish, with the understanding that as soon as we were settled in our new house she would subsidize me. I didn't feel guilty to be paid off in this way; it seemed an appropriate salary. With the birthday money my grandparents had sent, I bought a fifty-gallon aquarium and a wrought iron stand I painted neon blue. After the deal for the house in Austin fell through, I dragged a garden hose in through the kitchen window and filled up the aquarium, then swirled in a bag of scientifically concocted sea salts. Upon a bed of beige gravel flecked with rose, I placed pieces of coral, conch shells, and the fluted half of a giant clam. These had come from boxes my mother pulled down from the back of her closet, where I found them still wrapped in the ancient tissue paper she'd first used as a girl when collecting the shells from the beaches of Panama. I arranged them in as natural a constellation as my imagination could manage, and then I waited. The sea water required a curing period of two weeks in order to achieve the invisible chemical balance necessary to support life. At night I turned off all the lights in the kitchen except for the aquarium's fluorescent tube and sat alone in the dark, gazing into the aquatic world I'd created. Even without the life it begged to contain, it promised me a doorway.

From the ads in back of *Tropical Fish Hobbyist* magazine, I'd sent away to fish suppliers for lists of their stock, and from these I made my own lists of the fish that would commune here in the perfect aquarium. One of the stock lists from a supplier based in Singapore looked particularly promising. For the astonishing price of fifty cents each, even those fish that cost tens or even hundreds of dollars at the store seemed to be available. I fired off an order for the handful that would stun any observer with their vibrancy of pattern and color: the silver and orange copperband butterfly, the goofily spotted clown triggerfish, the brilliant yellow lemonpeel, the dragonlike mandarin. The Singapore supplier didn't reply, and though I'd known all along that it was a long shot, I still felt disappointed.

The aquarium was still awaiting the introduction of fish on the evening that my sister came shrieking into my room. Because of a long history of destruction, Celeste was not allowed over the threshold of my doorway, a rule she generally obeyed, so I knew something was up. I bolted downstairs, where I heard a sound like a waterfall.

My mother and I arrived in the kitchen at the same moment, and we stood immobilized by what we saw: from the seams of the aquarium gushed a cascade of water; a quarter of the tank had emptied; the floor was flooded. Then, as though we'd rehearsed for this eventuality, we leapt into action. We set out buckets to catch the cascade, she grabbed a mop, and I bailed out the aquarium to prevent the kitchen from flooding further. Toting the water to the sink I felt heartbreak enough, because the salt mixture alone had cost nearly as much as the aquarium; I was literally pouring her money down the drain. Trying to stop this tide was like trying to stop the Flood, and at some point we crossed the line separating hopeless disaster from hilarity. "The Lord sure has a funny way of telling you to mop your kitchen," my mother howled. We couldn't stop laughing. The torrent continued.

The empty aquarium was relocated to the back patio while we considered our options. Since both my mother and I were out of cash, fixing the leak struck us as highly preferable to buying another tank, but neither of us had the faintest notion how. "I'm going out with Hank Dixon tonight," my mother told me. "Maybe he'll have an idea what we could do." This caught my attention. Recently she'd been set up with a blind date, but amid the furor over the aquarium and losing the house in Austin, I hadn't paid much mind. But this was the third time she'd seen Hank, and I couldn't prevent a blossoming hope that it might lead to something more than the previous dead-end dates.

When Hank arrived that evening I took extra notice of him. He was broad, with dark hair, an aquiline nose, and a beautifully high forehead. Though he wore the requisite dark suit of the suitor, employing the same hands-in-pocket stance, he was not made of cardboard; beneath his urbane surface lay a hint of lithe animality. Hank had been introduced to me as a man whose realm of knowledge encompassed all things, even aquarium repair, and it was a good beginning. Wearing a t-shirt, I hugged myself in the chill of that fall evening, the three of us standing over the tank while my mother and I laughingly recounted the flood. We were a natural team, but tonight our timing was especially good, as though we both knew we were auditioning for the most important roles of our lives. Hank listened attentively; all my shyness evaporated beneath the serious, blue-eyed gaze that took me in and did not discount me.

"Have you thought about liquid epoxy?" he finally said.

My mother and I looked at each other. "Actually," I said, "we haven't."

"You could pour a layer of it to seal the bottom."

"Wouldn't that be toxic?"

"There are nontoxic types, I'm sure."

I liked Hank enough to consider his suggestion viable, and the next day in the hardware store my mother admitted she'd had a good time with him. We mixed the epoxy and poured a layer half-an-inch thick into the tank, then waited hopefully for it to perform its magic. Over the following days, the epoxy hardened into the color of a callus and curled up at one edge like a breaking wave. My mother and I converted the tank into a terrarium coffee table and on our next trip to Neptune's bought a new one, avoiding each other's eyes.

The process was repeated. I filled the tank, though this time waiting several days to check for leaks before I mixed in the salt, placed the coral and shells in reeflike position, and switched on the filter. Weeks passed. Specks of algae bloomed upon the glass. The child support check from my father was late as usual, my mother told me, but as soon as it came she promised to buy some fish, just a couple, and after that we'd add slowly.

A dozen roses were delivered to the house. They'd come from Hank, whom my mother had begun seeing two or three times a week. At first she masked her delight, but arranging the flowers she broke into a grin and laughed out loud. To think, she told me, if we'd moved to Austin she never would have met him. Her happiness infected me, but quite suddenly she became sharp. "The only time your father ever sent me roses," she said, "was on the day our divorce became final."

A smile remained on my face in order to mask my shock. I wasn't so naive as to think that my parents weren't divorced. Of course they were; my father had remarried. But in the three years since he'd gone, this was the first time I'd heard the word actually spoken: *divorce.* Later in my life, in college and after, I would often find myself in a group of peers, not one of whom could claim a family still intact. On the rare occasion someone admitted having parents who'd never divorced, I would say with the cool, knowing cynicism I wrapped about me like a cloak, "Why are they kidding themselves?" Divorce had become so common I forgot to think of it as painful. But when I was a child, it was a word we whispered in schoolroom corners, hugging to our chests the binders we'd plastered with POW and MIA stickers. We considered the children whose parents were divorcing as the victims of a tragedy more real than Vietnam. They didn't have to give details; they simply said, "My parents are getting divorced," and the heartbreak inherent in the statement was acknowledged with respectful silence by those who'd heard. Until the word was spoken by my mother, I had exempted myself from their ranks.

One night in late November, my mother's friend Bill came over for dinner, bringing with him the tape I'd begged to listen to, the one of the screaming rabbits. After we ate, he put the tape on the stereo, which led to my discovery that rabbits, normally so mild, could emit bloodcurdling, nearly human, screams.

The tape chilled me. I went up to bed, but a knock on my door interrupted my attempt to fall asleep. "The airport just called," my mother said, her expression amused and slightly perturbed. "Did you by any chance order some fish from Singapore?"

I leapt up. "They're here?"

"It's eleven o'clock and I have to drive out to the airport."

"I'm sorry."

"You are a very crazy boy."

My excitement transformed pulling on my pants into a slapstick routine, but she stopped me. "It's so late. Bill will come with me. You try to sleep and I'll wake you up when we get back."

Of course, after she left I lay awake in an agony of expectation. I couldn't remember what I'd ordered and flipped through my fish books to refresh my memory. When at last I heard them return, I raced to the kitchen, where I found my mother holding a large packing crate. Inside it were three water-filled bags, the plastic distorting their contents. The water was icy. What resembled a rock in the first bag turned out to be a piece of living coral. The second held the psychedelic mandarin fish, and in the third was a fish I hadn't ordered, velvety black with a filamentous, electric blue line along its back. When I released them into the aquarium, the fish behaved as though they were stunned. Their fins drooped. Their gills pumped with rapid, desperate breaths. The mandarin sank to the sand, while the other swam in the upward spiral of a daredevil pilot. "Maybe they have jet lag," I said, but the joke was made to cover my sadness. I didn't think they'd live through the night. I finally trudged off to bed, where I found myself in spontaneous, fervent prayer to God, and in the morning I entered the kitchen fully resigned. I was greeted by a miracle. The fish darted about the tank, regenerated.

For Christmas I received two orange clownfish and an anemone with purple-tipped tentacles. The fish required frequent and varied meals; they ate all the polyps from the live coral, but also relished Medusalike tubifex worms and live brine shrimp, which bore a remarkable resemblance to the sea monkeys I'd kept several years earlier. For the vegetarians, I poured a syrup of algal cells into the tank to encourage greenery. Its growth was explosive. In February, near the end of a mild winter, I was standing on a chair over the aquarium scraping extra algae from the glass when my mother entered the kitchen. John sat at the table with his homework, and she leaned against the counter watching us. After a while, we both looked up at her. Nick pushed open the kitchen door, and as it swung shut behind him, she said, "Hank has asked me to marry him."

She braced herself against the counter and looked at us, as though seeking our approval. A grin pulled across my face. This was the moment for which we'd been preparing for years.

Nick said, "Are you going to?"

"I've told him that I would."

"You've only known him six months."

John tapped a pencil on his homework. "That's good, Mom."

Dizzy, I stepped down from the chair and sat, where for the first time I allowed myself to admit how close a call we'd had. I pictured in my mind a family forming a circle. For such a long time our circle had been broken, vulnerable to all varieties of God-sent trials, but soon, Hank would seal that gap. The circle would connect again. My mother still watched us, her posture tentative, almost frightened. John sat pensively, Nick appeared lost in his glum version of the world. I thought: *at last.* We didn't have to worry about money anymore. She'd found someone to take care of her. At last I could rest.

KINGDOM: ANIMAL

9

On a gray Saturday in March, Hank drove into our driveway with a Thunderbird full of children. There were only three of them, my mother had counseled, but as the doors opened and legs and heads emerged, I entertained the possibility that they might keep flooding out of the car like circus clowns. They stood in a line beside their father, two girls and a boy, and we faced them in our own delegation. Quite suddenly, I felt the strangeness and enormity of being asked to take these three strangers into my heart. No doubt they felt on even shakier ground than I—they were outnumbered, after all, and on our turf—so we all stared woodenly at one another until Hank catalyzed the introductions: here was Jake, about Nick's age but as physically mature as a man, muscularly built, a blur of stubble on his jaw, an obvious wastrel; next was Ginny, on whom my gaze caught, slightly younger than John, with dark, beautiful eyes and cascading hair that she tossed around to best advantage; and finally Kiki, five months younger than I, with blond hair to her shoulders and a round, agreeable face. The plaid jumper she wore made her appear childish, but I gave her the benefit of the doubt. It was a costume worn for the occasion rather than a true reflection of her character.

Hank had not arrived without an official program; he'd come to prepare a *brunch*—a word which had previously held no meaning for me—of blackberry crepes. While he worked, Jake and Ginny displayed their good manners by getting acquainted with my mother. I took it for granted they would immediately love her, even though, try as she might to listen, she stood stupefied at the sight of a man cooking in her kitchen. Kiki remained close to her father, much as Celeste and Scotty backed shyly into my mother's skirted legs, while Nick and John recovered from its attic storage the leaf to the dining room table. As the three of us inserted the leaf, I realized happily that the larger version of the table would now become permanent.

Hank orchestrated not only the cooking but the progress of the meal as well. He drew us out with questions about our interests so that we could each learn about the others. Having recently returned from living in Virginia for five years, he was nearly as exotic a sight to his own children as he was to us. Their clear adoration and their delight in his playful, affectionate banter substantiated my own positive regard for him. In the first few hours of our acquaintance these shared feelings inspired a comfort among us that felt genuine, more real than simple blood kinship. The four older kids soon discovered they all went to the same high school, which led to comparisons of their different sufferings and boredoms. Jake spoke with the smiling cockiness granted him by long-standing familiarity with his own good looks. Ginny often burst into deep, infectious laughter. They talked about their unbearable mother, we about our unbearable father. I certainly did not take it for granted, but this bonhomie seemed to me a natural result of our parents' wedding plans.

After the meal, we drifted outside. Jake threw a football in long bombs across the front yard to John. Nick sauntered over to Ginny and cracked a few jokes, to which she responded with her hearty laugh, and I predicted that his busy schedule might soon free up to allow him more time with the family. Having brought the eight of us together, Hank and my mother observed from the sidelines what organic reactions might be produced, and we plunged into the project of liking one another. I watched them watching us. Since their engagement, Hank had been coming over in the evenings, playing with Celeste and Scotty until they went to bed, and then talking with my mother. Remaining nearby, but far enough that I did not interrupt, I wanted simply to witness. In his presence my mother laughed often, and it shocked me to recognize this as a new trait. Her face had always shone with expectant hope—that was how she greeted the world—and countless times I'd seen her light up with the deep love she felt for us her children, which I understood to be a form of happiness, but I'd never heard her truly laugh, certainly not with such luxury, as though she trusted it.

In the afternoon, after a silent consensus that it had been a successful first meeting, the older kids dispersed to jobs and friends. My mother dropped me and Kiki off at the Galleria to go ice-skating, and there, no longer under the eyes of our parents, we managed to escape some of the artificiality of the situation and loosen up. On the ice, Kiki displayed the daring and aggressive moves of a roller derby queen, though finesse was not her strong point. I wasn't very good either. We collapsed to the rink helicoptering our arms, and to slow our speed we slammed headlong into the barrier at the side. While loudspeakers energized the air with Karen Carpenter's crystalline voice, Kiki shot past me, her body bent forward at the waist as though pulled by a rope. Her skates sent her into an accidental but flawlessly executed U-turn. Anticipating impact, we flew toward each other, our arms outstretched with adolescent grace, and shockingly, in this public arena, Kiki let out a screech to shake the rafters. The power of that screech was transformative; I knew that I could love her. We collided, gripped, and held on as we maintained a shaky balance.

The wedding was set for the end of May. During those prenuptial months, my daily life suffered little change; I wasted time with my best friend Paul after school, pursued my private ichthyological studies, and watched an inordinate amount of television. These activities seemed to lie across my day in lazy configuration, but I anticipated that with Hank's arrival they would become fixed, as the real and correct version of my life began. He would give us purpose, validity. Until that time, I was only going through the motions.

While I remained focused on the date that Hank would officially join my family, there was a man already living in our house. Jorge was the husband of a woman my mother had hired to help with Celeste and

Scotty, and they were staying with us at her insistence while they looked for an apartment. Jorge was handsome, cultured, with a Zorro mustache, a dash of the Old World in our suburban American lives. He worked as a freelance photographer and appeared to have a lot of time on his hands. On occasion when I cleaned my aquarium he flattered me by taking a seat nearby and listening without overt boredom to my elaborations on the different personalities of the fish. Once, he asked to take photographs, and as he set up his camera and lights, I took the opportunity to question him. "Did you also take pictures in Mexico City?"

"Please, I'm from Guadalajara."

"Is that on the coast?"

"En las montañas." His English was without accent, but he sometimes slipped into Spanish because he knew the romantic, foreign sound of it delighted me. "You'll go there someday." He looked through the camera and snapped a shot of a clownfish. "The reason I'm interested in your friends here is that when I'm diving I want so much to take photographs, but I do not have an underwater camera."

"You're a scuba diver!"

"Didn't I tell you that?"

"Never."

"Well, I'll tell you something else. As soon as the weather warms up, I'll bring my gear over and teach you how to use it in the swimming pool."

"You promise?"

"Of course, *amiguíto.*" He patted my back, then looked again through his camera. I also watched the fish, proud of my accomplishment of having confined a beautiful fraction of the ocean for view behind glass, but I knew this to be a pale spectacle compared to what lay beneath the ocean itself, where a world, with Jorge's help, awaited me. For the first time in my life, I felt capable of solitary and self-sufficient adventure. A future materialized before me in which famous coral reefs figured prominently; I would dive Palancar in the Caribbean, the Great Barrier down under, the Red Sea, and the atolls of the South Pacific.

Returning home from school one afternoon, I found Jorge in the driveway conducting a photo session with Celeste perched on a bar stool. From behind his camera and tripod he was coaching her. "Show me love, sweetheart. That's right. That's good. Now, show me madness." She mugged and hammed, peeked through her bangs in mock timidity, screamed mutely in fear. When I later saw the photographs, her alphabet of expressions seemed to extend to me a promise: stores of vital and previously unknown qualities could be unlocked from the depths of one's own character by the rare touch of kindness.

But as much as I liked Jorge, throughout his brief tenure I considered him no more than a premonition. Having found an apartment, he left our house after a month, and though the season had not yet sufficiently changed to allow us to test his scuba gear, my disappointment was mild. I didn't miss his aquariumside company. I believed that a much more vast amount of the same commodity was coming our way, and the embarrassment of riches made me cavalier.

Every Sunday, Hank arrived with his three children to fulfill my mother's secret hope that we become a churchgoing family. At the time of their wedding announcement, I knew him only as the man who'd suggested using epoxy to fix my leaky aquarium, but after having successfully wooed her, he soon went to work wooing her children. I was shocked to find myself leaping from bed early each Sunday morning, especially since the contemplation of my fish transported me to a religious state of mind far more directly than did the teachings of the Bible. Two cars were necessary to carry the ten of us, which provided opportunity for endless combinations and dynamics, and then we filtered into the vestibule among several hundred other Caucasian middle-class families of west Houston. Though impressive as an architectural feature, the vaulted immensity of the church did not move me to grand emotion, nor did I listen too energetically to the cozy words served up to us by a minister on a bar stool. Instead, the sight of our group filling an entire pew made me worshipful, and for the sound of my mother singing tremblingly, jubilant, I sent my thanks to God.

Then we zoomed home for brunch. We told stories, some of them racy, and made plans for the summer. Hank proposed that his children move in with us after the wedding, and consensus settled this as a necessary, even urgent, course of action. In May, we spent a weekend at the beach house in Galveston owned by Hank's corporation, where Kiki and I spent all day in the waves, burning our skin bright pink. At night the living room became a patchwork of cots and sleeping bags. In the center, among us, my mother slept. Her hand dangled over the side of the cot, firmly held all night by Hank, who lay on a pallet beside her. Back at home, the pool warmed up for swimming parties. Hank gave a slide show; we saw Jake and Ginny splashing each other with paddles in a canoe on a Virginia river and Kiki's first view of the Pacific. The sense of invitation was so propulsive it boggled my senses.

From my bedroom window I witnessed a tableau: my mother was seated in a chair while Hank stood before her, one hand in his pocket and the other in midgesticulation. His expression was serious, intent, and though hers was polite, she owned a hint of a smile as though she were keeping a secret. An hour later they hadn't moved from these poses; another hour passed and they were still there, Hank pacing and orating like Caesar. Finally, after dark, I heard them come inside. Seeking out my mother, I found her alone in the kitchen. "What was that all about?" I asked. She smiled and rolled her eyes. "Child rearing." My mother and I shared an amused understanding that Hank was an occasional, though inoffensive, pedant, but to parade knowledge in an area where she was so clearly expert was too much. We laughed out loud, then set to work fixing dinner.

During those days, she and I communicated with brief smiles and quick glances that checked to assure no major disturbances, all that we could afford under circumstances that with each day flew forward in accelerating motion: church, crepes, beach, slide shows, flipping past at breakneck speed. The wedding hung before us like a red bull's-eye, and we were arrows shot from the bow, traveling toward it, supersonic.

The minister was late for the ceremony. As usual, we'd come in two cars. Driving the station wagon, my mother looked serene and beautiful, while I pulled at my tie and ill-fitting jacket, a maroon double-breasted business I'd inherited from one of my older brothers, or perhaps, being third in line, from both of them. In her simple blue wedding dress she had trimmed my hair earlier that morning, and bits still scratched inside my collar. Unable to sit still, Celeste and Scotty giggled in the front seat; Nick and John each looked silently out a window. In my customary position in the back, I was beyond anticipation or excitement. I felt swept along by the events of history.

Directed down corridors and past small courtyards, we entered a tiny chapel with only three or four pews. While we waited for the minister, the poverty of the room worked to deflate my spirits, until I could no longer prevent myself from expressing disappointment to my mother. This provoked a discussion among us all, and when the minister finally arrived, flustered and attempting to launch immediately into the ceremony, my mother interrupted. She asked with a touch of embarrassment if we could move to the large building where the Sunday service was held. "The children," she explained, nodding toward us. The minister had a worried, boyish face shadowed by a shelf of hair projecting from his forehead, and her request seemed to relax him a bit, as though he were much more comfortable in the realm of human vanity than with his own tardiness. He led us back through the corridors. We tread on the stones with the whispering steps of those whose shoes are made of satin. In the courtyards, spring had recently sprung, making us privy to brilliant squares of light and greenery, of flowers, bees, cicadas, and birdsong. Entering the darkness of the church momentarily washed me of sight. I had craved the physical grandness of the space I now felt surrounding me, the weight and celebrity it would bestow upon this union. On the dais where he usually sat on his bar stool, the minister turned to face us. We eight children gathered in a semicircle around our parents, our shoulders touching to form a nest for them, urging them forward with our hope and goodwill. The high roof beams dwarfed our small congregation, and, used to speaking to larger hordes in this room than ours, the minister wandered over several powerful decibel levels before landing on an appropriately softer one. The ceremony was brief. Hank spoke his vows in a perfectly modulated voice. Then it was my mother's turn. Until this point she'd appeared in absolute self-possession, but repeating the minister's words, her voice became tiny. It whispered and trembled as she plighted her troth, and at that moment I felt so precisely that she was the child and I her parent that a fiercely protective and proud love for her rushed through me with tempestuous force. In my mind, I began repeating the vows along with her, and in that way I silently coached my mother through to the end.

10

It was 1974 and, at my house, it was the summer of love. In the front yard we held family games—softball, volleyball, badminton—in which even Hank and my mother took part, playing until the heat of the day drove us to continue aquatic versions in the pool. There were outings north of Houston to piney lakes whitecapped by the wakes of speedboats, and weekends at the beach house in Galveston, where we water-skied, surfed, and swam until our bodies held no remaining reserves of energy. Best of all, every night we had dinner together, an hours-long banquet presided over by a parent at both ends of the table, where each child held an important voice. The democracy of that environment was richly organic, encouraging self-expression. Previously mute, Scotty became loquacious at these meals, mixing non sequiturs with observations of precocious acuity. Celeste luxuriated in having sisters at last to dilute the presence of so many boys, and the older kids lingered before taking off into the humid summer night for their various assignations. Reassembled from the pieces of broken homes, this was no ordinary family. We all knew we'd hit the jackpot.

Near the end of dinner one evening several weeks after they'd married, Hank requested that we make ourselves available at nine o'clock the following night for a family meeting. He left the table without giving details, and throughout the next day I was in an agony of suspense, wondering what might be said or done at this meeting, the concept of which was to me so alien. My imagination began to treat it as a kind of awards ceremony, picturing all of us crowned with laurels, laughing and toasting one another with goblets, so I arrived as early as I might have done on Christmas morning in order to get a good seat. The others wandered in at various intervals, and when our number reached a critical capacity of about five or six, there was an onset of jostling and rabble-rousing. By the time Hank ambled in, handsomely tousled in his boxers and undershirt, I was engineering a seat closer to Ginny, and Scotty was climbing onto Kiki's lap. We settled down while Hank took a seat, threw one leg over the arm of his chair, flipped through the papers he'd brought on a clipboard, and at last called the meeting to order.

"During the last month or so," he began, "even before I moved in, I've been trying to keep an eye on things. I'm very interested in how this family runs, and how it might run more smoothly. It seemed to me to be a good idea to have a forum tonight where we could all talk and make sure everyone understands what's going on. Now that we're a team, we need to pull together like a team." The caring tones Hank used made me even more than usually susceptible to this rhetoric, and I found myself responding with adrenalinized spirits. I felt important. He then spoke about the huge transition in our lives, how we were going to have to rely on one another more than we ever had, how the old way we did things might not work so well anymore. A new way, though difficult, must be found. Hank repeated the concepts of teamwork, strategy, and challenge. A reorganization of responsibilities was necessary, he said, but we could do it, we could tackle it, if we put our noses to the grindstone and got to work. Again: work, team spirit, new responsibilities. It was then that I realized our family meeting was about chores.

From his clipboard, Hank read off our names in descending order by age and explained the duties he'd penciled beside them, generally of the household maintenance variety—gather trash, wash windows, clean pool—nearly all of which were now accomplished by my mother. Other tasks seemed to have required a strenuous exercise of the imagination to create. Sweep the roof? Polish the doorknobs? By the time Hank reached me—cut-the-grass rake-the-yard wash-the-dishes-Tuesday-Thursday-Saturday clean-your-room—the droning quality of his voice had long since bemused me. It was certainly true my mother had never asked any of us to lift a finger around the house, but I felt something insistent and punitive about this roll call. Even my frustration confused me. I couldn't admit to it. I wanted Hank to like me.

After he finished listing off Scotty's duties, he asked if there were any questions.

"Are we done yet?" Nick said.

Hank gave only a polite smile as answer, and no one else breathed a word. Perhaps we'd forgotten how, since Hank had been speaking continuously for over an hour, but there were several frowns and a few angry expressions. "I've written all this down so no one will be confused," Hank said. "I'll post the charts up in the kitchen." He went on to give some concluding remarks about how my mother couldn't be expected to do all the work anymore; things had to change, and if there were any problems he'd be glad to talk about it. My focus shifted to my mother, who hadn't uttered a word all evening but sat beside her husband with a Mona Lisa smile. If only she had spoken, simply to agree with him or add her own thoughts, I would have accepted the new rules wholeheartedly, but she had become mysteriously voiceless. Before their marriage, I had thought of Hank only as a figurehead, and the possible rearrangements of our domestic lives had never once crossed my mind. Now, as I saw my mother ceding her position as head of the house, I berated myself for being surprised. The number of times I'd heard her scoff at women's lib and bra burning, exclaiming that the Bible clearly stated a woman should obey the man she's married to, was countless.

The family meeting had been a bust. Inside me swirled unsettling emotions: offense at Hank's militarism, anger at my mother's passivity, a suspicion of my own selfishness. Wanting to soothe these hurts alone, I gathered myself up and stood to leave the room.

"Michael?"

I turned to face my stepfather.

"Don't I get a goodnight kiss?"

I moved toward him. Hank's arms went around me and I lost my balance, falling into his chest, where he held me against the solid warmth of his body and planted a kiss on my cheek, an act that stunned me now as much as it had the first time he'd done it on the night of their wedding. In these last weeks he'd shown himself to be liberal with affection and unashamed of physicality, catching me up bodily in our games, inviting me to hurl myself into his arms. He did not shy away from my obvious joy in this attention.

Now, stumbling away from him to my room, my mind cleared. If Hank thought we needed a more disciplined environment, then I was ready to rise to the challenge, even if it was not to be painless. I also believed that the ten of us did not simply happen to live together by chance; we'd come together by mutual agreement, each of our own will, to create this family. The possibilities it offered us were as precious as magic wishes, and if we had to work hard or suffer the eccentricities of one another's character it was because, as Hank had said, we were now a team poised for victory.

The team had several new players, whose strengths and abilities had yet to be evaluated. They intercalated themselves into our closets, bathrooms, and dresser drawers, just as their father shared our mother's, and their arrival shifted alignments; Jake moved into Nick's room, Kiki into mine, and Celeste was pushed into Scotty's. Of all of us, Jake was perhaps the least invested in the family. He had just graduated from high school, and having decided to enlist in the navy in the fall, as well as being a fellow of red and burly blood, he was intent on indulging in several bacchanalian months. To this end, Jake disappeared every evening after dinner to mysterious, iniquitous haunts, returned between the hours of three and four in the morning to hurl a shoe at Nick's window, climbed drunkenly inside, and slept until noon. His chores were infrequently, and with half a heart, accomplished.

Ginny, however, quickly adapted to using our house as a base of operations. Each day after brushing down the sides of the pool, she worked on her tan upon its cerulean steps, from which point her presence called out like the song of a siren, ensnaring my brothers and their friends, as well as any visitors who might be passing through the neighborhood, in a circle around her. Quite often I found that my wandering down the corridors of our house corresponded precisely to her own. Behind a high screen of bushes outside her bedroom was situated the air-conditioning compressor, and there I would find Ginny in the early evening after her shower, drying her long hair over the artificial sci-rocco generated by the compressor's large fan. She didn't appear to mind my intrusion into the small arena of peace she'd managed to eke out in our overpopulated home, but would allow me to bum a cigarette off her, and then we'd talk about what was on her mind. Her mother had announced wedding plans to a man she'd known two months, only weeks after Hank and my mother were married, and this lay heavily on Ginny's heart. She had also just broken up with her boy-friend. She took a drag on her cigarette and sang, "You're no good, you're no good, you're no good, baby, you're no good," then she told me, "I just sent him that record. He was a pig."

"Good riddance," I said.

"What do you think about Nick?"

"Nick who?"

"Your brother, silly."

"He's okay," I said, by which I meant that he was not.

"I think he's funny."

"He can be."

"What I like about you," Ginny said, running her fingers through her billowing hair, "is that I can really speak to you like a friend, like an adult."

Out of modesty I kept my response to a nod, but inside I soared.

Nearly all of my time, however, I spent with Kiki. I adored her. We shared a room, woke together, ate breakfast, swam, rode bicycles, and explored together, then watched late night movies until we lost consciousness. We were companions as inseparable as the pair of twins to which I had once imagined belonging. She and I even looked alike, and we communicated in such a specific and idiosyncratic manner it was as though the private language of twins had sprung forth fully developed between us. She was crass and uninhibitedly weird, and her lack of inhibition set free my own more subdued eccentricities. After dinner, when the older kids left on their nocturnal forays, Kiki and I performed shows for our parents. She gave a rendition of Charo's Vegas nightclub act and I recited mock-beatnik poetry. We wrote skits and takeoffs on television commercials, which regardless of the quality of their humor sent us all into drunken laughter. Hank traveled in his work, and on his return from business trips Kiki and I accompanied my mother to the airport, so eager were we for the reunion.

Friends and interests outside of the family often took us away from each other. Every weekend, Nick drove to a distant part of Texas to race motorcycles. John traveled by river through Idaho, then Ginny went to Chicago for a week and fell in love with a boy whose hair was as long as her own. Kiki left for camp in the middle of the summer, and I spent several weeks with my father, during which time she and I wrote to each other furiously. But even this coming and going added to the brightness in our house, like sparks from flint on stone. The games, shouts, laughter, fights, and reconciliations wove us into a way of being I felt I'd dreamed of all my life, dreams that I had carried in my bones.

For their honeymoon, Hank had chartered a boat and taken my mother sailing in the Virgin Islands. Despite her maternal, homebound history, I'd always imagined her rightful place to be Paris in springtime, the African savannah, or some South Pacific isle, and so I was immensely grateful to Hank for allowing her true nature, until now obscured, to become realized. In a sense, I felt that I'd handed her over to him. Drafted into this larger family, I did not often seek to spend time alone with her, though I knew where she could be found. My mother rarely left the laundry room or kitchen after she returned from her honeymoon, in spite of our new work regimen and chores. I saw her in passing, when I came inside to slake my summer thirst with a Coke or was looking for an unstained t-shirt, and at those times she looked up at me with a weary smile. Every glance that passed between us confirmed that this was the way it should be. It was a relief to slip into the traditional roles of sacrificing, enslaved mother and ungrateful son; now that she had a husband, I had only to look out for myself. I took her for granted and gave up my days to the pursuit of pleasure.

11

"Goddamn it, son, are you going to be a fairy your whole life?" My father stood at the edge of the pool yelling at Scotty, who paddled across the shallow end inside the donut of a float. Scotty looked up at him impassively but began paddling with swifter strokes. On the front of the float bobbed a plastic giraffe's head. My father yelled a little more, encouraging, then impatient, finally angry, unable to abide that Scotty, almost five, still couldn't swim. I'd just come around the corner of the bay house, and the tone of my father's voice stopped me in my tracks. I wanted to protect Scotty, but I didn't move a muscle until my father went inside; standing up to him I placed on par with jumping in front of a lion.

Already barefoot, I sat beside the pool and plunged my legs into the cool water, watching Scotty and various relations—cousins, my sister, and stepsiblings from my father's marriage—play Marco Polo. The red hair he'd inherited from our mother glinted in the sun like metal, and he was smiling the broad smile that had earned him the nickname Football Mouth. Scotty had come to be considered the problem child of the family. His premature birth had already subjected him to several corrective surgeries, for blocked tear ducts, a wandering eye, and double hernias. Though tall for his age, he was somewhat clumsy, with the motor coordination of a child several years younger. Because he was already having difficulty in school he'd been tested for learning disabilities, but none were discovered, which only added further mystery to his problems. He was the kind of child who often made himself invisible, so quiet, so still could he become; yet he was also frustrating to deal with, recalcitrant and stubborn, occasionally infuriating; and in rare instances, when pushed, he threw tantrums so extreme they were frightening. Several times I'd tried to teach Scotty to swim without the float, but it was not simply my inelegant method that escalated his initial refusal into fist-swinging hysterics.

Most of the time I kept my distance. Though Scotty was seven years younger than I, his age was not the reason for this. What was already recognizable as his unhappiness, complicated and deeply rooted, scared me off. The responsibility to help him was a constant weight on my shoulders—perhaps if I were more encouraging and patient, more loving, rather than frustrated by him—but I did nothing. My lack of will inspired such severe self-reprimand that at times I was convinced Scotty's problems were the result of my own inattention.

"Hey, Michael," my stepbrother Howie called from the house. "You want to go fishing?"

I yelled back that I did and left the younger kids to their games. With fishing poles, some frozen shrimp, and a net, Howie and I hiked down to the pier, where we fished for a couple of hours, finally growing bored of catching nothing but catfish, a junk fish you couldn't eat but the only thing we ever hooked, and took to casting our lines into the sky in attempts to reel in a seagull. To no avail. We took a seat, counted waves, hoped for some unusual behavior from one of the many sailboats out on the water. In the distance, gray freighters chugged along the shipping lanes to the port of Houston.

I'd come here for several weeks every summer of my life. Each June, there migrated to this bay, just twenty-five miles east of downtown, the Houston equivalent of Asian colonials repairing to the mountains for summer, my father among them. Here they played racquet games, lounged by the pool, and drank Bloody Marys in the morning, beer in the afternoon, and tonic with either vodka or gin in the evening. We stayed in one of the houses built by the rich family my father's sister had married into, who owned a sizable piece of coastline. Also in this compound were two swimming pools, a tennis court, a pecan orchard, several other houses filled with distant relatives, and the pier Howie and I currently inhabited which extended a hundred yards over choppy brown water. The opportunities for children were immense, and I had always loved the bay because I loved the freedom and heat of summer, I loved fishing, and I loved my brother John, who, outside of the hierarchical structure of home, would allow me to be his constant companion and would even repay my devotions with what appeared to be enjoyment in my company.

But this summer I hadn't wanted to come to the bay. John had remained in Houston to work, and I knew I was missing out on all the fun at home. Though plenty of kids were around with whom to play games, to swim, fish, run, and soak up the sun and earth, my heart wasn't in it. Here, I was on the outside of things. I missed what I hadn't been aware that I lacked before Hank joined my family, the feeling of being included.

By evening, Howie and I had traded fishing for hurling crab apples at each other beside the tennis court, while Celeste and my stepsister Lauren played a jump rope game nearby and Scotty scratched patterns into the sidewalk with a rock. My father came ambling up the path from my aunt's house, heedless of a crab apple Howie had just lobbed in his direction. It struck the ground at his feet, narrowly missing him, but my father continued on unaware. He put a hand each on Scotty's and Celeste's heads. "How are my babies?" he said with the easy, expansive emotion that was proof he'd been drinking. In a mix of confusion and delight they hugged his waist, holding on even as he turned to go inside, but then released him when he reeled suddenly back. "Son," my father said to Scotty, his voice harsh, almost amused, with disbelief, "where the hell did you get that shirt?"

Scotty looked up at him with wide, autistic eyes. A fanciful pink butterfly flew across the front of the shirt, one of his favorites, which he wore at home on a daily basis until it became grubby and gray. My father put out his hand. "Give it to me."

Scotty didn't move.

"Take it off."

My father took hold of the shirt's hem and roughly pulled it over Scotty's head. "I don't know what your mother is thinking," he said, then tore up the shirt in his fists. Scotty had turned to stone. So had I. I stood apart as hatred welled up in me, hatred for myself.

For the joint celebration of Scotty's and my birthdays, which fell one day after the other, my stepmother kept the two of us back in the house while the family gathered by the pool. I watched them out the window as they milled around the table laden with presents, siblings and cousins, my aunt and father, and others for whom there was no word to describe our relationship, such as the stepnephew of my uncle. Finally my stepmother led us outside to make our formal entrance. It was not so distantly in the past when my mother had been among this poolside group that I did not feel her absence. One summer she was there with a tennis racquet at her side, and the next my stepmother Helen sat in her place. Though always comfortable and friendly with me, Helen was absolutely different from my mother. She was strict where my mother was casual, a conformist where my mother was eccentric, reserved where my mother was loving. My mother's beauty was one of softness, and Helen's was finely drawn, with high cheekbones, a straight nose, a strong chin. My mother yielded. Helen put up with no fuss, a quality my father admired. He liked spirit and feistiness, particularly in women.

Helen now arranged the presents on the table to her liking, and the other adults' interest in the party began to drift. Also in attendance were Helen's three children by her first marriage, whom I had known since toddlerhood as occasional playmates: Beth, a girl my age whose fair skin and manner was the antithesis of Kiki's; Howie, with a dark, feral, but not unhandsome face, the kind of hellion my father admired, though younger than I by enough margin that he allowed me to boss him around; and Lauren, a blond, impish girl Scotty's age, who made frequent use of her unrestricted access to my father's lap. This was my father's new family, the circle he had joined after detaching himself from ours. He was much less awkward with them, natural and full of humor and affection, which particularly seemed to pain Celeste. She nearly always came home weeping from these visits.

Helen raised her voice to corral everyone's interest back to the matter at hand. A giant chocolate cake she'd spent all afternoon creating now lay in the center of the table, but this my eyes quickly passed over as they scanned the wrapped packages for a particular, tell-tale shape. I was victimized by a gnatty buzz of anticipation I didn't fully want to acknowledge. At twelve, my age today, Nick and John had each received a twenty-gauge shotgun from my father, and though I knew a lot of things had changed since that time, and though I had never been able to aim a gun at any living thing, I wanted that shotgun. Unfortunately, not one of the presents drew my attention. They were all too truncated or round. I told myself that I didn't really mind, that I'd suspected all along I wasn't going to get it, but my hope maintained flickering life.

Scotty opened a box containing three new shirts, each with a little green alligator sewn on the front. "We'll get you dressed right," my father said, pulling Scotty into his lap and nuzzling him. I received three similar shirts in larger sizes, for which I gave my strangely humiliated thanks. More boxes produced more clothes: a pair of shoes, a leather belt, tennis shorts. Before I had a chance to open my aunt's present, she said, "I hope you like the book, Michael." The deep Alabama countryside of her voice had always entranced me, the vowels drawn out like syrup poured from the bottle. At a restaurant I would hang on the edge of my seat to hear her order the *shreeimps* cocktail.

"I love all books," I told her, but I hardly saw what lay inside the wrapping, so glum did I feel that the gun hadn't materialized.

Later, after birthday cake and a night's sleep, after the disappointment had run its course, I lay on the couch in the sunporch watching sailboats tack across the bay and leafed through the book my aunt had given me, titled *Very Special People.* It chilled me to my bones. The most famous freaks of all time were presented on its musty pages: the original Siamese twins Chang and Eng; Prince Randian, the caterpillar man; the Ugliest Woman in the World; and the spectacularly tiny Tom Thumb, who married another midget and sired a handful of six-foot children. A moldy, rotten smell emanated from its spine, but the gruesome photographs kept me riveted. I viewed a woman with two pelvises who'd given birth through each, a painted hermaphrodite, the grotesque Elephant Man, and scores of other human oddities. I pored over this gallery of the malformed, shrunken, and limbless until my stomach turned. Gorged on freaks, I threw the book away from me.

But I couldn't leave it alone for long. A few days later I was reading about a boy with no arms who could play the piano and eat ice cream from a spoon using only his toes. Testing out my own toes, I found that they moved in unison and were barely dexterous enough to pick up a single pebble. Afternoon shadows lengthened as I read. The usual shrieking came from the pool nearby, where the younger children performed flips and cannonballs from the diving board. This being the time adults gathered at the watering hole, I found myself among several of them fresh off the tennis court and ready for their lime-laced drinks. Wet children were soon drawn to parents' sides, men traded jokes, a backgammon board was unfolded. Within minutes a community of ten or twelve had congregated around me.

"Hey, Mickey," my father said, holding up his empty glass and tinkling the ice that remained, "get me a refill, will you?"

I took the glass to the outdoor bar and splashed in tonic and gin, erring on the side of too much gin. "Do you ever go hunting anymore?" I asked him.

"Not very often."

"Do you still have all those guns?" I handed him the drink and leaned against the back of the chair, my chin nearly resting on his head.

"Of course." He sipped the drink and coughed. "Your bartending sure does pack a punch, Mickey."

Five or six people were approaching down the walk, normally unremarkable except that this group included a man about whom my stepmother had recently warned me. His name was Joey, the stepson of someone or other. And he was mentally retarded, she didn't know how severely. Helen told me this because part of her friendliness with me included gossip, but she was also preparing me so that I would make no social gaffes. As the group neared the pool, I had no problem picking out Joey, a large man of about twenty. They arrived, greetings were made, drinks mixed and handed out. Joey was introduced and then seated in a chair, where he was promptly ignored. There are qualities that identify those who are different from us, though it is often difficult to know what they are; we sense only that a connection between us and them must not be considered. Joey's clothes were perhaps untidy, his beard poorly shaved, his hair disheveled. He had the look of being tended by someone other than himself. But his physical appearance was not so noticeable as to draw attention. His difference seemed to lie in his face, or more specifically, in the vacancy of his eyes. People were scared of it.

My uncle called to me, asking if I wanted to join him for a fishing trip the next morning. They were leaving at dawn.

I told him he was crazy.

Joey occupied a chair beside the couch where I'd been reading, and, horrified, I saw that *Very Special People* lay no more than two feet away from him. As nonchalantly as possible, I moved to the couch and sat upon the book. At such close range, I was unable not to stare at Joey, simultaneously fascinated and repelled by him, and he offered me an unthreatening profile for study. Every few minutes he took a sip from a beer someone had placed in his hand, then rested the cup on his knee. He did not speak. No one spoke to him. I studied harder. His eyes were not utterly vacant, after all. I was sure they disguised some sort of intelligence held, maybe by his choice, in reserve.

My father asked if I wanted to challenge him to backgammon.

Later, I told him.

The hand holding the beer had gone slack, and a rivulet had run down Joey's leg, droplets standing out on the hairs of his thigh. A wave of disgust swept over me. I wanted to get away from him. But I also wanted to know what thoughts lay quiescent behind those eyes, newly gripped as I was by a belief in the mystic and visionary capabilities of idiots: perhaps Joey could see the truth. We hadn't been introduced. If he were Betty's stepson, then that made him the stepcousin of my cousin, no relation to me at all. But I wanted him to know we were allies.

Howie tapped my shoulder and made the motion of swinging a tennis racquet. I got up to follow him, pulling the book from beneath me and holding it close to my body as I walked away. I didn't take a last look at Joey. Howie was a better tennis player than I, but he let his anger get the better of him. He didn't concentrate, made wild shots, flung his racquet into the pecan orchard where it lodged in some high branches. Keeping my emotion under wraps, I gathered momentum, aced him on a serve for the winning shot, and in the sweetness of victory Joey slipped easily from my mind.

A week later, my stepmother handed me a letter. "This came for you. It's from Joey." I looked at her uncomprehendingly and didn't move to take it. "You remember," she said, "Betty's stepson. It's a very nice letter. I already wrote back to thank him."

Then I snatched the blue envelope from her hand. The seal of it had been cleanly broken, and I stared at the letter with battling emotions, anger and disbelief at Helen's violation, as well as an unwillingness to read the letter's contents.

The handwriting was an almost illegible scrawl, childish, but the sentiment was not. *I know this is strange,* Joey wrote, *but of all the people I met I felt closest to you, even though we didn't talk. I'm back home in Colorado now. Maybe you could write me and tell me about yourself?*

My first reaction was to feel sorry that he'd received my stepmother's crisp thank you letter rather than the heartfelt one he craved. I realized that Helen hadn't trusted me to respond in an appropriate manner, especially in a situation that required true finesse. Good form was her hallmark. But I began to feel that her intercession had been purposeful, a severing, in order to nip in the bud any possible connection between us, and for this I even felt some gratitude. For many years I kept Joey's letter in the drawer that held my most valued possessions, but I never wrote him back.

Two days before we were to leave, Scotty pulled off the yellow triangular floats he usually wore on his upper arms and dove into the pool. He swam thrashingly to the far side while a group of us looked on, as speechless as witnesses to a miracle. "That's my son," my father whooped. "Maybe you won't be a fairy your whole life after all." One freestyle event had apparently been enough for the time being, but as Scotty pulled himself out of the pool, he beamed, as proud of himself as I'd ever seen. Water dripped off him and evaporated instantly from the hot cement. He said to no one in particular, "Maybe I *won't* be a fairy my whole life."

Packing to go home, I didn't want to bring the book my aunt had given me. I wanted to throw it away or simply leave it, but I knew that would be the very worst form. I buried *Very Special People* at the bottom of my duffel bag.

12

It was late July, high summer. I was home, Kiki had returned from camp at last, and the sun had baked us terra-cotta; things were as they should be. In a knee-length t-shirt with a Campbell's Soup logo across the front, Kiki lay on her bed flipping through *Very Special People*. The book had been moving around my room like a virus I couldn't shake, first on the dresser, then splayed on the floor at the foot of the bed, then on the night table. I was trying to read *The Water World*, a century-old leather-bound book of ocean exploration that my mother had given me for my birthday, but every few minutes Kiki made another snort of disgust, and I looked over to see what page she was on. By now I knew all the freaks by heart.

"This book really grosses me out," she said. "And it's mean to call someone the ugliest woman in the world. Anyway, she's not all that ugly." She showed me the picture I'd already seen a hundred times of a tiny woman with dark skin and an apish, hairy face. According to the caption, she'd been discovered in Mexico and was initially believed to be the missing link. The next photograph was of a woman whose partial, undeveloped twin protruded from her stomach, a headless sack with arms and legs. "Now *that's* ugly," Kiki said, and we writhed in queasy laughter.

A knock on the door heralded Hank, who entered wearing his regulation boxers and undershirt and took a seat on the floor with his back against the wall, as though he wanted to rap for a while. I loved the homey casualness of his manner and dress. Kiki and I lay in our beds, our two reading lamps softly illuminating the room, and when we caught each other's eye we started laughing again. Then we saw the disappointment filtering across Hank's face and hushed ourselves. "I thought we had a deal," he said. "I thought we'd agreed your bedtime was eleven."

The time, I saw, was 11:05. I shared another fleeting glance with Kiki. Hank had recently called a second family meeting to suggest some fine tuning in the performance of our chores, and for good measure he'd added a few more to the list. Then, in order to test our understanding of what was expected of us, he asked a few sample questions, such as, "Michael, what does *weed the garden* mean to you?" Finally, he didn't think it was a good idea for us to be sleeping so late, so he was instituting bedtimes that would go into effect the following week.

His attitude unsettled me, but because I didn't quite know what to make of it, my incomprehension focused on the bedtime. I appealed to my mother; in summer she'd never given me a bedtime, and now she said, "I know, honey, I'm sorry," as though this were one of God's trials I had to rise to, but on her face was an expression that maddened me: *he's the man and he makes the rules.* At last I went to Hank. He answered reasonably that if I cared to read for a while after the bedtime, that was fine. I found it hard to believe he could sit before me now denying he'd ever made such a compromise.

"We're in bed," I said. "You said we could read for a while after eleven."

"That's not what we agreed to. We decided lights out at eleven."

To have misunderstood a matter this simple was not possible, but tendrils of self-doubt were creeping into my certainty so that I no longer knew what to believe. "Fine," I said, "okay," and turned out my lamp. Kiki did the same. After he left the room I experienced a sensation like an enormous weight pressing against my temples.

"What a jerk," Kiki whispered in the dark. "He did too say we could read."

"I thought I was crazy."

"He's as bad as Mom sometimes."

I pushed Hank from my mind.

"Hey," Kiki said, "I learned something at camp."

"What?"

She produced a long, fluttering fart.

"That's attractive," I said primly.

"But I'm not passing gas." Again I heard the farting noise. "I'm pulling air in."

"What do you mean in?"

She giggled.

"In where?"

"You know," she said. "Down there."

"No way. Do it again."

She did it.

"You're a very special person," I said.

"And you're very spasmodic."

We continued in this vein, made illicit by the transgression of our bedtime, until sleep overtook us.

A sailboat on violet, dusk-reflecting water: this was the slide already projected on the screen as we filed into the darkened living room. Steel drums played on the stereo. Hank handed each of us a piña colada, rumless for the younger kids, alcoholic for the older, and allowed the image to settle over us before he began the slide show he'd prepared of their honeymoon. "What you're about to see on screen you're all going to see for yourselves," he announced, then paused, letting our curiosity simmer. "We're going to charter a sailboat in the Virgin Islands every summer, at least for the next few years," he explained, "and each year some of you will come along." Next summer he'd take the older ones; the year after, Kiki and I would go, then Celeste and Scotty. My mother called to me across the room, "You're going to think you've gone to heaven. The fish are out of this world."

We embarked. Hank provided a running commentary on the slides. There was the day he was chased by a barricuda, the episode of seasickness suffered by my mother, the night in an isolated cove when they heard drums on the island and locked themselves in the hold of the boat. There my mother was now in a big straw hat at the helm of the sailboat, and there in snorkling gear about to plunge into crystalline water. There again, lying on the purest, whitest sand. The names—the Baths on Virgin Gorda, Charlotte Amalie, Stanley's at Cane Garden Bay, Jost Van Dyke—I committed instantly to memory, imagining myself in the midst of that scenery, among those beautiful droplet islands and water of delicately shading blues. These slides were proof of a realm as lost to me as Atlantis. Palms arched over beaches, fresh mangoes could be picked from the trees, and most extraordinary of all, coral reefs encrusted the coves and teemed with tropical fish. I envisioned myself in the Virgin Islands as the person I wanted most to become: worldly, adventurous, self-sustaining. As fantastic as this might be, Hank promised to take me there.

He served us another round of piña coladas, and then at everyone's insistence, we watched the three carousels of slides a second time, following the story as if we'd all been there ourselves. A slide he'd passed quickly over on the first showing, one of the few of him, showed Hank with his mouth clamped shut, his eyes icy, nothing behind him but the gauzy blue sky of morning. Nick said, "Hey, what flew up your butt?"

"I surprised him there," my mother said, laughing. "That was after we'd had such a huge fight Hank wouldn't talk to me until the next day."

"Newlyweds," Ginny teased, and we all laughed. It wasn't difficult to find the incident cute, an expression of the awkward, clumsy love of newlyweds, especially with that tropical backdrop: aqua waters, palm trees, and sunsets, the ingredients of storybook romance. After the slide show, we dispersed happily, Kiki and I to the pool for one last swim, where Hank, fueled by the slide show, photographed us in submarine poses. My mother waved to me from her bedroom window, and after Hank went inside, she closed the shutters. I saw him pass behind her just as the light was extinguished.

The closing of shutters and doors was new. Before she'd married Hank, access to my mother was a palpable feeling in the house; at any time I had only to follow the line that connected us to bring myself to her side. But now, every few nights I felt the distinct, sharp sensation of her absence, and I knew that if I crept down the hall I would find her bedroom door closed and Hank's voice running, controlled but forceful. Like Ginny, we all joked about this, what Hank referred to as their discussions. They were no secret. Still, some nights, I sat on the stairs outside their door to listen, and once or twice Hank spoke loudly enough that I could hear accusations: Nick had come in at three in the morning in defiance of his one o'clock curfew; we were performing our chores sloppily and my mother wasn't watching us to make sure we did them correctly; she did not enforce the rules when he was out of town on business. She tried to respond to these charges with humor, but his voice bulldozed over hers.

My other complaints—the bedtime, the chores—I was easily distracted from by the next thought that occupied my mind, but these discussions were different. Hank was attacking my mother, and it made me regard him distrustfully. Since my nature was not a deeply suspicious one, this distrust would have been transient had Hank not begun to exhibit other inconsistencies. In family games and weekend trips he obviously enjoyed being the king of fun, but every so often without provocation he slipped into the role of grand inquisitor. Not long after the slide show, Hank began a project of silent surveillance. While I cut the grass, he watched me from the front porch, and later, as I washed the dishes, he stood to the side and evaluated my method and thoroughness. We did not exchange words. I pretended he wasn't there, though my heart hammered in my chest as though every movement I made were evidence of my ineptitude.

At a third family meeting, Hank ran down his list, by now familiar, giving personal critiques: Scotty wasn't keeping his shoes in the closet or his bed satisfactorily made; Ginny was leaving stripes of algae when she brushed down the sides of the pool; Nick wasn't sweeping off the gravel at the very top of the driveway; there were blades of grass escaping my lawn mower's scythe. Even my mother was included. From now on dinner was to be ready at six o'clock precisely every night, rather than at variable times between six and seven. She tried to catch my attention, but I felt impatient with her, and instead I rolled my eyes for Kiki's benefit.

"We're moving back to Mom's when school starts," Kiki told me the next day, and Ginny added, "I never knew Dad was such an asshole." I was devastated by the news. The knowing look on their mother's face when I'd helped them move out at the beginning of the summer came back to me. She'd waved, smiling. *Bon voyage and I'll see you when you get back.* Even before Kiki left, I began to miss her wrenchingly. But my mother collapsed into a chair, privately thankful at the prospect of returning to a kind of normalcy. Three fewer children in the house meant a saner life for her, and less pressure from their father.

At the end of August, we went to the beach house in Galveston for a last week-long family beach party. Friends pushed the total to over twenty people, and Hank was in grand form, barbequeing, playing frisbee, drinking beer with the older boys. He attached a fishing line to his chest, splashed his shirt with catsup, and pretended to be a creature Kiki and I reeled in from the sea. She and I bodysurfed in the waves, went on long, moonlit walks to smoke cigarettes and search for luminescence, and fell into our beds each night exhausted. A nostalgic finality perfused those days. Summer was ending, Jake would soon leave for the navy, Ginny and Kiki would return to their mother's. The previous months were already burning themselves into a static, golden picture in my memory. One evening, as I helped my mother prepare dinner, she nudged me and I followed her gaze to the couch. Hank held Celeste in his lap, reading from a children's book. "What is up there on top of that tree? A dog party! A big dog party!" My mother looked almost stunned at this manifestation of her most private, fervent prayers. For the life he made possible, I too was willing to suffer Hank's disappointment in my filial performance. The instances he made me feel low and battered were countered by at least as many others when I felt that I could soar to the sun, and this, I understood for the first time in my life, was the meaning of compromise.

13

I lay in bed reading ***Finches and Soft-Billed Birds*** until late in the morning when hunger finally drove me downstairs. It was my spring break, and I was using it as an opportunity for languor. En route to the kitchen I happened upon my mother, who stood gazing out the glass panels of the front door, statuesque. Startled, she spun to face me. She was dressed in a serious-colored suit with big shoulders, a style I'd seen her wear only for travel on trains or airplanes, for public appearances, a First Lady sort of suit. On her head sat a Russian-looking hat of checkered tweed. It didn't look bad, but a hat! She was fidgety, excited.

"What on earth are you doing?" I asked.

My mother straightened the fine leather gloves she wore as naturally as if they were her dirt-encrusted gardening gloves. "Hank is picking me up. We have an appointment."

"You look nice."

She smiled but didn't explain further. Hank's car swung into the driveway, and my mother bounded out the door, waving to me through the car window as they drove off.

A mysterious exuberance carried me on to the kitchen, lifted my arm to pour cereal into a bowl, and infected the quotidian routine of my day. It had been many months since I'd seen my mother happy, and I knew that something specific, and probably enormous, was emerging to cause her change of mood. The suit, the smile. The appointment almost certainly was with a doctor, and that could only mean one thing. I danced a celebratory jig in the privacy of my room.

When my mother returned in the early afternoon, I kept my hope private. I did not ask how the appointment had gone. She changed out of the suit into her usual garb, an ethnic and flowing dress that covered the outlines of her body in its folds, while Celeste, Scotty, and I kept her company in her room. My mother and I grinned at each other every so often, as though no words needed to pass between us in order to share the secret.

Throughout the fall and winter, hopefulness had been available in limited quantities. For one thing, my fish had begun dying. I found first the queen angel, then a wrasse, then a blue damsel lying on its side nearly drained of color, rapidly pumping its gills, and I watched helplessly until the fish finally gave up fighting to live. Studying my books again, I saw that the answer lay in the miasma of saltwater chemistry, chapters I had previously glossed over, and as many times as I read them now the discussions of nitrate and nitrite balance remained impenetrable. It did not occur to me to ask for help. So I continued the regimen of feeding and cleaning I did understand, and each dead fish I scooped out with a net, then dropped into a plastic bag in the freezer. Despite the soaring cost, my mother dutifully replaced them until I finally asked her to stop. At night, she sat with me in the dark, watching the aquarium as its population dwindled. I did not tell her it was my fault the fish were dying.

My silence echoed the silence of my mother; she did not speak to me about her marriage. More and more often, I sat on the stairs outside the closed bedroom door that muffled what could no longer be laughed off as discussions, as though somehow my proximity might protect her from her husband's awful disappointment. A secret passageway led from an upstairs closet into the attic, and from there I could slide across beams and position myself above their room. Hank never shouted, but his words came clearly through the light fixture in the ceiling. The disgust in his voice was too painful to endure for long.

"John is lazy. He doesn't lift a finger around the house. You haven't taught any of them to respect you." Another time: "Nick is running loose. He takes advantage of you and you don't even see it."

"I raised my children on trust," my mother protested.

"Don't be ridiculous. You can't trust them. Every child will lie. They'll get away with as much as you let them. They have to be controlled, that's all they understand."

And once, my mother's cry: "I am not a country club wife."

Rules multiplied, governing our table manners, comportment, personal hygiene, dress, and study habits; breaking them was taken by Hank as a personal injury. Our first Christmas together was a disaster. In compliance with his wishes, my mother had gotten a job, working through the autumn to finance her gift giving. She was proud of herself, but as we opened our presents, he proclaimed her to be extravagant and undisciplined, closing his eyes and putting a hand to his stomach as though he were truly going to be ill. Afterward, he lectured me for not affecting enough sincerity in my thank-yous. He'd once been a force that pulled us together, but after that first summer Hank spun us away centrifugally. Nick and John worked late nearly every night, Ginny rarely spent time with us, Celeste and Scotty played in their rooms, and I nearly lived at the house of my best friend Paul. Paul had a tame cockatiel for a pet, an elegant gray bird with a yellow crest, which spurred me into getting my own, and so I leapt, swinging from one vine to the next, from aquatic to avian pursuits. My mother leapt with me, and in several months the aquariums were replaced with birdcages.

Fortunately, Kiki continued to spend every weekend at our house. With her it was a remarkably simple feat to recapture the headlong joy of the previous summer, and usually for her visits Hank reverted to the freewheeling, fun-loving personality my mother had married. When my stepfather was bad, he was terrible, but when he was good, he was so very, very good that he made us blind to the bad, or rather, we became willing to be blinded.

In this way we passed two hundred days.

At dinner, my suspicions about my mother's appointment were confirmed. Halfway around the world on that March evening, Jake's aircraft carrier was plowing through the Indian Ocean, but the remaining nine of us had gathered here for the weekend, another I hoped was present in embryonic form, and we were having one of our dinners in the old, rowdy style. We lingered at the table, laughing and telling stories, and talk drifted to the upcoming trip to the Virgin Islands. This summer only the older kids were going, but it was still a topic that got me worked up probably more than was advisable. In contrast, I noticed, my mother was quiet, somewhat removed. I asked her if she wasn't looking forward to it.

"I don't think I'll be going this year, honey." My throat seized before I could ask her about this revelation, made more dramatic by the fact she hardly appeared disappointed. Instead, she possessed a knowing, calmly authoritative power. She raised her voice and addressed the table. "Before anyone leaves, I have an announcement to make."

Faces like sunflowers turned toward her. I saw that I was fiercely pinching my own arms.

"I'm going to have a baby," my mother said.

A supernova exploded inside me. I had never in my life felt such happiness. A din of shouts and celebratory noise erupted, then the questions rained down on my mother, who sat radiant at the head of the table. Ginny: "When is it due?" "I'm already three months pregnant, so sometime in October." John: "What will you name it?" "We haven't chosen names yet. Since I'm such an old lady—" "You're not old," I cried. "Since I'm forty and at a higher risk than I used to be, I'm going to have a test that will show if the baby has any birth defects, and it will also tell us whether it's a boy or a girl." Celeste: "A girl!"

There were some silences at the table, Kiki's for one, but my heart was tumbling too joyfully to pay attention. Only when my mother made entreaties to Nick did I notice that he sat mutely against the back wall, his mouth drawn tight in an attitude not unlike my father's. "You haven't said much," she called softly.

"I knew already." He threw his words like punches. "I have eyes. I can see."

Our collective high spirits could not be dashed by his single note of discord. We made toasts, came up with outlandish names for the baby, and put our ears to my mother's stomach. But later as I was washing the dishes, I overheard her catch up to Nick in the hallway. "Honey," she said, "are you alright?"

"I think it's just crazy to have a kid."

"Oh, honey."

"No, it's stupid. Do you understand what you're doing?"

"I've certainly had enough children by now—"

"Do you see what you're doing to yourself?"

She laughed. "This isn't about *me*."

"Do you really believe a baby will help?"

In my room I covered the cages with towels for the night; the birds rustled and peeped, then settled down. Pounding music began to thrum the wall that separated my room from Nick's, then he poked his head in my door to ask if the music was too loud. Curtly I answered no, but he turned it down anyway. I was furious, draconian; I did not think I could ever forgive him. Years would pass before I admitted that only Nick had called attention to what the rest of us, though we also had eyes, refused to see.

Hank sought me out for a little talk. Now that my mother was going to have a baby, he said, she really had to take it easy. I could help by taking over some of her work. Certainly I could do my own laundry and make my lunch for school, and while I was at it, I could also make lunch for Celeste and Scotty. Where I could really make a difference, though, was with the grocery shopping, since it was an errand that kept her on her feet for hours. Hank's voice was as smooth as cake frosting, but he was losing his subtlety. The joy he took in regulating my behavior was too evident to be misread. He stood over me, talking on while I kept my face absolutely blank to hide my fury. I would not give him the pleasure of cultivating my anger.

I also would never let him know that I enjoyed the jobs, especially the grocery shopping. Performing an errand so vital to our family made me feel even more connected to my mother, as well as to the baby she carried. One or two afternoons a week, the trek to Rice Food Market took me through the undulating hills behind our house where I'd played as a child. Sometimes I'd rest there or dawdle on the bridge over the bayou, trying to spot in the shallow water one of the water moccasins or alligators we'd scared each other with, then I moved on. Over time I grew to know the topography of the grocery and the contents of its aisles as intimately as the layout of those hills. Filling my cart, I experienced a satisfying sense of adult purpose, and the familiar names—Oscar Mayer, Sara Lee, Mrs. Baird's—I regarded as warmly as old friends.

The supermarket was not a place of loneliness, unlike my own house. I had been used to leisurely mornings with my mother in the kitchen before I walked to school, but now Hank kept her confined in the bedroom. Alone, I ate a bowl of cereal, made three lunches, then, steeling myself, traveled the length of the house to where my mother lay in bed, as though she were delicate or sickly, still in her nightgown, her legs raised up on pillows to ease the pressure on her varicose veins. Her stomach grew rounder by the week. I kissed her good-bye and tried not to catch Hank's notice, because then he would demand a kiss also, once the sweetest of rules he'd instituted, now torture.

Between me and my older brothers there was a minor generation gap. I was still a child, my mind filled with thoughts of games, the miseries of homework, and my home, which was the center of the world, but they both had jobs that kept them away from the house until past dinnertime, John in a restaurant and Nick in a motorcycle shop. And though he made sure to load me down with chores, Hank took extra care in the few hours they were available to confront them, especially Nick, who by nature was more rebellious, and therefore more tempting bait. One Friday night as Nick was leaving the house, Hank caught up with him. "Hey, where're you going?" he asked, with the casual interest of a buddy.

"Over to Ed's," Nick said.

"What're you going to do there?"

"Hang out."

Hank's laugh came out like a whisper. "No, really, where are you going?"

"I said over to Ed's house."

"Right."

Nick got into his car.

"Well," Hank said. "It's about ten right now. I think twelve is a reasonable time for you to be home, don't you?"

"No, I don't." Nick slammed the car door shut, backed his Toyota out of the garage, and hot-rodded across the front yard to the street, while Hank maintained his practiced stoniness. It was, perhaps, Nick's sweetest victory, though it was not long-lasting. Several weeks later Jake came home on leave. Over a welcoming dinner of roast duck and goose, hunted by Hank the previous winter, he entertained us with bawdy tales of navy life, hinting at girls in every Oriental port. In the past six months, Jake had become even brawnier and was now sporting a dark mustache that gave him a rakishly unsavory air, prompting his father to announce he'd grow one also. "I thought we'd have a big barbeque tomorrow," Hank said as dinner was winding up, then called down to Nick at the opposite end of the table. "Do you think you could pick up some things at the store for me?"

"I'm leaving at six in the morning for a motocross race," Nick said.

"Then you could go tonight."

"I need to get ready for the race tonight. Also, I'm going over to my dad's to see my grandmother. She's only here for the weekend. Maybe someone else could go to the store."

"I asked you to go."

"Well, I'm sorry, I can't."

Their talk was interspersed with laughs, the clattering of plates, other simultaneous dramatics. Kiki was admiring the present Jake had brought her, a carved wooden cup from Haiti, but Ginny was trying to escape his notice. Before Jake's arrival, she and I had engaged in lengthy conferences over what she should do: in her older brother's absence she'd begun dating his best friend.

Hank had not taken his eyes off Nick. "So, you're going over to Ed's tonight, did you say?"

"I said I'm going to my father's."

"Right. To see your grandmother."

"That's what I said."

"Your grandmother is very important to you, isn't she?"

"As a matter of fact, she is."

"You just can't wait to go see her."

"Would you get off my back?" Nick's shout stunned the rest of us into silence. "I am so sick of your bullshit."

Hank raised his voice, but even so it was level, cool, maddening. "I'm afraid it's your bullshit we need to talk about."

"What bullshit is that?" Nick cried.

"Your mother buys it, but I don't."

"Buys what?"

"I know what you're trying to pull."

"Tell me what I'm trying to pull."

Nick was up to no good with his friends, Hank accused, the veins on his forehead suddenly prominent. Nick never accounted for his whereabouts. He drove his car across the lawn. He didn't do enough around the house. He still didn't sweep the pebbles from the top of the driveway.

And Hank was a tyrant, Nick countered. He was petty, controlling. He was talking out his ass.

They struck their volley back and forth across the length of the dining room table, shocking for its volume and its publicity, while the rest of us excused ourselves one by one until only my mother remained. Ginny, Kiki, and I conferred in the kitchen: we should have seen this coming; Hank had been pushing Nick for a long time. Peeking back through the door, I saw my mother's face cast down in such profound misery that I returned and pulled her from the room. As I washed the dishes, she leaned against the counter with her arms folded across her chest and her eyes on the floor. The shouting continued. A half hour passed, an hour, and the heat in their voices had not diminished. I wanted to tell her, It's just a fight, nothing serious, Nick has always been the one who bucked authority; but I didn't believe it myself. To my amazement, however, after two hours the battle finally diffused into laughter and ribbing, but still, I knew there was no going back. Nick was not prevented, either by Hank or his own resentments, from going on the sailing trip to the Virgin Islands several weeks later, but within days of their return he'd packed his bags into his Toyota. He traveled to California with his friend Ed for the rest of the summer, then to college, and to Europe the summer after. He never lived with us again.

But Nick was eighteen, ready to take flight from the nest, and there was nothing unusual in that. We didn't have to examine too closely the circumstances surrounding his departure, and after he left, we resettled into a halcyon period. At night Hank pored over the baby books he'd purchased, marking relevant passages with a yellow highlighter, and my mother looked on hopefully, buoyed by the unheard-of prospect of a husband interested in helping her with child care. To celebrate their first anniversary, they went out to dinner alone, leaving the house as hushed as a museum. Soon enough, the door to their bedroom was closed in the evenings. When I had the fortitude, I listened from my attic perch to Hank's charges, occasionally as ridiculous and baseless as that my mother was having an affair with Kirby, the Christian singer who'd gone to Hollywood and recently returned, but more often he struck the same tired notes: her unsuitability as a mother and the insubstantiveness of her character. She rarely defended herself. My mother emerged from these sessions stretching her hands out to the solidity of the walls for support. Her pregnancy suffused her with a rosy physical strength that belied the erosion of her spirit, but her deepening unhappiness seeped through the house, a pall too frightening for me to face. I could not talk about it, not to my mother, nor to Kiki or John. And so I turned away from her.

My friend Paul lived a bicycle ride away. In the super-eight movies that he and I had begun producing every day after school, our own versions of *Frankenstein,* the Battle of the Alamo, and silent films with rapacious landlords, Paul was always the director. I didn't mind. His tastes were far more sophisticated than mine—he loved the Marx Brothers, Buster Keaton, and other classics that I found old-fashioned or boring—and I respected his critical sense. Besides, all the equipment was his. On location at the San Jacinto monument and the battleship *Texas,* Paul told me to perform certain actions and gestures, and to these I could add my own personal embellishments, passions and angers that otherwise found no expression. From the roof of a downtown skyscraper I threw fluttering into the sky two bags of money I'd stolen from a bank. I took potshots at Texas Rangers, emerged from a fiery car wreck unscathed. Paul costumed me as a Mexican *bandido* with a handlebar mustache, a hunchbacked laboratory assistant, a rock band groupie in hot pants and an Afro wig. Bending myself to his artistic will allowed me a heady, if indirect, freedom.

The climactic scene of our latest movie was a wedding, in which I was to marry a bronze bust he'd taken from a pedestal in his mother's garden. Paul wanted me to be the bride. He had the veil, he said, but I would need to find a dress and appropriate shoes.

I told him I didn't want to.

He asked me what I meant.

I told him there was no way I was going to wear a dress.

Paul said nothing. He just shook his head sadly with an awful look on his face. The next afternoon while my mother was out of the house, I pilfered from her closet a plain white dress and a pair of white sandals with moderately high heels. I stuffed them into a paper sack and waited for Paul and his mother to pick me up. We drove to an open field not far from my house that was slated to be bulldozed for the construction of a fancy hotel, and in the backseat I slipped the dress over my head, keeping on my blue jean cutoffs beneath it. Checking for possible witnesses to my humiliation as we walked out into the center of the field, I slipped in a patch of mud, which oozed up between my toes, and my mind raced frantically to determine how I might clean the sandals before my mother noticed they were missing.

Paul set up the camera, described his vision of the scene, blocked out the steps, and we ran through it a couple of times. The rehearsal began to unravel the cords of my anxiety, and I started having fun. Lugging the classically featured bronze head to a cardboard altar, I enjoyed the light feel of the dress, how it fluttered at my knees. I felt light myself, suddenly unburdened of the weights of my old life. Under Paul's direction, I threw back my veil and planted a lingering kiss on cool, bronze lips. A passerby stared, and I waved hello, feeling wicked in my tranvestism. By the time we finished shooting the scene, I finally inhabited that dress, and risky as I knew it was, I was still wearing it when Paul's mother dropped me off at home.

From the back door to the stairs my sandals clacked against the wooden floor, but the first carpeted stair silenced them. Relief made me weak. I stood still for a moment, smiling to myself.

"What on earth are you doing?"

I whipped around to face my mother. She looked as though she were witness to unspeakable horror, her eyes signaling disapproval so dark and deep that it sliced through me like a blade. I mumbled something about the movie, Paul, a wedding.

"That's not funny." Her words were stones striking me.

I went up the stairs to my room and removed the dress, which could not have stung me more had it been dipped in acid. While my mother cooked dinner, I replaced the dress and sandals, polished clean of mud, precisely where I'd found them in her closet. Throughout the meal I could not meet her gaze. I ached as if with fever. Afterward I stood outside her bedroom door, closer than usual, wanting to be near her. Hank's voice ran monotonously low and controlled, and once or twice she interrupted in plaintive defense. I could imagine his complaints too clearly: we children couldn't be trusted, she spoiled us, she was subversive in his efforts to discipline us, our table manners were embarrassing, we never said *yes sir* or *yes ma'am,* our clothes were ratty, our fingernails were dirty, our minds full of undisciplined, shameful thoughts. We were guilty. She was guilty.

I returned to my room and lay on the bed, where my pet cockatiel flew to my shoulder. She tucked her head beneath my chin and sat immobile while I scratched her neck. Now that Nick was gone, I missed the raucous edge of his music, the nightly lullaby that had launched me into animal dreams. "Tommy can you hear me?" I sang softly to my bird. "Tommy can you feel me?"

My mother was trapped; she would never accept the failure of her marriage, never move to dissolve it. In the equation of this family, our happiness was a negligible quantity; it was the price she and I were both willing to pay. A man was necessary to reconnect the circle. He made us whole, even if to keep him we'd sacrificed a home in which we were allowed to be ourselves. No matter; this I knew I could survive. What made me fearful, I realized now, and what was not survivable, was that Hank severed the bond I shared with my mother. She anchored me to the world. Only through her did I understand how to live in a way that was good or, at the very least, honest and trusting and well intentioned. She alone had sown in me a belief in my abilities, the power to reveal beauty hidden all around us, and a dogged faith to follow what I loved. Without her, I saw no beauty, I had no faith. When she drew away from me as she had done tonight, or when she became lost herself, which was happening more and more of the time, everything I had ever known or felt or believed fell into darkness.

14

At the far end of the house, in the study beyond my mother's bedroom, John and Hank were engaged in battle. For three days, ever since my mother had gone to Alabama to be by her father's hospital bedside, their voices had carried upstairs to my room. The fight concerned a work project Hank had given John. In addition to our regular chores, Hank's vision of home improvement had grown to include more arduous, large-scale industries. I'd helped grade a swampy section of the back lawn, Nick had refinished the playroom floor, and on their return from the Caribbean sailing trip, Hank concocted a similar plan for John. Running across the front of our house was a porch about seventy feet in length of Saltillo tile, which had darkened over the years with stains of various origin. The porch would be scrubbed clean by John, Hank proposed, then sealed so that it wouldn't stain again; and since families were partnerships, he, Hank, would do the sealing. John did not find the terms unreasonable, and he immediately set to work. Unlike our oldest brother, he was no rebel, and unlike me, he had his feet firmly planted on the ground, by far the most serious and unselfish of us children. For weeks he brushed the tiles on his knees, in the hours before work and on his days off, using an acid solution that burned his hands right through the gloves he wore. Methodically, he advanced from one end of the porch to the other, and at the end of July he reached his goal. The pale yellow and rose shadings of the tiles were beautifully restored. Weeks passed, and Hank did not find time to apply the sealant. Summer thunderstorms raged. Mildew crept over the tiles with remarkable speed, obscuring all of John's work. Hours after my mother left for Alabama, Hank ordered him to clean the tiles again.

John refused.

Hank escorted him back to the study. "I didn't ask you. I told you. You will clean them again."

"We had a deal."

"I don't know what you're talking about."

"And you didn't fulfill your part of the bargain."

"We didn't have a deal."

"Yes, we did." John's voice shot high with disbelief.

"It doesn't matter whether we did or not. The porch needs to be cleaned again."

"You clean it. I cleaned it once and you reneged."

"You'll clean it again."

"I won't."

"You will, or else you will leave this house."

When I couldn't stand the fighting any longer, I went outside to my aviary. In six months, my avian population had grown explosively, fueled primarily by my mother's enthusiasm, as well as by some minor breeding successes, until the cages containing finches, lovebirds, and cockatiels overflowed from my bedroom to the bathroom down the hall. In May I'd sprung on her an idea I'd been nursing: why not build an aviary and move all the birds outside? Her eyes grew wide and she clapped her hands together. "Yes!" she exclaimed, and I knew I'd tapped into that old nerve of hers, the one that fired up when confronted with a visionary plan. "Of course we'll have to ask Hank," she said on further consideration, and I felt my hopes dashed. He would say no just to spite me. But one evening I determinedly made my case before him, presenting the drawings I'd sketched and pacing off the site in the side yard where I wanted to build, twenty-five feet by twelve feet. He said he didn't have any problem with the plan and good luck. My mother was thrilled and bought a pair of fire finches to celebrate. In usual fashion, she subsidized my trips to the lumberyard and did not question my design or judgment, though at age thirteen I had never once in my life laid saw to timber. I let my vision guide my hand. While

John scrubbed the porch, I was nailing beams together, laying wire over the frame of the structure, and with the aid of frequent hammer blows to my thumb, becoming very comfortable with blue language. The completed aviary was six feet tall, with an open flight area larger than my bedroom and a smaller, enclosed space to protect the birds from inclement weather, though in spite of the pride I'd earned in its construction, I felt the truth of my mother's pronouncement when she first saw it. "Well, it won't win any beauty contests." She laughed and hugged me, and we spent the next few days landscaping with bushes, honeysuckle vines, and even a banana tree, until its interior was lush and brambly, full of beckoning perches. Together we brought the cages outside to the aviary and set free my finches, birds no more than four inches long from tropical forests and savannahs: fire, lavender, and strawberry finches, green avadavats, goldbreasted and red-eared waxbills, cordon bleus, and tricolored nuns. Motionless in the corner of the aviary, I spent many summer hours observing the birds fly, eat, preen their multicolored feathers, bathe, sing, and eventually mate and raise their young, a population as alive and communal as the family that had inhabited my house only one year earlier. In this microcosmic jungle I'd created, my mind swung open like a door in a breeze, and I felt the barrier that separated me from the external world dissolve. An entire afternoon could pass without my notice. I was free of myself.

Back inside the house, the fight continued without much variation; Hank's strategy employed repetition to wear down his opponent. After a week, my mother returned from Alabama drawn and tired, sunk in private grief. She adored her father. Though he was recuperating from this operation, his health had been steadily declining for some time. Within an hour of her arrival, John spoke to her alone. He explained the circumstances, how Hank had told him he must leave the house if he wouldn't clean the porch again, so he had called my father and was moving out as soon as possible. To my surprise, my mother didn't try to convince him to stay. Hank was furious. "I don't give you permission to go," he shouted. "You will live here and do as I tell you." But two days later John was gone.

Seven months pregnant and exhausted by her father's illness, my mother spat fire, challenging her husband for the first and only time.

"How dare you force my children out of my house? This is my house, in case you've forgotten. They are my children. They belong here."

But that was as much as she could muster, and Hank managed to get in the last word. "Children have to be controlled," he said. "That's all they understand. Without confrontation, there can be no control. You just don't get it, do you?"

On the floor of John's bedroom I lay down and ran my hand over the blue carpet, the fact of the room's emptiness too huge to contemplate. I searched his closet and drawers for relics, but he'd been very thorough, leaving only a pair of dress shoes that didn't fit me. Inside the left one, my hand ran over the altered heel and arch support. A brief bout of polio as an infant had left John with a left foot half a size smaller than the right, an imperfection I'd always found exotic but that, years later, John admitted had grieved him terribly his entire life. This admission helped me to understand at last how closely he held his wounds and that Hank, in going back on their deal, had stung him deeply and forever. But at the time, John's defection was unbelievable to me. I could not comprehend how he found it possible to leave and break our mother's heart. In three months both Nick and John had gone, and I swore to myself that no matter how bad things became, because I knew that Hank would now turn his gaze upon me, I would never abandon her.

At dinner there were now five of us. The table had become too expansive, so we removed the center leaf and I carried it back up to the attic. John's absence was sharply painful, but nearly subsuming it was a restless expectancy. In only weeks, my mother was going to have a baby. Her amniocentesis had shown it to be a boy, who would be named Henry, after his father.

I forced myself down the hall to their bedroom to say good night. Hank sat on the bed alone in his undershirt and boxers, and from the dressing room, I heard the sound of running water. I stared at my stepfather for a moment, then he held out his arms. He wrapped me up in them and drew me to his chest, but I kept my arms at my sides. Hank tightened his grip, my feet left the ground, and he tossed me to the bed, tickling me. I writhed, trying to escape his hands, but my own laughter betrayed me. We began wrestling, rough, tumbling. I threw myself at him. He pinned me down. I jumped on his back with my arms around his neck. He flipped me over and pinned me again. Begging him to release me, I gave myself over to a delight that weakened my body like a drug. My mother had come out of the dressing room and stood beside the bed watching, and the brief look that passed between us said as plainly as words, *Not all is lost.* But was I a traitor to play along, I wondered, to love this man who made me feel for the first time in my life that I belonged?

15

From the window I watched my mother. The white nightgown made her appear beautifully wraithlike in the October twilight as she drifted around the edge of the property, studying the garden as if to anchor herself after her absence. When she'd arrived home from the hospital that afternoon, I hadn't been quite prepared for the distinct humanness of the baby, his thatch of black hair and squashed red face, his fingers with perfectly formed and minute nails, nor was I prepared for the ferocious animal love that possessed me.

I left the window and went out to my mother. She put her arm across my shoulders, letting me support some of her weight, and asked, "What do you think of your new brother?"

"He's beautiful," I said, "and he's so tiny. Is he asleep?"

She nodded. "But not for long." Facing the garden, I could feel her gaze upon me. "You know, don't you," she said, "that Henry is going to take up almost all of my time?"

"Yes." The moment of peace we were sharing now might very well be our last, at least for a while.

"You're going to be a huge help to me."

"I know." I smiled at the rightness of this.

We walked together around the border of the garden. "Maybe this weekend you can help me with some weeding," she said. "It's been a long time since we've done any of that." Then she gave a soft laugh. I looked at her quickly because her laugh had contained that edge of roughness that signaled hurt. "Honey," she asked, "why didn't you come say good-bye to me?"

I understood immediately what she meant: why hadn't I come back to her bedroom to say I was leaving for school, as was my habit, on the morning she'd gone to the hospital?

"I knew I was about to have Henry," she said. "And I was waiting for you to come back so that I could tell you."

"I'm sorry." I put my arm around her and squeezed, but I didn't say that as I was fixing my breakfast that morning, Hank had come into the kitchen and told me to follow him back to their room, and I'd known she was in labor. I watched him saunter down the hall, and I'd gathered my books and gone quietly out the backdoor. In Latin class several hours later, I suddenly said aloud, to no one in particular, "My mom is having a baby now."

Night had fallen fully upon us. My mother kissed the top of my head and told me that she loved me very much.

She hadn't exaggerated; the baby consumed her. Late into the day she stayed in her nightgown and robe, and for months she hardly left the back part of the house where the nursery lay. Her hair grew long as a girl's, and a higher, more saccharine pitch invaded her voice. She used diminutives to excess. I had to admit she'd grown a little boring.

But I didn't mind. The baby was a genuine marvel, and he was never boring. His face bloomed from the scrunched newborn look to one that was handsome and open. His skin was buttery soft to my touch. He grew with what seemed the speed of a vine in the tropics, presenting us regularly with milestones by which we could measure his progress, such as the loss of his beetlelike, shiny black umbilical cord.

After school, I sat with my mother while she nursed Henry, and then she placed him in my arms, a hot, snuggling weight. She taught me how to pick him up with a hand supporting his delicate neck and head. I watched his heartbeat in the soft spot on his cranium where the bones had not fully met. In my opinion, he was an extremely well-behaved baby. He never had colic, he rarely cried, and he smiled frequently, which I refused to believe, though my mother assured me it was true, was the result of gas; he could see that I loved him. She taught me, too, how to fold and pin his diapers. I managed to change them without suffering too much revulsion, but I worried about crib death and often slipped into the nursery to watch Henry sleep. He looked so uncomfortable. His face was mashed sideways into the foam mattress, and he made muffled cries, his eyes twitching in wordless dreams I could not begin to imagine.

With Henry's birth, our house underwent a tectonic shift. This resulted not only from the baby's constant need for attention, but also from the departure of the four older kids. During the first part of my mother's marriage to Hank, they had commanded center stage, but with them out of the picture, the younger population emerged. I still regarded Celeste and Scotty as entities not dissimilar to the furniture, necessary to the household but hardly interesting enough to contemplate, but they flourished under Hank's new attentions. He'd battled to control the older kids, but he was good with Celeste and Scotty, stern but affectionate. He didn't bother with me too often, and besides, he was often away, either on business or at sailing races, his new passion. When my mother and I were with Henry in the nursery, Hank felt as distant as a shadow that occasionally flew over us.

The extra jobs he'd given me during my mother's pregnancy were not rescinded, as I'd known all along they wouldn't be. Instead, with my mother so busy, I gained several more. On winter nights I lit the kerosene heater for the greenhouse, bathed in petrochemical fumes for half an hour until the flames died down and I could place it in with the plants. Two afternoons a week I trod the mile or so to the office of Scotty's speech therapist in order to escort him home. He and I didn't speak much on the walk. Perhaps Scotty's mouth was tired from the hour of trying to cure the stutter he'd recently developed, or maybe my fears for him made me awkward and mute. The speech therapist had recently advised he see a child psychiatrist. Most of the physical problems related to his premature birth had cleared up and so no longer camouflaged the stubborn tantrums or his difficulty in school, signs of a deeper and more disturbing emotional distress. By the time we finally turned the corner onto our street and came into view of the house, I walked toward it gladly. These days I didn't mind so much being home, where I could spend time with my mother and Henry and caring for my birds. Though often frantic, we had achieved a new kind of peacefulness. Scotty and I stepped onto the porch. After John had gone I'd suspected that Hank would reassign the cleaning of the bricks to me, but apparently he'd lost interest. He didn't clean them either, and so they remained mildewed and stained.

My mother had to drive Hank to the airport; he was flying to Virginia for a week of corporate real estate deal making. Kiki and I followed them out to the car, where Hank formally bid us good night.

"We're coming with you," Kiki told him.

"What for?"

"Because we want to keep Mom company," I said. "It's a special occasion."

"But it's almost ten o'clock, and you won't be home before your bedtime."

"Oh, Hank," my mother said, smiling, "just this once. They want to come."

He leveled upon her a look of arctic ice.

"But it's Mom's birthday," I said.

"That doesn't mean you get to change the rules." He got into the car and held his briefcase on his lap, waiting for my mother to join him. She quickly kissed me and Kiki, then slid behind the steering wheel. As they drove off, a simple thing clicked in me, not painful, like the sudden recollection of a necessary errand. I saw that in the two years of their marriage Hank had never honored the pact I thought we'd made, for him to take over responsibility for my mother. He made the money, certainly, but I realized now that the pact had been one-sided.

Kiki and I looked at each other and at the same instant said, "A cake!" We raced inside, excited by the limitation of the hour and ten minutes it would take my mother to drive a round trip to the airport, and there we had the good fortune to find all the ingredients we required. We mixed them with brutal haste and set the cake to bake. Just in case she returned early, we turned the kitchen lights off and sat in the dark, keeping an eye on the street and singing top-forty lyrics to each other. "Loving you is easy 'cause you're beautiful," Kiki sang as she removed the cake from the oven. "Hey, it actually looks half decent." I was searching drawers and cabinets for any candles they could yield, including a votive candle with a mosquito congealed in its wax. Just as the lights of the station wagon swept into the driveway, we finished with a great flinging of pots and pans into the sink.

My mother entered the house and passed only feet away from where Kiki and I stood like topiary children beside an assortment of houseplants. Silently we stole behind her. She poked her head into the nursery to check on Henry, then continued through her bedroom to the dressing room, where at last she turned and found us at the door. Startled, she put a hand to her heart. "You two should be in bed," she admonished, "or else I'll get in trouble." From behind my back I produced the cake, and her mouth fell open. Kiki and I sang out, "Happy Birthday." Momentarily my mother acted confused, first reaching for the cake and then for Kiki to give her a hug, and suddenly she burst out sobbing, grabbing at me as if at a life preserver. Then she snapped up, wiping her eyes, and said, "I don't know what's gotten into me." From the bathroom counter she took a nail file and deftly sliced three pieces of cake. We ate them over the sink.

16

My mother gave me a book about the birds and the bees. Nick and John had each read it when they were my age, she said, handing me a rather slim blue volume called *For Boys Only,* and she believed it had helped them both. Helped them with what? I wanted to know, though I was grateful the inevitable sex talk had arrived in printed form so that we didn't have to speak about it.

For as long as I could remember, I'd been ashamed of my body; it was too small, too skinny, too uncoordinated, a far cry from meeting the expectations of my father, a hearty sporting man. For several years, kids at school had talked of spin-the-bottle parties and been caught French-kissing behind classroom dividers, but these hormonal forays still felt to me, at thirteen, as far beyond my experience as interplanetary exploration. Instead, I engaged in surreptitious, bookish research. The *Cosmopolitan* magazines in my mother's room I secretly read cover to cover. Whenever I visited a particular friend's house, I pulled *Everything You Always Wanted to Know About Sex** from the bookshelf and spirited it away to backrooms. I acquired a taste for trashy literature, reading *The Adventurers* and *The Other Side of Midnight* way past my bedtime in search of mysteries revealed. I'd heard that a book called *The Joy of Sex* contained actual pictures, and hoped against hope that it would miraculously make itself available to me. These studies had made me fairly well versed among my peers in the information of sex, but learned as I was, the biology of reproduction, anatomical names, and the concepts of foreplay and simultaneous orgasm hardly scratched the surface of my cravings. I was trying for the impossible, to reach, with words, the feel of taut skin beneath my hand, the hot flower of another mouth upon my own.

I read *For Boys Only* in one sitting. In some areas it was helpfully candid; the sore lumps around my nipples were not the cancer I had privately dreaded. It also served as a surprisingly explicit guidebook for masturbation, of which my inert sexual imagination had provided me with no previous knowledge. But most of the book was maddeningly veiled. Intercourse was described only as an act in which male elements left the body, and was to be performed only after marriage, which was its natural and normal place. Outside of marriage, sexual intercourse became "unlawful, dangerous, and terribly selfish," for reasons not specified in the text. I read that even deep kissing should best be reserved for after the wedding, at such time when children were wanted. Occasionally the book drifted into lurid territory. Abortion frequently killed women, it reported; pornography was a million-dollar industry aimed at debauching young people and should be reported to government agents; and homosexuals were described as "thirty- or forty-year-old sex offenders . . . whispering dirty suggestions to others like themselves, or to innocent kids they can get hold of."

A lot of this I found preposterous. In response to my mother's gullibility to written tracts, especially the Bible, books of pop psychology, and any form of advertising, I had developed a healthy dose of skepticism for those same sources. But I was also impressionable. On one level, I understood that my mother had responded favorably to the book because of its religious timbre, its directness in the absence of my real father, and its adamant upholding of such old-fashioned standbys as no sex before marriage. On another, less reasonable level, I was disturbed by the book and felt a heightened shamefulness about my sexual curiosity. My mother didn't mention the book to me again; she assumed I had read it and, a good student, digested its contents. For me, though, *For Boys Only* was another dead end. I returned to *Jaws*, where two people were embarking on an extramarital affair, the woman described as glisteningly open, the man stiff as a flagpole. For weeks my heart raced to this image. I followed the masturbatory guidelines to the letter.

As soon as school let out, Kiki and I were in the pool practicing our snorkling technique: dive, surface, blow hard like a whale, breathe with even breaths. After two years of anticipation, only weeks now separated us from our sailing trip to the Virgin Islands. The approaching trip and the lazy sumptuousness of summer's heat put a rosy spin on family life. Our practice turned into a performance of water ballet for Hank and my mother, who called out pointers from the pool steps, Henry in my mother's lap. As if also in preparation for the islands, they drank piña coladas out of plastic tumblers, and my mother wore a bathing suit Hank had brought back to her from the previous trip, a scandalous, loosely woven macramé number that covered only the most private parts.

Kiki and I threw a dog food bowl, a brick, and some sticks into the deep end to serve as simulated reef and treasure, but that didn't sustain our interest for long. During a contest to see which of us could stay underwater longest, we watched each other's face through our masks, then kicked to the surface among the air bubbles of our laughter. Kiki pressed her mask against my chest and burst up shrieking, "There are little hairs around your nipple!" In a fit of embarrassment I accidentally socked her in the jaw. She accused me of doing it on purpose and ran inside, then returned, taking the baby from our parents to a shady spot in the yard. She ignored me, and feeling guilty, I resumed my snorkling practice in solitary penance, diving to collect the objects from the bottom of the pool, expelling the water from my snorkle, listening to my own hoarse breaths.

Lying on the cement floor of the pool as still as a sting ray, I noticed my mother and Hank moving from the steps into the shallow end. The clear underwater vision granted me by the mask gave me something of a shock: two virtually naked bodies without heads, a woman's legs straddling a man's waist and her arms around his shoulders. Nonchalantly, I surfaced, took breath, and paddled around the pool with my heart in my throat, intermittently glancing over at them when courage allowed. They were pressed up against the pool wall, where they murmured and laughed softly. I was appalled. Hank caught my eye with a look that told me to get lost, but I was incapable of leaving. On several instances during my aquarium days, the electric current of the fluorescent light had inexplicably been conducted into the water itself, where the fish swam jerkily, agitated, in electric shock. That was how I felt now. A haze seemed to have fallen across my vision. Could they actually be having sex, I wondered, even through their swimsuits?

At last they untangled themselves and emerged from the water. "Could you two take care of Henry for a while?" my mother called. "We're going inside for a nap." Kiki shot me a stare that warned not to come close. As soon as the door shut behind Hank and my mother, I raced dripping into the house and headed upstairs. In the closet of John's old room, I pulled away the panel to my secret passageway and climbed into the hot, dark atmosphere of the attic. Cracks of light shone through the shingles above me, enough to guide my tiptoeing steps along the slender attic beams. Over their room I stifled my rough breathing. I felt faint, almost sick. I could hear nothing. A sheet rustled, then nothing again. When at last my heart slowed, I inched back along the beam away from my espionage. My sweat smelled of chlorine.

"Where is Martha's Vineyard?" I asked the next day.

"Massachusetts," my mother said. She spoke to the sink as she washed dishes. "It's an island."

"Sounds cold."

"That's where they're filming *Jaws*," Kiki said.

"They're using three mechanical sharks." I couldn't approach this topic without performing mildly spasmodic movements, adrenaline pumping in my veins. "You'll let us see it, won't you, even if it's rated R?"

My mother knew I wasn't referring to the violence, though it included the bloody chomping deaths of several children. While Kiki and I were flying through the book, some extrasensory maternal perception informed her of its sexual content, and though she hadn't prohibited us from reading it, she'd been vocally disapproving. She sighed. "Oh, honey, I don't know."

"Please, you have to."

"There isn't really that much sex in it," Kiki promised.

"Hardly any," I said.

"It's not even described, only implied."

My mother turned to face us. "It saddens me, to be honest, to have you hear those kinds of messages. I know it's not your fault. Sex is everywhere these days, so of course you don't want to listen to some old lady like your mother. But it's such a wonderful thing between a man and a woman who love each other, who are married. A truly beautiful thing." Rarely had I seen her so impassioned, and though chiding thoughts blossomed in my head out of discomfort with her speaking about sex even in such veiled terms, as well as from believing her out of touch with changing times, her conviction came from a private knowledge that I certainly did not possess. It commanded respect.

"But I know what it is," Kiki said. She laid a hand over her heart. "I know here that it's just as you say. A movie isn't going to teach me to believe something else."

My mother put her palm to Kiki's cheek, her expression amused and loving, but when she looked at me, I shrugged. I wasn't making any claims that I understood the shifting, hurricane forces of physical and spiritual passions, within marriage or without. But I wanted to understand. Her talk of sex as something as pure and beautiful as the white light of the Lord only deepened this wish. I felt grateful that in the sexual arena Hank and my mother could find this connection; he was certainly a physical creature, easy and spontaneous with his touch, inhabiting his body as thoroughly as an animal. But if their sexual life were powerful enough to counter the enmity I had been witness to, then contrary to my mother's words, there was, I felt sure, an element of darkness to it.

"Maybe," Hank said, "Kiki and Michael could take off from school, and we could all sail around the world for a year."

"Yes," Kiki and I cried.

"Wouldn't that be a dream?" my mother said.

It was evening, our first night on the boat, and we were watching the sunset from a private cove on Norman Island. In the previous days Hank had escorted us through a rain forest in Puerto Rico, through the cobbled streets of Old San Juan, and on a propeller plane over the Sargasso Sea. Already I'd experienced the rush of more tropical adventure than my entire life had previously afforded me, and I saw nothing to prevent the plan he'd just proposed from reaching fruition.

For the next week we sailed among the Virgin Islands, both American and British, the names like those from pirate's logs—Tortola, Virgin Gorda, Mosquito. By day we snorkled above coral reefs diademed with rock beauties, beau gregories, French angels, and sparkling others I identified in the fish books I'd brought from home, and by night our laughs echoed over the coves we'd anchored in, heard only by whatever mongoose, frangipani, or puffer fish caught the sound. We attempted to make a cake in the sailboat's kerosene oven, only to scoop out a gelatinous slop for dessert. After running aground in a shallow passage, Hank sent me and Kiki inching out along the boom, hanging over the water like trapeze artists in order to rock the boat off the sandbar. Diving beneath one of the magnificent boulders strewn about the beach at the Baths, I discovered a barracuda inspecting me at such close range that my mother heard my snorkled shouts a hundred yards away. When it was time to return home, I not only brought back a t-shirt from Stanley's restaurant in Cane Garden Bay and a box of what I thought were Cuban cigars for my father; I also carried a new belief that I was heir to the extraordinary possibilities of the world. It seemed to me my family was not unlike the fanworms, barnacles, or coral polyps we'd gazed at beneath the clear Caribbean water, which, when danger passed, shyly flowered from their shells into glorious, brilliant life.

And so, on the afternoon in late August when my mother approached the aviary, where I was planting a new extension, and stared at me through the wire, I was not prepared for her brittle words.

"Hank is leaving me," she said.

17

"What did you say?" The words, foolish as they sounded, were flung out of my mouth, as though I'd been smacked in the head by a great fist. Physical sensations of astonishment rushed up to confound me. I stood leaning heavily on a shovel, but my body plummeted through infinite space. Sounds of birds and cicadas vibrated harshly in my ears, and my vision tricked me into seeing the aviary walls fall away, leaving my mother and me to face each other alone, not two feet distant.

"He's not happy in the marriage." She was grim but matter-of-fact. "I've been telling him for a long time that if he wanted a divorce he'd have to be the one to ask for it. I wasn't going to. He just told me he'd made up his mind."

"Just now?"

"Yes."

"He wants a divorce?"

"Yes."

"He wasn't happy?"

"No."

"And you were?"

She didn't answer, her face bland while I felt mine hardening into granite. We continued to stare at each other through the wire mesh. It was there after all, a silver fabric between us. At last she said, "I haven't told anyone else," and returned to the house.

The door closed, and after a pause, I continued with my

work. The August heat invigorated me. Sodden with sweat, my shirt kept my skin cool as I hacked at dry dirt with the shovel, hefted shrubs into the excavations, and buried their bundles of roots. I dragged a hose in to water the plants, then found myself sitting with the gurgling hose still in my hand while the birds flitted through the branches of their new territory and pecked at the overturned soil. I didn't know how long I'd been there. I was stupid, really, to be surprised; any idiot could have seen this coming for miles. It had been a miserable marriage from the beginning. I pressed my thumb to the nozzle, and in the falling mist the finches bathed ecstatically.

Stealthily I entered the house and ascended the stairs to my room, where my cockatiel Bok Choy flew to my shoulder. I saw Jake, recently set free from the navy, and some of his friends roughhousing in the pool below, their play sloshing waves over the sides. Fans of water crept over the hot cement, evaporating at the edges. Just beyond the reach of their splashes Hank lay on a chaise with his eyes closed, sunning himself like a snake on a rock. I pretended to shoot him. My mother came out of the house, still dressed in the shorts and t-shirt I'd seen her in earlier, but a purse dangled from one elbow and she'd put on lipstick. Her stride was informed by purpose. As she spoke to Hank, he shaded his eyes with a hand to his brow, and I could see only his mouth breaking into a laugh. Then my mother bent down and gave him a deep, prolonged kiss.

Dark confusion and anger crowded upon me. I pushed away from the window just as Jake and his friends began to whoop. If she could kiss him like that, then I understood nothing of human motivation, and any answer to the questions that skittered about my mind like roadside trash—when was he leaving? where would he live? how would we get money?—could not help me. Bok Choy bit my ear to get attention. I scratched her head until the afternoon light dimmed into evening and I heard my mother calling me down to dinner.

At the table, Jake and his two pals, one tall and big-nosed, the other stern and rather handsome, were already assembled. Hank sauntered in and said, "Hey guys."

"Hey, Big H," the big-nosed one said.

All of my energy was required to say nothing. In my eyes, Hank now wore the uniform of an intruder.

"So tell us about this new school you're going to," he said halfway through the meal.

I looked up. Hank was addressing me. "St. John's," I said. "Not much to tell."

"I hear there are lots of rich kids there."

"Just like me." Monosyllables helped. I may have even whispered. The surface of our lives was so fragile we had to tread in satin shoes.

Big-nose said, "I hear the girls there are all pretty doggy."

"What a terrible thing to say," my mother said, but she laughed with the rest of them.

Jake and his father began conferring about the roads his future might take, and I took the chance to escape. In my room I contemplated the possibility that I was the crazy one, that I lived in an otherwise normal family. The next evening Hank didn't come home from work.

"So he's gone?" I asked my mother.

She was feeding dinner to Henry, who banged his fists on the sides of his high chair. "He's on a trip," she said. "He'll be back on Thursday."

If he's going to leave, I wanted to scream, then he must leave. I forced myself to contain the words; they wanted to split me open, explode me into shards. Hank returned several days later and maintained his regular schedule. Each morning he dressed and went to work. Each evening we ate dinner together at six o'clock. My mother cared for Henry, worked in her garden, ran errands. I felt dangerous, mad.

At last I confronted her.

"He's decided to stay," she said.

"What do you mean stay? He said he was going."

"He changed his mind."

"He's not asking for a divorce anymore?"

"No, he's not."

"Why?"

"Because he's decided not to leave."

"Is that what you want?"

"We're going to try to work it out."

"Is that what you want?"

"Yes."

In her opacity I saw reflected my own hard, polished anger. A coldness seeped into my heart, freezing me. I became untouchable. From that distance, I could offer my mother neither support nor forgiveness, not one word of understanding. Then she put her hand on my arm, and I wished fiercely to break the spell, to crack apart my icy self and show her how much I loved her. I longed to recapture the time when I could lay my head in my mother's lap, with her hand stroking my hair, and all the problems of the world would vanish. "I'm sorry I told you he was leaving," she said. "I shouldn't have told you that. He's not leaving."

A week earlier I'd received an offer of admission from St. John's School, which my father had been pressing me to attend for several years, not only for its rigorous academics but also because, in his words, "Anybody who's anybody in this town sends their kids to St. John's." I dreaded going there. My mother was especially sympathetic; the school represented for both of us all of my father's values—the snobbery and elitism—we despised, but it also seemed to take on responsibility for everything oppressive in our lives. At a meeting with one of the school administrators, she actually laughed in his face because he'd suggested I might have a more difficult time at St. John's than I'd had at my previous school.

The administrator's warning proved to be well founded. School began, and my grades plummeted. My mind was not on my work. I was wrested of friends. In the rigid social hierarchy of my new school, I'd been delegated by an unseen committee to join a group of bookish, unathletic types only one step up from the true, calculator-toting nerds. One of my classmates happened to be my stepsister Beth, with whom I enjoyed a warm familiarity at my father's house, but under the roof of St. John's we did not exchange a word. She had spent three unhappy years climbing the school social ladder, and though I despised the popular kids, vocal in my abuse of them both at home and at school, secretly I planned how I would rise, like Beth, to take my place among them. For the time being, I went doggedly through classes with my energy focused on making no egregious gaffes that might jeopardize this plan.

My old school had been within easy walking distance of home, but St. John's commanded a corner in the ritzy part of town, not far from my father's house. Though my mother found a car pool for me in the morning, Hank would not allow her to pick me up in the afternoons, insisting instead that I take the bus. At first I liked how public transportation took me into the great maw of city life. I got to be on familiar terms with one of the bus drivers, a stocky ex-GI who told me stories of playing soccer with steel-toed boots against German soldiers and the satisfying crunch from the well-placed kick to a shin. One afternoon during a thunderstorm my mother was waiting for me outside the school gates, and when Hank found out he had a fit of near apoplexy, forbidding her ever to pick me up again. From then on I was resolute in my decision not to ride the bus. As fall turned crisply cool, I began walking the six miles home. I passed through residential neighborhoods, over the railroad tracks, under the freeway, cut south at the Galleria, and across the last two open fields left in the area, where billboards advertised the imminent construction of a skyscraper complex. In early evening I arrived home and went straight to my room, where Bok Choy greeted me with the flutter of wings and a beaky kiss.

There was no further mention of my stepfather leaving, but neither was there evidence of their redoubled effort to save the marriage. Now they fought openly with cutting, sarcastic words, or else they were grimly silent. Once, when Kiki was visiting for the weekend, Hank took hold of my mother's shoulders and forcibly shoved her from their bedroom, and afterward I listened to Kiki's tearful reaction. Impatient, I restrained myself from telling her that her father had nearly called it quits already, but not because I believed he was really staying. I had heard the truth in my mother's first announcement by the aviary, that the marriage was over. They would move toward that conclusion as inexorably, as slowly, as planets in their orbits. Nothing I could do would hurry them. I hunkered down and waited.

18

I was obsessed with birds. My three aviaries supported a population of over fifty finches, cockatiels, and lovebirds. From the ads in the back of *American Cagebird* magazine, I struck up correspondence with breeders around the country. Aviary maintenance required much of my free time, including the preparation of a diet that consisted not only of seeds, but of fruits and vegetables, mealworms, grubs of any variety I could gather, fruit flies, thistle, millet sprays, the backbone of cuttlefish, and, somewhat disturbingly, hard-boiled eggs. For nesting materials, I offered grass shoots, lint from the dryer, and the cuttings of my own hair.

At night I lay in bed planning big plans. I would sell a clutch of lovebird nestlings to raise the $175 I needed for a pair of Lady Goulds. From Australia, these were the most brilliant of finches, their plumage a painter's palette of colors. My first parrot aviary would be built of steel pipe and hurricane fence to withstand their powerful beaks, and inside, like Noah, I would place one pair of grand eclectus, the male, a plain green, outshone by a startling female of purple, blue, red, and black. They cost over a thousand dollars, and I had no idea how I would raise the money, but I had faith that somehow, perhaps with my mother's help, these birds would come into my possession.

In sleep, I slipped into dreams inhabited by birds, dreams of worry and disaster. I stepped outside to find that all of my finches had escaped from the aviary and were flitting about the trees, their survival impossible without my care. Cats caught them through the wire, and rats broke in, tearing the birds apart in their teeth. The worst dreams were those in which I forgot to feed them or give them water, and my own carelessness resulted in their deaths.

The rustle of feathered wings woke me each morning; then I felt the light steps of Bok Choy padding up the length of my bed. She nibbled my hair, gave me kisses to my lips until I roused myself. Dressed in my St. John's uniform, I went out into the humid beginning of day to give the birds fresh water. One fall morning, just as I heard the honk of the car pool, I noticed that two of the fledglings recently raised by the strawberry finches appeared to be missing. In the afternoon I made a thorough search to find that they had disappeared without a trace. I inspected the aviary for holes and fortified any suspicious or weak points through which they might have escaped, but two days later a lavender and a green singing finch were gone, and two days after that a pair of fire finches. By then, I knew I was up against a predator, most likely a snake squeezing through the half-inch mesh at night, and when I stepped into the yard the next morning, there it was, a four-foot-long sinuous form climbing up the inside of the wire, the two lumps in its gut preventing it from escaping. I swept up a shovel, threw open the aviary door, knocked the snake to the ground, and only after I'd chopped off its head did I stop yelling. After school I split the snake open with a knife, using scientific care to recover my birds. I found them entire and undigested, their feathers slick as if they'd just bathed, and gave them a proper burial in the corner of the yard. The snake I burned.

Defeating the enemy, I'd incurred heavy losses; it hardly felt like victory. Nor could I fully believe the danger to be past. My instinct proved correct. Word had apparently gotten out in snake town, because several days later I looked through the hole of a nest box to see a wall of reddish scales. My thoughts on execution, I slowly removed the nest box from the aviary, took up the shovel, and dropped the box to the ground. A snake bigger than the last slithered out, five feet long and fat with the nestlings and parents it had just swallowed. As I pinned the snake with the shovel, its length coiled and wrapped upward along my leg. I jumped and landed with both feet upon the shovel's blade, and the snake fell limp.

On Saturday, my mother packed up Henry with extra diapers and a bottle of juice and buckled him into the baby seat in the station wagon. Because of the duration of the drive and the exotic atmosphere of our destination, the trip, which took us beyond the port and the ship channel to far eastern Houston, held the thrill of minor adventure. We were going to the house of Georgia Rosencutter, a woman I'd met at a bird show during the summer, who was renowned among Houston bird circles. Initially we had begun visiting Georgia for the fun of it, then she became my supplier of seed, and later, after much discussion on the topic of her deteriorating health, my mother suggested that I work for her. I wasn't without qualms at the prospect of mixing friendship with employment, but I liked the idea of no longer having to rely wholly on my mother to finance my avian life, so I agreed.

Sometime in late morning, we pulled up to the Rosencutters', a small, flattened, rust-colored house whose lawn was overgrown with grasses, shrubs, and the rusted parts of abandoned machinery. Georgia greeted us at the door, a woman hardly bigger than a bird herself. She had a kind, prematurely wrinkled face, close-cropped hair, and eyes made owlish by thick glasses. She was diabetic and nearly blind.

"Georgia," my mother cried. "What have you done now?" She was speaking about the splint on Georgia's right hand, which held two fingers extended. This was a new injury, but by no means a new occurrence. She nearly always had a cast or sling of some sort, recuperating from something recently broken; the diabetes made her bones brittle.

"I snapped it on something," Georgia said. "I don't even know how."

"Oh, Lord," my mother said. "He certainly gives you your share."

"That He does."

"But He'll see you through."

"I'm sure He will."

The house smelled overpoweringly of cigarette smoke and the mustiness of birds. Different calls spiked the air: a parrot's screech, a mynah's piercing bell tone, the chattering of lorikeets. Little dogs scurried under our feet scattering birdseed hulls, and every planar surface was jammed with figurines and bird-show trophies. Though politeness forbade her from saying so, even to me, it was the kind of house that horrified my mother, the kind that reflected something undisciplined and disordered in herself.

My mother murmured encouragement to Georgia, repeatedly citing the grace of the Lord, and Georgia voiced hope that her health would not force her to give up her birds. She made admiring comments about Henry, whose eyes grew large taking in the chaotic scene, but she maintained the distance of one who had decided not to make the same purchase herself. Then my mother left, and I went to work.

Georgia's aviaries were very nearly the size of her house; they filled the backyard, with only a narrow pathway around them for access. Like me, she concentrated on finches, but she also had several rare soft-bills, including a pair of endangered white mynahs for which she had a special permit. She'd been loaned the mynahs by a zoo to try her hand at breeding them. One aviary was filled with fiery orange weaver birds from Africa, and another held an injured hawk that a neighborhood boy had shot with a pellet gun. The finch aviary contained five breeding pairs each of roughly the same ten species I owned, but unlike mine, this was no dreamy-eyed operation. A pair of finches sold for an average price of $50, and in a good season she might produce three hundred birds.

The aviaries had large interior sections, well-built structures with insulated walls and cement floors. Armed with a paint scraper, I cleaned every surface—the walls, floor, and wooden beams—of bird droppings, then mopped them with an antiseptic wash. It was not arduous work, but it lacked significant redeeming features. The interior of the aviary reliably maintained a temperature of ninety degrees throughout the seasons. The droppings atomized into dust clouds that, in a space without ventilation, I could not help but inhale for several hours. The birds fled into the outdoor flight, so I did not even have the consolation of watching them, though of course, being other people's birds, they held substantially less interest than my own.

When I'd finished scraping and inhaling, I telephoned my mother, who promised to bundle Henry up that minute and return to pick me up, but I knew it would be at least an hour and a half before she arrived. While I waited, I kept company with Georgia, drinking Cokes and discussing new happenings in the bird world.

"We got the autopsy results back," she told me.

A pair of tricolored nuns I'd bought from her had died the day after I'd taken them home; she promised to replace them, but she wanted to know the cause. "What happened?" I asked.

"They ate rancid seed. It's hard to know where they ate it. Maybe in the shipping container. Are you sure you're cleaning out all the old seed?"

I nodded, but it wasn't true. In fact, I hadn't known that seed, uneaten, could transform into poison. On her part, Georgia sat unaware that the African gray parrot perched behind her kept stretching to grab her cigarette in its beak. It made a particularly passionate lunge just as she brought the cigarette to her own lips and nearly fell off its perch. This little drama was only one reason for my discomfort, however. Dwarfed in the big La-Z-Boy chair as if in a throne, Georgia was ruler of this messy kingdom. I was eager to absorb her knowledge, enthusiastic in my ambitions to reach the same flourishing level of business operations as she, but I did not want to end up like her, divorced from the world, broken boned. I pretended to offer myself as a convert, all the while obscuring my true nature so that she couldn't see I was just an ordinary pillager.

Later in the afternoon her husband Carl lumbered into the house and interrupted our conference. He popped open a beer and to my relief took a seat beside us. They were an unlikely pair. He looked fifteen years younger than his wife, lean and muscular, with thick black hair and a broad grin that revealed one black front tooth. Carl cracked jokes until my mother arrived, and then, after Georgia led her into the room, he became suddenly shy.

Georgia and my mother repeated the scene of our morning arrival. The Lord would surely give Georgia strength through her diabetic struggle, my mother softly promised, and Georgia gave a throaty, smoke-soaked laugh in concurrence. Meanwhile, Carl nudged me with an elbow. "How old are you again?" he asked.

"Fourteen."

"I guess we'll still be seeing you for another year or so. That's good. But after that, you'll be going on *dates*. You like birds now, but just wait. I've seen it happen."

At last we backed out of the house and got into the station wagon for the trip home, the Rosencutters waving to us from their doorway. Years later, long after I'd given up birds, Georgia's wizened face leapt out at me from the pages of the Houston newspaper. I read that Carl had left her; she was alone now, virtually blind; she'd sold off all her birds; but still she took in injured raptors and owls for the Park Service and nursed them back to health. If I hadn't known her, I would have dismissed her as one of those crazy little old ladies unconnected to another soul who pass from this life unremembered.

In the car, palpable exhaustion settled upon us. I was exhausted from the heat and work, Henry fussed from being confined so long in his car seat, and while at home my mother seemed to have soaked in a bath of exhaustion. Her movements were as tentative and achingly slow as a sloth's, her body slumped as if too heavy to bear. We entered the freeway, and the part of the drive I most dreaded began.

"It's unbelievable," she said. "I can't take it anymore. I don't know how much longer I can last." She spoke in a monotone, almost detached. "If he wants the marriage over, he's got to be the one to do it. I refuse. I asked for a divorce once in my life. I won't do it again."

I could not bear to look at her. At one time I'd thought she wanted a response, and I felt keenly my failure to provide possible solutions. By now I understood she only wanted me as an audience, her faithful confidante. For the rest of the trip home, she relived terrible moments of her marriage to Hank, both recent and past. Her misery was like a venom; it so paralyzed her it was a miracle she could drive at all.

"Before we were married, he told me that he loved me more than anything in the world. He wanted to live together, but I didn't believe in it." She laughed bitterly. "If we had, I never would have married him. I told John when he left that I understood he had to go, that I'd go with him if I could."

I felt myself becoming pitiless. I wanted to shout at the top of my lungs: Do not lay your life in my hands! This must stop! At the same time I was on the verge of cracking from the impossibility of letting myself feel angry at her. Even more, I felt for Hank a pure, viscous hatred for propelling me away from my mother.

My mother and I were back in the car, on our way to see my pediatrician. We weren't going to Dr. Curtis's office, however, but to his house. Though I hadn't seen him in several years, my mother still took Henry for pediatric care nearly once a week. On one of her recent visits she'd mentioned my birds, and Dr. Curtis admitted to being a bird fancier himself, if only a casual one. He kept ringneck doves and offered to give me a few if I was interested.

My mother loved a bargain, and free things especially. It gave her proof that she was not as extravagant as she'd been accused, so she was in a good mood. My own thoughts surprised me by beginning to travel an extremely familiar, but long overgrown, path. "Dr. Curtis isn't married, is he?" I said.

"No."

"I didn't think so."

"Why do you ask?"

"No reason." I smiled to myself. Maybe after all this time something really would work out between them.

As we got out of the car in front of his house, Dr. Curtis was already coming down the walk to welcome us, and I felt a mild shock at the intimacy of this contact. Gone was his hygienic white doctor's coat. He wore Birkenstocks with thick blue socks, and a tuft of dark hair extruded at the neck of his cotton, Mexican-style shirt. He had a thick, squarish build and was not much taller than my mother, nor for that matter much taller than I. Dr. Curtis greeted us warmly in the hoarse inflections that recalled to me feelings of childish helplessness, but it was an unthreatening memory, even pleasant.

He led us around the house to the backyard, where my mother gushed at its size and lushness, its beautiful old trees, and the lovely garden. "Do you mind if I look around?" she asked.

"Not at all."

Dr. Curtis and I continued to the dove aviary, a cube about eight feet in each dimension nearly engulfed by ivy. We stepped inside. In the dim light, twenty or so doves perched cooing on branches. "How many do you want?" he said.

"I don't know. A couple, I guess."

He moved toward one of the perches and gingerly captured a dove with his bare hand. The birds to either side hardly ruffled their feathers. Dr. Curtis put the dove in a paper grocery sack he'd brought out with him. "I've had these birds a long time," he said. "Lately, rats are getting in here. I'll find a few feathers on the ground where they've dragged the bird out." He placed his hand upon the back of another dove, and as he dropped it into the sack, my attention strayed to his forearm, which was feathered with dark hair. "You can see they don't try to get away."

"I've had a problem with snakes myself," I said. Since I'd last seen him, Dr. Curtis had gone silver at the temples. He had sad, dark eyes, and a gentleness that seemed like a kind of loneliness. He was so similar to my mother, I realized; as a child I must have picked that up. I saw her approaching the aviary from the far corner of the garden.

"How's school going?" he said.

"Fine," I said, then risked truthfulness. "Actually, I hate it. I just started at a new high school."

He nodded. "New schools are tough." He looked me in the eye, sympathetic. "What sort of things are you interested in?"

I shrugged, embarrassed to admit I liked anything. "Birds, I guess. And I love reading."

"Books about birds?"

We laughed.

"He loves to read everything." My mother stood close to the aviary, looking through the wire into the gloom. "When he's reading a book, he may as well be on another planet."

Dr. Curtis and I watched her. It was strange how she was suddenly the outsider, but stranger to me still was speaking to a man without fear, or anger, or suspicion. I felt at ease with myself.

"Well," he said. "I feed them wild birdseed, and grit, of course. They don't need heat in the winter, though it's good to provide a lamp of some sort if they need the warmth. But you know that." He handed me the grocery sack. I hadn't paid attention to how many doves he'd put inside it.

Dr. Curtis stood on the curb as we drove away, and I kept my eyes on him until we turned the corner far down the block, wondering if I would see him again like this, without the professional distance of the white coat. Then I peered into the sack. "He gave me six," I said, looking up at my mother to share my delight, but she was lost in reverie.

"He hasn't spoken to me in three days," she finally said, speaking as if through a haze. "Not a word. I ask him a question and he pretends he doesn't hear me. I keep asking him, 'Hank, what did I do wrong? Why are you punishing me?' and he just gives me that awful look."

Again, I bent close to the bag. The doves sat calmly, occasionally blinking their black, liquid eyes, which caught what little light there was and shone.

"Maybe I changed Henry's diaper the wrong way," she said. I looked up quickly. She was smiling at me. I had never in my life been so grateful for her humor.

"Maybe you forgot to put your napkin in your lap," I said.

"Maybe I served dinner at one minute past six."

"Or maybe I'm not supposed to ride the bus anymore, I'm supposed to carry it."

We were laughing by the time we reached home. My mother followed me to the side yard, where I set to work finishing the last touches on the dove cage, tacking on wire netting and attaching perches. When I was a child, this had been the play yard. The remnants of a sandbox still lay in one corner, and while I worked, my mother sat on the swing set, dividing her attention between me and the aviaries, where finches warbled and where Bok Choy was raising her first brood with a mate that, out of jealousy, I had given no name. A peacefulness settled upon us, as when I had worked beside her in the garden.

"Sometimes when you're at school, I come out here and sit," my mother said. "I could watch the birds for hours. It's heavenly what you've made here." Her voice changed, took on momentum and energy. "Maybe we should get some Lady Goulds," she said. "They're so exquisite."

"You think?"

"I was talking to Georgia, and I think she can find us some. Maybe two pairs."

"But they're so expensive." I didn't really believe that would prevent us; her momentum was infectious.

"We'll find a way." For a moment I stopped my work, and we both looked into space. "I've always dreamed of Lady Goulds," she said.

19

Beneath a low, rainy sky, we shared the freeway with light traffic on our way to visit my mother in the hospital. I listened to Nick respond without rancor to Hank's questions about college, and to Hank's chatty comments, but their talk didn't puncture the stillness of the car. I felt deeply forested in the night. My mother hadn't told me why she was having surgery; she said only that she'd be fine, back on her feet in a couple of days, and I let it go at that. Perhaps I was too frightened to ask for details, but I didn't feel frightened. I simply believed her.

Once we reached the hospital, Nick and I followed Hank down hushed, empty halls with carpeted walls, and for once I was grateful for him. This protective authority was what I expected from a father. An unnerving quality pervaded the hospital air, an attempted freshness that instead held the liquid weight of mercury. I didn't want to pull it into my lungs. We reached a door indistinguishable from the others, and with the care of a cat burglar Hank turned the knob and pushed it open on darkness.

I began to make out my mother's form on the bed. She lay still, as if asleep, but then I saw that she'd been watching us enter the room. Her eyes were open, glinting with the small degree of available light like those of a dove in a sack, and she smiled. Hank put a hand to her shoulder and kissed her forehead. I wanted to cry out at his gentleness. Why now, when it was too late?

"You've come," she said weakly, her words hardly more

than a breath. She tried to sit up, but the effort cost her. She winced in pain, then gave up, unable even to raise her head from the pillow.

Hank took her hand. "Yes," he said. "We're here."

"Hi, Mom," Nick said.

"Hi, honey." She looked at me and smiled, but I couldn't speak. "I feel as though I've been drinking too much Tanqueray gin," she said.

"Mom," I pleaded, but I laughed.

Still, her smile disturbed me. It wasn't her own; it was the result of the anaesthesia, something devilish in her veins. As often as I'd been subject to the turmoil of my mother's emotional life, I considered her physical being no more frail than an ox. Days after Henry was born she was active, indefatigable. She could dip her hands into boiling water without ill effect, cut down a tree with a chain saw. I'd seen her do it. Now I stood witness to the unimaginable truth: she could be brought down.

"I thank the Lord you're boys," she said, the smile still creeping across her face. "You'll never have to have a hysterectomy."

There it was, the reason she was here. Because it had not previously been spoken, the word was shocking, but after a moment I settled down. The operation was a standard, uncomplicated one, I reasoned, and she would recover as quickly as she'd promised. My mother closed her eyes and lay still, as if she'd fallen deeply asleep. Hank asked if we'd mind giving them some time alone. Happy to, I told him.

Nick and I wandered a considerable distance down the hall, then slid with our backs against the wall to the floor. We sat facing each other. "I hate hospitals," he said.

The hallway was deserted, bathed in the half-light of tasteful but dim lamps. "They are pretty depressing," I agreed. Nick kept his eyes on the floor. I hadn't seen him since Christmas four months earlier, and he seemed foreign to me. His hair had been cut short. Whenever he came home from college he treated me with such friendly interest that it made me suspicious. Still, I thought of him as holding on to the end of an escape rope. Not that I wanted to escape quite yet, but he was proof that when I was ready to follow him, I could be sure the other side existed. I wanted to impress him, my college-age brother, so I said, "I can't believe she said that about the gin."

"She's drugged out of her mind."

"It was a big scandal at New Year's. Didn't Mom tell you?"

He shook his head.

Kiki and I had decided that we were going to have a New Year's Eve blowout, I told him, to celebrate the end of the Bicentennial. She stole a bottle of gin from her mother's liquor cabinet, and I took samplings of rum and vodka from ours. As midnight neared, we gagged down the straight booze in the woods beside our house; then, having achieved a state of moderate drunkenness, we took off into the neighborhood, where we stood a Christmas tree up in the middle of the street and waited until a station wagon full of teenagers came hauling along and rammed into it. Then we crashed a keg party, sang loud songs in the street, walked home, and jumped on the trampoline.

In the morning, Hank took Kiki into one room, and my mother took me into another. When Hank had gone out to get the paper that morning, she explained, he'd found a bottle of gin in the ditch, and she wanted to know if I knew anything about it. What she didn't mention was that beside the gin lay two glasses we'd taken from the cupboard, with a pattern easily identifiable as our own. Of course I knew something about it; we were caught red handed. I told her I wasn't going to lie, and she said she didn't expect me to. I admitted the gin was ours.

She and Hank left to go sailing for the day. But Kiki had told her father she didn't know anything about the gin, and he'd believed her. She was in tears when they returned about an hour later. "They'd gotten all the way to the yacht club," I told Nick, whose attention I'd finally captured, "before they compared their stories and found out Kiki had lied and I hadn't."

Down the hall, Hank emerged from my mother's room. Nick and I stood up from the floor, awaiting our stepfather. "So I guess Mom finally won," Nick said.

A month later I was on my way to the hospital again, this time to see my friend Clay, who'd just had an emergency appendectomy. The visit was my mother's idea. She'd bounced back so quickly from her own surgery that I found it easy to put from my mind. On the way we picked up Gloria, Clay's girlfriend and my best friend at St. John's. My mother parked at the hospital entrance but remained in her seat as we got out of the car. She held up a book and said she'd read until we got back.

"Well, we won't be long. Thirty minutes or so," I joked.

"That's fine."

"I'm not serious. I wouldn't stay that long."

I stayed three hours. Once inside, I lost sense of the world beyond Clay's hospital room. Gloria and Clay were in love, and they were my two best friends. The stability of our threesome was hugely gratifying to me. We talked, watched two situation comedies on television, and for a while I played with the controls of Clay's hospital bed, bending and contorting it until he angrily informed us that visiting hours were over.

Gloria and I rode the elevator down making nervous jokes about having made my mother wait all this time. Hers was the only remaining car in the parking lot. As we approached, I saw that my mother's head lay against the window as though she were asleep. The engine was running. I knocked on the hood to rouse her, and she looked up, streetlights catching the tears on her face.

Gloria and I got into the car without a sound. "What were you thinking?" my mother said, putting the car into reverse. "I was waiting down here all that time." She began to cry again. "I just don't know what you were thinking."

"I'm sorry," I said, but I wondered why she hadn't called Clay's room and told us to get downstairs. No more than twenty-five feet had separated her from the receptionist's desk. Still, I knew that my thoughtlessness outweighed any mistake she may have committed.

"I'm sorry to be acting like this," she said to Gloria, "but in case Michael didn't tell you, I was in the hospital myself not long ago, and I'm not really over it."

Then I realized the awful magnitude of my crime. It was not that I had made her wait so long; it was that I had not bothered to understand her grief over the hysterectomy. To me, they'd removed a part of her she didn't need anymore, as unnecessary as an appendix, but to her, I saw now, she had lost her very essence.

After her operation, my mother changed. Hank's accusations lost their power against her. She made light of him to his face, and in the middle of a tirade she stood and walked away.

"Where are you going?" he demanded.

"I just realized that I don't have to sit here and listen to you anymore. You are a ridiculous man."

"And you," he said, "you have a zit on your nose!"

One Saturday, on the way home from the Rosencutters', she pulled off the freeway and parked at a dilapidated building with a two-story facade advertising antiques for sale. "Do you mind if we stop?" she said. "I've been dying to go into this place."

I said of course I didn't mind. We walked across the oyster shell parking lot, the cars on the highway zooming past close enough to kick up a breeze. We left the glaring summer afternoon and stepped inside the cool building, and immediately I was propelled back across years to the days of my childhood adventuring with my mother.

The store was labyrinthine, dark, and dusty. My mother steered one way among chairs and tables, and I another. I squeezed between cabinets filled with antique porcelain and turn-of-the-century bottles of smoky blue glass. On the walls hung rusted branding irons, saddles, and cow skulls. After a while I heard my mother speaking to someone, then there came a male voice in answer. By the time I reached her, she was already writing a check.

She pulled the station wagon close to the entrance and directed me as I loaded chairs into the back. We lashed two tables to the roof, and when there was no more space, she turned with a beaming smile to the store owner. "I guess we'll have to come back for the rest."

"No problem," he said.

"How much more is there?" I asked.

She laughed. "This might be half."

Back on the freeway, I looked over her booty: three sets of four chairs each. One was a delicate carved wood with needlepoint cushions, another of heavier wood, and the last was straight backed with woven cane seats. "What are you going to do with all these?"

She laughed again, in soaring spirits. "I always wanted to sell antiques myself. So why not sell them out of my house? Make some extra money. These were such a good deal I couldn't pass them up."

I appraised the chairs again. It seemed to me they must have come at rock-bottom prices to have qualified as a good deal.

At home, while I was unloading the car, Hank appeared and leaned against a wall to watch me. I brought the chairs into the playroom and began stacking them in a corner, trying to ignore him. Since New Year's, he'd taken extra care to make life difficult for me, questioning everything I did, heckling me at dinner. He hated me for telling the truth about the gin.

I untied the rope and lugged in one of the tables. "What are you doing?" Hank said.

To that same question he would have answered, "What does it look like I'm doing?" his words laced with acid sarcasm, but I said, "Unloading the car," then went outside and hauled in the second table.

"Who told you to put it there?"

"Nobody told me," I said.

"Then why did you?"

I kept my voice even. "I thought it was a good place."

His words came down like hammer blows. "You are not to think. You do only what you are told. You do what I tell you to do."

I still held the table upright, balancing it on my toes. One push with my finger would have sent it crashing to the floor. The molecules of my body had gone into furious motion, expanding, rushing into collisions, converging upon a single point to produce a big bang that would send me splattering into every crevice of the room. So this was the moment of confrontation, I thought. To confront and then control. This was how he had pushed both Nick and John until they could not bear it another moment. But I was not so easily manipulated as they. I breathed in and clamped an iron lid upon my anger, looking Hank in the eye. I would relish the pleasure of frustrating him.

"So, tell me where to stack the furniture," I said.

He pointed to the corner on the opposite side of the room. "Put them there!"

In June I asked my mother if Hank still lived with us, and with a surprised look she said, "Of course he does. He's traveling a lot these days." I hadn't seen him in over a week.

His presence had become vaporous, as though we'd thrown open all the windows to air out the house, and he lingered, slowly diluting. It seemed to me that one day, testing the air, we would decide to close the windows again. This finally occurred at the end of July, when Kiki returned from camp. Jake brought her over that night, and when they arrived my mother was on the telephone. Hank hadn't been home in several days. Kiki took a long look at my mother, then said to me, breathless, "She's not wearing her wedding ring."

I hadn't noticed the absent wedding ring myself, but I supposed that officially decided it. "Well, we knew it would happen," I said.

"No!"

"I don't see why you're surprised." I felt impatient, almost cruel. Kiki was crying now. She ran back toward my mother in the kitchen, but Jake intercepted and led her down the hall. I waited for my mother to get off the phone. At last she hung up.

"Kiki noticed you're not wearing your wedding ring," I said.

"I am too." I heard the same note of hardness in her voice as had set into mine. She held up her hand and showed me the ring.

"Well, she knows, anyway."

"You told her?"

I nodded.

"I went to a lawyer to start divorce proceedings," she said. "I couldn't stand it any longer." She looked at me for a while. We could hear Kiki's cries from a distant part of the house. "He didn't even have the guts to tell his own kids. I'll go talk to her."

"She's with Jake now."

We continued to look at each other, not moving. So Hank was gone at last. For at least a year I'd been unable to think beyond the point of his expulsion from our house, but now that we were free, I saw that the world would quickly, necessarily, rush in upon us. We were arrows that had missed their targets, and now, exhausting our trajectories, we must fall back to earth and land, striking sand, or swamp, or dank humus. I braced myself.

CITY OF GOLD

20

Hefting her scuba tank to the pool's edge, my mother looked like one of those fashionably tough and independent women in television advertisements, with her hair tied back in a ponytail and a weight belt cinched around the waist of her sleek swimsuit like a wide Parisian sash. Then I said, "Mom, you always attach the regulator upside down," and she backed away to let me correct it. For three months we'd been coming to the local YMCA twice a week, to the classroom on Tuesday nights for lectures on first aid, the decompression tables, and poisonous fishes, and to the pool on Thursdays to learn the use of the equipment. This evening, our last class, we were to be put through a series of exercises that would not only test our individual knowledge but also, since no diver was to venture underwater without a buddy, prove how well my mother and I had developed trust and reliance on each other. I set my tank beside hers and began donning my gear, my bare skin sensing the first cool taint of fall in the air. From the garblings of the twenty classmates around us several words repeatedly sprang clear: *regulator, buoyancy compensator, o-ring,* and *Elvis.* On the way to class we'd heard over the radio that Elvis Presley was dead.

At the instructor's signal, I fell back into the water. This was my favorite moment, first the lifting of gravity from my burdened frame, the disorientation among the bubbles of my plunge, and then righting myself as the air bubbles cleared, understanding anew that I was able to draw breath underwater. The initial tests included extended periods of swimming, treading water, and assuming the dead man's float, skills that would enable me to survive being stranded in the open ocean. Under observation for two laps, my mother and I displayed the buddy breathing technique, by which we took breaths from each other's regulator; then I pulled her to safety after discovering her in a feigned state of unconsciousness on the pool floor. For the final test I was to sink fifteen feet to the greatest depth of the pool, remove all of my equipment, come up for breath, then dive down to suit up again in my tank, mask, fins, weight belt, and buoyancy compensator. Leaving my gear in a tangled mess on the bottom, I surfaced and nearly collided into one of my classmates, a big, ursine fellow hanging furtively onto the pool's edge. "Hello," he said, and smiled.

"Hi." I gulped air too soon and dove, searching for my regulator like a man who'd lost his glasses. Once I'd found it, I drew in deep breaths.

At the class break, I found my mother talking to the furtive smiler. "This is Bob," she told me.

"We met."

Bob sat with my mother on the lawn beside the pool, and I sat several feet away, hearing the demure and smiling charm she assumed in the presence of a man who found her attractive. I had forgotten those cadences, but their familiarity came rushing back to me. I stared at the shifting surface of the pool while they chatted, steaming mad.

"Isn't that right, honey?" my mother said, touching my arm.

"Isn't what right?"

"That you and I are going on a diving trip to Mexico as soon as we get certified."

"If you say so."

"Don't you think that would be fun?"

"I'd like to know where you're going to get the money."

Laughing, she said, "I see you didn't forget to take your grump pill tonight."

Holding a roll of aluminum foil up for view, the instructor announced that for the second half of class we were going to have a little fun. We were to cover the inside of our masks with a piece of foil so that no light could intrude, and with our partner decide upon a signal and a specific location in the pool so that we could find each other by tactile means alone.

My mother and I determined our signal, chose a corner in the deep end of the pool, slipped on our masks, and, in perfect blackness, entered the water separately. In my rapid exhalations I heard a spark of fear, but soon I settled into the rhythm of swimming blind, guided by the feel of rough cement beneath my fingers. The downward slope of the pool took me to our corner, and there, tapping twice on my left shoulder and tugging once on my hair, my mother was waiting for me. We clasped hands and set forth. I held one arm out for protection against walls and other divers, moving with her through the water with slow, scissoring beats of our fins.

My forearm was gripped by an outside agent. My mother's hand was ripped from mine. I understood the game at once, but panic spurted through my chest, sending me speedily, carelessly along the bottom to our corner, where I bumped into several other bodies. A hand pulled on my ear. A fist knocked on my mask. Other wrong signals assailed me. I found a shoulder, tapped two times, tugged hair, and then, as the sequence was reiterated upon me, water began leaking into my mouthpiece until I realized I was grinning. My mother and I gripped hands determinedly as we swam off into the black universe.

But after a few moments I sensed another presence churning the water like a Tasmanian devil, and for the second time my mother was pulled away. This devil twirled me in circles and propelled me in some fathomless direction. Stretching my arms to reach for the floor, my hands instead broke through the surface into cold, shocking air. I reoriented myself and returned to our corner, ran through false signals, an arm pinch, a forehead knock, until I discovered my mother. Each of the ten or twelve times we became separated, she was always there when I arrived, and the delight of finding her was as sharp and unexpected as my first underwater breath.

Those of us who gathered at Luther's barbeque restaurant after class were in a celebratory mood. Even my mother had a mug of beer to toast to the end of our course. Elsie, whose hoarse voice I found sexy, sat beside our mop-haired instructor, a rather dim bulb. Bob saved a chair for my mother. In the light I saw that he had a kind and swarthily handsome face, though the large size of his head recalled previous hominids in earth's history. His small, round glasses lent him the look of a bohemian Cro-Magnon. I took a seat beside a man and his two teenage daughters. Still excited from swimming sightless, we were all talking over one another to describe the experience. "The two of you were amazing," the instructor told me and my mother. "Every time I looked over you were together again, stuck like clams. I kept having to pull you apart."

"Like clams?" Elsie teased.

"Well, you know, stuck together."

"Like peas in a pod, maybe."

"Maybe." Their lips curled into smiles.

"Hey," Elsie said, turning to my mother. "Am I crazy or did I see your husband at the beginning of the course in July? Did he quit the class?"

"He quit the marriage," my mother nearly shouted, and brayed a laugh as though this were the punch line to the funniest joke she knew.

Elsie clapped a hand over her mouth and tried to stifle her own laughter. "Oh, God," she cried. "Pardon my big trap." She gulped down half of her beer, then kicked in with a topic fresh on everyone's mind. "I heard Elvis died on the pot. They found him on the bathroom floor. What a way to go."

"Poor soul," my mother said. "He destroyed his life."

"I never understood why he was such a big deal," I said. "When I saw him—"

Elsie swiveled to face me. "You saw Elvis?"

"At the rodeo. When I was little."

"And? Come on. What was he like?"

"I could barely see him. He was on one of those rotating stages way out in the middle of the Astrodome. I could sort of see the sequins on his suit. It was blue."

She dug around for more information—which songs did he sing? did he really shake it up?—but I was unable to unearth much, and she finally returned her attention to the instructor for more interesting fare. Perhaps I remembered so little of Elvis, I might have told her, because I hadn't faced the stage but away from it, unable to take my eyes off the sight of Mrs. Stone and Mrs. Seward, the two neighborhood moms who'd brought the bunch of us kids, screaming, shrieking, and actually pulling their hair with both hands for the entire length of Elvis's show. I was immensely glad not to have to witness the spectacle of my mother doing the same. Turning now, I found her in conversation with Bob. I overheard him say that he'd recently been separated from his wife as well.

It was nearly eleven by the time we left the restaurant, and green lights stretched into the distance, beckoning me to race along the deserted streets all the way home. I kept my speed in check. Now that I had my learner's permit, my mother rarely drove.

"Some people are coming to look at the house tomorrow," she said. "Could you make sure the upstairs looks okay?"

I nodded.

"Honey," she cried. "Would you please answer me when I ask you a question?"

"I nodded my head. That meant yes."

"I can't see you nod your head in the dark. Honestly. If I don't sell the house soon, we're sunk."

Her monologue of money woes had begun as soon as Hank had moved out, and though these worries had a tired familiarity—I'd heard them most of my life—they possessed a new and frightening immediacy. The roof of our house had begun developing leaks and needed to be reshingled. The columns along the front porch were rotting at their bases. These and other forms of dilapidation struck me as the direct, erosive work of fatherlessness, and at night I was kept awake by sounds I was certain were the creakings of housebreakers. I sandwiched my head with a pillow to block out the noise. On the wall of the living room hung a portrait of my mother that looked nothing like her—she stood in a field, wearing a white dress and holding a rose—and every so often Hank had referred to the woman in the painting as Scarlett, a remark that stung from the combined effect of its purposeful cruelty and its accuracy. "All that's missing is Tara burning in the background," he said, but that was missing no longer. Tara had burned. We were living in the rubble.

An orange Volkswagen bug was parked in our driveway. I pulled up behind it and waited for my mother to comment on the car. At last I said, "Who's that, do you think?"

"That's the boarder," she said. "He moved in today."

"The what!"

"Honey, I had to. Marsha had a friend who needed a place to stay, and I had to take him in. I just don't have the money to say no."

It was not obstinacy that muted me. At this confirmation of my worst fears, that even our home offered us no protection, I sank into true despair. "Where is he staying?" I asked quietly.

"In Nick's old room."

"That's right next to mine."

We lugged our scuba gear into the house, and after my mother sent off the baby-sitter, we said good night. "We really will go to Mexico," she promised. "You have helped me so much." Then I ascended the stairs as slowly and effortfully as if the dark were a viscous substance; he was up there, the boarder. Running the length of the second story was one long hallway from which the bedrooms branched off, first John's, then mine, finally Nick's at the end. At the topmost stair I viewed down the narrow tunnel of that hallway an open door, the room warmly illuminated by a lamp. To reach my own room, I began moving toward that door, when, surprisingly, a little dog leapt into the doorway and watched me with alert eyes and ears. I almost laughed in relief and came forward. Then the torso of a man moved into view. He had shaggy brown hair, a mustache, and he was not wearing a shirt. The boarder's eyes locked on to mine, and I halted, immobilized. Then he scooped up the dog with one hand and quickly withdrew. I hurried into my room and locked the door.

By breakfast time the next morning, the boarder had moved out. "He didn't realize there were so many children," my mother said. "Actually, I'm glad. I didn't like having a stranger in the house."

21

My mother was sitting meditatively over a cup of tea when I came in with the groceries. Though only fifteen, I'd been awarded a hardship driver's license, so I no longer required her to fetch me from Rice Food Market after I'd done the shopping. As I carried in the last bags, she said, "I bought a house today."

In response I began putting away the groceries, my back to her. To acknowledge her statement was somehow to make real the events of the last six months. "How did you buy one if you haven't sold this one yet?" I said.

"I didn't have to put down much money, but I signed the papers, and I'm getting a loan."

"Is that wise?"

She was becoming animated. "It's an investment. It's on a hundred and fifty acres."

"Where did you possibly find that much land in Houston?"

"You're going to love it. It's beautiful, and odd, and it has lots of potential. It's perfect for us."

"But where is it?"

"Brookshire," she admitted.

"What's Brookshire?"

"It's a town, goony. About ten miles past Katy."

"Ten miles past Katy?" Disbelief calmed me. "Mom, that's an hour from here."

"More like forty miles. Thirty-eight to be exact. There

are two ponds, and a creek lined with the most beautiful old oaks. We can even have horses."

"You're moving us to the country?"

"I couldn't pass it up. Land out there is already going for twice what I'll pay for this property. We could sell it off immediately and be rich." She tapped her teacup with a fingernail, grinning. "Actually, I'm proud of myself."

We drove west the next weekend beneath grim February skies, my mother and I, Celeste, Scotty, and Henry, with a picnic basket and blanket tucked into the station wagon. While my mother manned the wheel, my place was up front managing Henry's constant activity and turning to keep an eye on Celeste and Scotty. I'd stood beside my mother when she told them Hank was leaving, but their reactions were imperceptible, blank faces, small voices. Not long after, she had gotten together the money to send Scotty to a psychiatrist, grateful and relieved to hand him over to an authority who, she trusted, would get to the root of his problems at last. But recently Celeste seemed to me the more worrisome child; she'd turned fearful of nearly everything, of thunderstorms and the dark, of being alone, and though she was only eleven, and had forever been as slim as a blade, she'd begun proclaiming she was fat.

Each mile along that freeway drive, past jumbled Houston suburbs, industrial parks, and finally fields of rice, I imagined the return journey I would have to make to school each morning for the next two years, and I repeated a private mantra: we will turn off at the next exit, we will turn off at the next exit. Finally, approaching Farm to Market Road 1489, my mother put on the blinker.

At the crossroads stood a truck stop crowded with growling eighteen-wheelers, a barbeque stand, some uninhabited ramshackle buildings, and, distantly across a field, what appeared to be a windowless factory. The town center of Brookshire was not visible to the unaided eye. We'd left far behind the satellites of Houston, but we had not left the coastal plains, which stretched away in all directions, virtually treeless, without a hint of topographic variance. We had arrived in hicksville. My mother followed F.M. 1489 for a couple of miles, then turned onto a dirt road, bumping over a cattle guard. "This is our driveway," she announced with pride. Several red buildings in varying degrees of dilapidation lay on our right, and a small corral crowded the driveway on the left. Ahead was a dingy, gray-yellow field, brought to a halt on the distant side by a thick stand of denuded oaks. In the blank expressions of my siblings I believed I caught the echo of my own low expectations.

"Are we really going to get horses?" Celeste asked, unconvinced.

"Yes, honey, I promise."

"Where's the house?" Scotty said.

"Just watch. I won't spoil the surprise."

Continuing along the field, we encountered what appeared to be a mud hole. "That's the small pond," my mother said brightly. "Isn't it sweet?" The driveway swung around a sharp angle, taking us through the trees, and as we emerged the house swept magnificently into view. It stood on a rise, as massive as a castle, with long, squarish sides of white stucco and arched windows in heavy wooden frames. Four copper-helmeted turrets stood sentry at its front.

"Oh my God," I cried. "You bought the Alamo!"

"Honey," she pleaded. "Please don't use that expression."

"The Alamo?"

The house had been built by a wheeler-dealer who'd gone bankrupt, my mother explained, and no one had lived in it for two years. So, of course, it needed a lot of work. She'd have the exterior painted because the white was excessive and glaring. Burglar bars would be installed on the windows and doors; we'd be very secluded out here, and she didn't want to be worried about our safety.

The heavy wooden door swung open at her push, and Henry took headlong steps across the red tile floor of the front hallway to the center of the house, which rose up to a high ceiling of paned glass. Weak winter sun dappled a twenty-foot-square plot of dirt in which anemic shrubs surrounded an inert cement fountain. "Isn't it unlike anything you've ever seen?" my mother said. "The atrium decided me. I had to have this house."

"Atrium," Henry repeated, his arm around my thigh. He was two, and new words bubbled out of him like springwater.

My mother took in the sweep of the house, which for those two uninhabited years appeared to have been thrown open to prairie whims. The floors were coated with dirt, and thick, grimy cobwebs hung from the ceiling. A tumbleweed had come to comfortable lodging in the corner. "I guess we'll just have to bring in a fire hose," my mother said, then she led us on a tour, outlining her plans. "Of course we'll patch that up," she said in the living room, where a gaping crack snaked across the wall, wide enough to permit a view of the field outside. Wind whistled through it. "And we'll get rid of that hideous thing," she said, pointing to the monstrous chandelier that hung like an iron wagon wheel in the dining room. In one room, a multitude of colored phone lines branched out of the wall like a nest of octopi, the legacy of the wheeler-dealer whose dream this house had been. "This was his office," my mother said, and we regarded the room silently in recognition of his precarious existence, so like our own. All of the bedrooms opened onto the atrium, except mine, which had a separate entrance, an architectural feature that appealed to me greatly. In Celeste's bedroom, one of the turrets formed a circular shower covered in ocean blue tile, like a Pompeian mosaic. "And in mine," my mother said, "there's a marble tub you step down into that is out of this world." We followed her there to view this spectacle, but at her bathroom door she abruptly halted. "Rats! They told me they were going to clean that out." We crowded around her. On the floor of the grotto-sized bathtub lay the carcass of an animal, withered and dry, hardly more than bones. "It's just a possum," she said as we groaned in disgust, then shooed us outside to the backyard, where the swimming pool lay half filled with black water. "I hope you all brought your bathing suits," she called, laughing. A high cinder-block wall enclosed the yard, obscuring the view of the countryside. "We'll knock that down first thing," my mother said. "Isn't it crazy to build a house out here where it's so beautiful and then hem yourself in?"

Drawn back into the house, she shifted into high gear. "Isn't it exciting, Michael? There's a stable right up the road that has some horses for sale. I always wanted a llama, too. And ostriches! We'll plant trees all around the house, big shade trees, and it will be paradise. This house was just waiting for the right person to fall in love with it." She knelt and dug her hand into the dirt of the atrium. "Of course we'll get rid of these terrible shrubs, but the soil's good. The fountain is a wonderful touch. Imagine it when we're done. We'll plant hibiscus and bougainvillea, frangipani, flamboyan, banana trees. Oh Michael, can't you see it?"

Her glittering eyes were able to see the fruition of her plans as clearly as mine viewed the ragged winter landscape through the crack in the wall. But I closed them on the dirty, forsaken rooms of this house, on the miles of freeway that separated me from everything I'd ever known, and for a moment I allowed her vision to filter into mine. The sight was stunning: the atrium grew as lushly dense and flowered as the Panamanian jungles of my mother's childhood, while the fountain jetted sparkling arcs of water, shot through with sunlight. It was her gift to me, that rapturous beauty, and I told her, yes, I could see exactly what she saw.

My mother had backed herself into a corner. She quickly discovered that owning two houses was an even greater financial burden than owning one, and in her desperation to sell the first she accepted an offer fifty thousand dollars less than she was asking, tendered by a couple from California. Tough negotiators, they also demanded she pay for several improvements, terms she felt in no position to dispute. The sale proved to be a stupendous error. The Californians bought our house for $300,000, a sum that left my mother little after settling the mortgage, and three years later, on the hyperinflated Houston real estate market, they sold it for over a million.

In April there appeared in our driveway a blue horse trailer. We didn't have the money to hire a moving company, my mother explained, and after all, it was only thirty-eight miles; we could accomplish the move ourselves. We were fortunate that the new owners were not moving to Texas until July. Attics, closets, cabinets, and wardrobes began to disgorge immense quantities of material, the accumulation of fifteen years of family life, which we loaded into the horse trailer, carried to Brookshire, and deposited. Since Nick was in Germany and John at college, it fell to me and my mother alone to roll up rugs, lug boxes, and single-handedly maneuver dressers down staircases.

Bob, from scuba class, took in these doings with an amused eye. He often arrived as we were returning from our daily trip to Brookshire and sat talking with my mother over a glass of wine, or sometimes not talking at all. Both of their divorces were proceeding at a torturously slow pace, and they countered this with their own quietly measured courtship. Once, I discovered them reclining in chaise longues by the pool beneath the night sky, perfectly silent, gazing up at the stars. An insurance salesman, Bob remained politely uninterested in me for the duration of our acquaintance, an example I emulated. Men were like gnats flying in my face; I could hardly be bothered to brush them away. There was too much work to do.

In June, Bob rented a van and helped to transport the heaviest of our appliances and furniture; in one afternoon, hardly speaking to each other, he and I moved the refrigerator, freezer, washing machine, couches, and beds. We worked well together. We had an understanding. Around that time, my mother switched insurance companies.

"He convinced me his policy was better," she told me without irony.

The day of the California family's arrival rapidly approached, and in the rush to empty the house there was no time to sort or throw anything away, so we carted off boxes of laughably unstylish clothes, moldy camping equipment unused for years, and kindling from the woodpile. My mother was determined to remove everything rather than leave it for the rapacious vultures moving in, and in a fit of anger she dug up all her favorite plants from the garden, virtually destroying years of work. In Brookshire, the plants were promptly eaten by cows. Late one night, driving on the rural freeway, her station wagon threw a piston rod and left her stranded with Henry and the dining room table. At midnight I received a call to rescue them. We lost a week of moving time shopping for a new car, and then the California family showed up three days early.

Two blond parents, three children, a smartly turned out grandmother, and an uncle in a minister's white collar viewed the house in horror; to the casually observing eye it appeared as though we had not even begun to pack. Their moving van idling in the street, all but the grandmother remained diplomatic, then they drafted themselves into hastening our expulsion, cramming boxes with whatever objects lay at hand. "I just don't understand why you're not out of this house," the grandmother spat as she swept into a box a collection of ancient glass vases, half of which my mother would later find broken, then set the box into Celeste's hands.

After we had packed up the last load, I slipped for once into the passenger seat of my mother's car, where I allowed ravenous exhaustion to feast upon me. I closed my eyes and did not give my old home, where my mother had spent two marriages and I my childhood, even a last look.

In spite of all her precautionary talk, money flew from my mother's hands like birds set free. Within the first month, she'd sunk fifteen thousand dollars into the new house. Just the right shade of Mediterranean pink was mixed to paint its exterior, and iron bars were custom wrought for every door and window to protect us from nocturnal prowlers. The cracks in the living room wall were cemented, the black water in the swimming pool replaced with fresh, and the dead possum was removed from my mother's bathtub. We planted the atrium with flowering tropical greenery.

While she directed the small army of workmen, wielding a paint roller herself to save money—one less man to hire—and bolting burglar bars to window frames, I was occupied with a creation of my own. My new aviary would correct all the faults of the old; a masterpiece of engineering, it would contain six large flights. In order to finish its construction before school started, I worked all day and into the evening. One afternoon, my mother came out of the house and watched me nail sheets of corrugated tin upon the aviary roof. "I've just had some terrible news," she said.

I stopped hammering.

"You know Howard Vole?"

I nodded. He was the real estate agent through whom she'd bought the house, and they'd become friendly.

"He just called," she said. "He's been diagnosed with melanoma. The doctors give him only two months to live."

As she looked up at me, she appeared small and unprotected, jarred from the project of this new house she'd thrown all her energy into, that had rooted her, given her such adamant purpose. I imagined the wind might lift her from the ground and spirit her away. Why then, at that moment, did I feel a relief so sweet it was nearly joy? Because a lightning bolt meant for us had been intercepted, and lightning did not strike twice in one place.

22

I could build a structure but I could not tame the elements. Within a week of their release into the completed aviary, most of my birds had vanished, by what specific means besides brutal nature I was never to discover. Rodents and snakes may have carried them off, though my only evidence was the discovery on the third morning of a large rat with its head squeezed through the wire of the floor, struggling to get free. I left it to strangle itself slowly. The hardier doves survived the relentless assault of the prairie wind, but the cockatiels huddled against it with ruffled feathers. When I found Bok Choy's mate dead, already covered with ants, I knew that I could wait no longer; I had to bring the remaining birds inside.

Jokingly, I had always referred to Bok Choy as my best friend, and yet my emotion for her was perhaps the only uncomplicated love I felt for any being on earth. I prepared a cage for her in my room, just as in the old days. As I entered the aviary, she regarded me with alert obsidian eyes, inching away on the perch. Raising her own young over the last two years she'd heard the trumpet of the wild—my human touch was not as captivating as it had once been—but still she stepped gingerly onto my offered finger. Speaking endearments, I tucked her beneath my chin and held one hand over her wings, then left the aviary and tread softly toward the house. At my door, I reached for the knob too quickly, spooking her. Bok broke free and ran up my shoulder with her wings extended. Then she was aloft.

I did not believe I'd lost her. I ran following into the field as she made a wide swooping circle, hearing in her anxious cries the desire to return to me, the one familiar thing in this foreign landscape. My carelessness was shocking to me; why had I not carried her in a cage, a bag, anything? Why had I not held her more tightly? But even as she headed for the trees along the creek I did not think she was leaving. She would land there, take stock, and return. Instead, she circled high above the trees, then aimed northward, and at last I understood she wasn't coming back. My body grew calm. Go, I thought, find others like yourself somewhere, be happy, my oldest friend. I watched until she was only a speck blending into particles of sky; and a part of me died. Numbly, I returned to the house.

My mother, in the middle of hanging a painting, saw my face and leapt down from her chair. "Bok flew away." I spoke evenly but without much force. "I was bringing her inside and she got away from me."

My mother flung the painting to the couch and rushed outside. I did not follow. She looked upward with intense concentration, as though trying to read a message in the sky. For a long time she scanned in every direction, a figure in a field. "She'll come back, I'm sure she will," my mother said when at last she'd come inside, but she was distraught, nearly in tears. She examined my face. "What's wrong with you?" she cried. "You don't even seem sad."

In the "Around Our Town" column of the *Brookshire Banner*, a local weekly with a distribution of two thousand, amid descriptions of bridge club luncheons, tea parties, and the weights of bass recently reeled ashore by town anglers, we read of our arrival in Brookshire. Over time, my family found its place in this town. Celeste and Scotty attended its schools, rode ponies down Main Street in annual parades; Henry was befriended by neighboring farm boys, the descendants of sharecroppers, both white and black. Even my mother, initially rumored to be a rich divorcée from Houston setting herself up for wild, bohemian life, hooked up with some of the townsfolk, rural hippie types, women with waist-length hair and turquoise jewelry, in whose homes animals had achieved an equal status with humans. Only I found no niche in that place. After enduring a long initiation at St. John's, I was unwilling to give up my hard-won friends by switching schools again, even if the price I paid was an hour and a half drive each morning and afternoon. My experience of Brookshire had little to do with the town, but rather with the land—I wandered its ravines, traveled its fence line on horseback—and the home that my mother and I created.

By September the workmen were gone, and, birdless, I threw myself into work for my mother. On the icebox she'd posted a list of home improvement projects that ranged from planting a vegetable garden to removing the three dilapidated barns from the front of the property. Arriving home each afternoon, I chose a task from the list and worked until suppertime. The motorized tiller bucked and kicked like a wild bronco in my arms as I cleared a space for the vegetable garden beside the empty aviary, then I fertilized the dirt with manure I collected from one of the barns. I hung paintings, removed the iron chandelier from the dining room, slid books onto shelves. I planted trees all around the house, flowering vines that would cling to its stucco walls, and two palms at its entrance. At last I tackled the cinder-block wall around the backyard, a project that carried me through the fall. Swinging a sledgehammer, I knocked down the wall block by block and carted away the shards. That is the memory my mother retains of me from our first full season in Brookshire, throwing all my weight into a sledgehammer to bring down that wall, day after day.

What I remember of her is the unflagging energy she wielded to realize her plans for the house, and also her exhaustion. Her divorce was stuck in quagmire. She was often in Houston conferring with lawyers or testifying in court, and at dinner she ranted; Hank was now demanding a share of the money from the sale of the house in Houston. During the day she worked alongside me, her enthusiasm fueling us both—we would plant orchards, build monuments—but in the evening her energy deserted her. She retired alone to her bedroom, and there, on the other side of a closed door, she watched television, an activity I found shocking. In daylight she seemed to shed twenty of her forty-four years, but at sundown she fell under a spell that bent her with old age; what she did not seem to recognize was that it was the spell of loneliness. She had no grown-up companions. The distance between Brookshire and Houston had proved too far for Bob. I could see, when she was deep in her plans, how intoxicated and robust she had become with her new freedom. For the first time in her life she felt powerful. But she suffered from that same freedom.

Then she met a man.

23

lung back in a chair, I squinted at the bright light in my eyes. "Tell your mother I want to set her up with someone," Dr. Musselwhite said, peering into my mouth. His breath fluttered across my face; his metal instruments mercilessly probed my teeth.

I attempted to answer, as I had his previous questions about school and Brookshire, but could produce no more than a honk, and even this was drowned by the coil slurping up saliva inside my cheek. I felt that I was behaving rudely. Here at last was a situation in which Hank could really be of use to me; what was the proper etiquette for conversations with the dentist?

"Who are you going to set her up with?" the dental hygienist asked. Throughout the years I'd been acquainted with this woman, I'd never known her name. Her starched white uniform had become an emblem of flouride and floss.

"You remember Emmett Davis?" Dr. Musselwhite said, scraping along my bicuspid.

"He lost his wife not long ago?"

"To cancer. It just about killed him."

"She was an angel on this earth, I heard."

"Yes, she was." With one of his pointed instruments he poked on a molar until I winced. "And so is your mother," he said to my mouth. "She's just what he needs. He'll fall for her in a minute."

Will he lose her, too? I wondered, but I kept this question to myself. Dr. Musselwhite was spraying a jet of water across my teeth.

"Spit," he ordered. Then to the dental hygienist, "Could we get another X ray of that back molar? There's a sticky spot I want to get a look at."

"Bite," she said, stuffing the cardboard-encased film far back along my jaw, and with her practiced foot she operated the chair. I began my ascent toward the metallic green X-ray machine that swung out on a long radius-and-ulna combination and tapered to a point like a fang. Meanwhile, she was asking Dr. Musselwhite about Emmett Davis; he'd lived in Costa Rica, hadn't he? He was sweet as could be, wasn't he, a real Christian gentleman?

The instrument tray was laid with picks and hooks and mirrors, all of which I could examine clearly because the tray was still situated about eight inches over my legs, a distance that was decreasing with mechanical precision as my chair continued to rise. A sort of stubbornness prevented me from calling the dental hygienist's attention, even when the bar supporting the tray began to press into my shins. "Ow," I said. This exclamation was muffled by the cardboard clamped in my jaw.

She swung the X-ray machine toward my head. Emmett had three children, didn't he? No, two, that's right. The chair bore me inexorably upward into the metal bar. I was fascinated by the resilient properties of my legs.

"Ouch," I said, loudly.

"Oh, Lord," the dental hygienist cried. She tried to pull away the tray, but it was held fast until she'd lowered the chair. As I rubbed my shins, I offered her assurances that I was fine, but she was too distressed to listen. She extracted the film from my mouth and escaped into the recesses of the dentist's office, where I overheard her berating herself.

"It's okay," I called. "Really, it is."

But I didn't see her again that day. Dr. Musselwhite returned with the X-ray results. "You're in luck," he said. "It's not a cavity. We'll see you in six months. And hey, remember to ask your mother if she wants to go on a blind date."

Perhaps she hadn't bargained for the extreme isolation country living provided. Perhaps she missed the vivifying, appreciative gaze of a man. Whatever the reason, my mother agreed to go on the date. I was at my desk working over some geometry problems on the evening Emmett arrived, and a waft of perfume accompanied my mother into my room.

"He's here," she said. "He seems very nice."

"So I've heard." I did not look up from my books.

She stood for a moment beside my desk, waiting shyly, but I was not going to offer to come into the house to meet him. She would have to ask me. What could a man possibly offer us now? "He's taking me to the Cotton Gin for dinner," she said.

"Brookshire's attempt at fine cuisine."

"You don't mind watching the children?" she asked after a minute more.

"Nope."

"There's a frozen pizza, if you don't feel like cooking." She kissed the top of my head, then left me.

The next morning, eating instant oatmeal in the half-light before dawn, I was joined by my mother, and she conferred with me in the dark kitchen. She'd had a nice time, she said, and had immediately felt comfortable and companionable with him. Emmett had led a very interesting life; he'd driven down the Pan-American Highway with his family, everything they owned tied on top of their car, all the way to Costa Rica, where he'd been a rancher for fifteen years. Now he built houses in the suburbs of Houston.

Heartened by this exotic streak in his past, I was more available when Emmett next arrived to escort my mother out on the town. His sturdy frame fit nicely in our front hall, but he carried it with the tentative uncertainty of a country farmer in the city, and I stumbled onto the surprising pleasure of intimidating him with my reserve. His hair was thinning, his sideburns and eyebrows bushy, like a tired, grim Lorne Greene from the last episodes of *Bonanza*. Emmett was as plain and enduring as soil. My eyes focused not on what he possessed but on what he lacked. The quality that distinguished all of the men my mother had previously been involved with, my father, Hank, even Bob—a forcefully male authority, a physical vibrance—was absent in Emmett. He was not a threat; nor was he a savior.

So began Emmett's tenure. It was not long before he occupied the sidelines of our house, watching the bustle and gazing longingly at my mother. He lavished more care and feeling on Celeste, Scotty, and Henry than their own fathers managed to muster, and in return they rewarded him with their attentions, even love. Still, I could never bring myself to discard my chilly cordiality, an attitude that continued to make Emmett nervous; I felt I couldn't be bothered. I was too busy, and too tired. In order to make it to school on time I woke at five in the morning. I didn't get home until late afternoon, and then Henry had to be picked up from child care, there were animals to be fed, chores to be done, cinder-block walls to level. I had no patience for Emmett's melancholic courtship of my mother. Out of the suspicion that his quest to win her heart was futile, he nagged her unremittingly; she spoiled her children, in his opinion, kept a messy house, and didn't comport herself as a woman should. He insisted that her appearance would be improved, and her femininity heightened, with a beehive hairdo and long, fake fingernails.

She laughed off these criticisms. At dinner, his presence didn't intrude upon Henry and Scotty's clowning, Celeste's colorful stories of country schooling, my mother's dreamy plans. "That's so unreasonable," Emmett told her after hearing her latest idea to build a roof of red tile over the house, and she began sketching her design on a napkin. "Michael," he scolded, "don't use so much salt," and I added an extra shake or two.

In spite of my unyielding stance, I was glad that Emmett had appeared. He was a balm to my mother's loneliness during that period, and his bumbling kindness was constant and genuine, the only paternal attention my younger siblings received. For Christmas, Emmett gave me a card with a check folded neatly inside, though the gesture embarrassed both of us. He didn't have much money, and I knew how hard he was trying to win even my grudging acceptance.

During the summer he hired me and my mother to landscape the houses he built in the suburbs. Houston was still growing swiftly, spreading out like a monstrous amoeba in all directions, and these developments at its edge hosted a cataclysm of architectural styles—Tudor, Italian villa, antebellum, Victorian—often incorporated into a single structure. The houses were crammed unattractively against one another on the treeless plain, and it was my mother's job to transform them with her garden designs, my job to dig, mulch, plant, and water. Each morning, she dropped me off to begin, then returned an hour later with the horse trailer full of vegetation, spindly treetops I could see coming from a mile away through the open spaces of the development. All day I labored in the hundred-degree heat, with a cooler full of ice and two cans of Hi-C my only sustenance. It was too hot to eat solid food. When she returned to pick me up in the evening, my mother paced the yard, admiring our work. We both had a particular fondness for these suburban tracts; as the pseudopods of Houston reached westward toward Brookshire, the value of our own land increased exponentially. We drove home with dollar signs in our eyes.

One spring morning about six months after Emmett's first date with my mother, I arose at five in the usual state of hammering unconsciousness, showered, and groggily dressed before I noticed that the state of the body report was sending rather urgent signals of distress. My temperature: 103°. The luxurious folds of my bed claimed me once again until much later in the morning when the sun had risen a respectable distance above the horizon. My mother offered me toast, on which I nibbled, then left the house on errands. I dozed again. A high-pitched whine began to insinuate itself into my dreams, a whine that took on momentum, grew louder until it became a continuous scream, and at last woke me. Through the bars on my window I glimpsed movement out in the distant field, a dark shape jogging through the grass.

Outside, I stood on the patio beside the pool, the cement cooling my bare feet. The day was bright, glaring, and my fever applied to it a wondrous, hallucinatory edge. The almost human scream rooted me while I gauged the strange creature's approach. Now I saw three separate animals, two of our dogs on either side of a third, their jaws clamped firmly upon its neck. But the third animal was not a dog at all. It was a pig with auburn hair, a pig that continued to reel out a piercing, violated scream. Over the rubble of the cinder-block wall and into the backyard they galloped, and at the corner of the swimming pool opposite me the dogs peeled away in concert, as if their movements were choreographed, and the pig, still screaming, leapt into the air and fell with a great cannonballing splash.

The line of its course did not waver. This pig paddled directly across the pool to the point below my feet, where I knelt, grabbed it by the forelimbs, and hefted it from the water. It had finally ceased screaming and momentarily rested in my arms while I crooned to it. The dogs had inflicted wounds on its neck. It began to struggle, and that decided me. Though not much older than a piglet, it was no sack of feathers. I carried this kicking, bleeding pig of mysterious origin to my empty aviary and shut it into one of the flights. Then I took to my bed.

My mother insisted on posting a notice at the local supermarket that we'd found a lost pig, and while she dithered over the thirteen responses, appalled that so many people might actually lie to acquire a free pig—"Free bacon," I corrected her—it fell to me to feed and care for our new charge, for whom Scotty suggested the interim name of Yolanda. Each afternoon I slammed a syringe of antibiotics into Yolanda's tough hide, and her wounds healed quickly, though she learned to run away at the sight of me. Finally my mother chose the claimant whose story most affected her heart—a little boy raising the pig for a Future Farmers of America event—and his family arrived to haul away Yolanda, who squealed with the human scream that first announced her arrival.

An auburn pig's brief appearance in our lives was not an unusual event in those days. Throughout the time we lived in the country a curious phenomenon occurred: farm animals mysteriously appeared at our door at regular intervals. We fed them, and often they would move on, but many of them stayed. Though we never bought the llama or ostrich my mother had envisioned owning, we managed to acquire an entire flock of chickens without a single purchase, a lame burro, an omnivorous billy goat, and a great, lumbering turkey. The turkey was tame and gentle, and when it became evident that he had installed himself in our backyard permanently, we named him Emmett. When we disclosed this to the human Emmett, his feelings didn't appear to be hurt, but he didn't think it was particularly funny either.

24

At the main crossroads in town squatted the Brookshire Post Office, where one gathered mail and gossip from the behemothic postmistress. Often I found our post office box jammed with the magazines my mother subscribed to: *Savvy, Working Woman, Money*. Thoughts of money—the lack of it and how to make more of it—fueled the busy machinery of my mother's mind. Without a man, she had taken the reins into her own hands to ensure for her children a home, food, and clothing. Our 150 acres were a smart investment, she proclaimed; we were going to ride the boom of the Houston real estate market into financial security. My mother stayed up late at night sketching plans, dividing up the land for prospective markets. Since the Brookshire town council had successfully lured several companies into building factories in the area, the front pasture, with its easy highway access, she zoned for light industry. The larger of our two ponds drained into a ravine that wound sinuously through the back fields. Though this ravine was little more than a ditch, in the algae that floated upon its pools my mother sighted the color of legal tender. She planned to excavate the pond and drainage system, create a long, winding waterway, and build a housing community along its shores. The land was going to make us rich.

To aid her in these plans, she enlisted Howard Vole, the local real estate agent who'd been diagnosed with melanoma. She had a good feeling about him—he was her kind of Lord-loving man—in spite of the virulent disease. This Christian soldier worked hard to strike the deal that would deliver my mother once and for all, and to this end he telephoned every afternoon and often called upon her unannounced, throwing compliments on the beauty of the property as liberally as flower petals, as though in practice to prospective buyers. At first I stood somewhat in awe of him, this unpretentious man who lived in the shadow of his own imminent death, a heroic figure, but over time the hyperbole of his compliments took on ridiculous proportions. His chatter became ingratiating, obsequious, and I felt the need to rebuff his insistent intrusion into our lives. Besides, he wasn't doing his job. A year passed and there was no sale, not even a significant nibble.

"Maybe you should think about getting another agent," I suggested to my mother. "He might have too many other things on his mind right now."

"But Howard specializes in rural real estate," she said hotly. "He's very well connected." Her defensiveness signaled me to mind my own business. We both knew that her loyalties were not based solely on business insight or real estate connections; this was a matter of Christian fellowship.

On an overcast, steamy afternoon in spring, around the time Emmett the turkey joined our household, my mother and I were fortifying the chicken coop after one of the dogs had decided to storm the citadel and carry away our best egg layer. We stood up from our work just as a truck turned off the road into our driveway with a strange jiggling contraption in tow. Howard Vole became visible behind the windshield of the nearing tow truck, and the contraption resolved into an ancient, rust-pitted hulk of a car, no longer intact. "Oh, my God," I said, then shot a look at my mother. "I mean, my gosh!"

She gave a hoot of laughter and clapped her hands. "It's that abandoned car that's been sitting off the side of the freeway ever since we moved here. I told Howard Vole the other day that I'd always loved it."

The tow truck rolled to a stop, and the big, rusted aqua sections of the car continued to bounce, suspended and bound up by chains. Clinging to the fenders were long spears of grass that grazed Howard Vole's jacket when he jumped down from the truck to present his offering to my delighted mother. It wasn't a permanent gift, he explained; he just wanted to get some pictures of her standing beside it. She ran inside to get a camera, and he turned to me.

Though his dark hair was natural, it had the badly cut appearance of a hairpiece. Black-rimmed glasses dwarfed his face, and the lapel of his coat was obscured by a flopping, winglike shirt collar. The quality he shared with Emmett, new among my mother's admirers, was a kind of browbeaten resignation. Perhaps this was the result of the cancer, but more likely my mother had started hanging out with nerds. Unlike Emmett, Howard Vole always wanted to involve himself in my concerns and doings, launching valiant attempts to engage me in conversation, but his tone of cahoots turned me cold.

"So, hey, Michael, what are you up to?"

"Not much."

"How's school?"

"Fine."

"And that traffic jam you fight every morning?"

"Still there."

"You sure do work hard. Are you reading anything good?"

"Nope."

My mother returned. He directed her to stand beside the car, where, enlivened, she struck a variety of poses. Howard snapped photos; my mother propped an elbow upon the remains of the car door and looked out across the verdant fields she was trying to divest herself of, the wind blowing her hair and fluttering the hem of her flower-patterned dress. Then it dawned on me: Howard Vole was capable of sabotage. Whether or not he was an ineffectual real estate agent, I realized he had no intention of helping my mother leave this town.

"That guy is crazy," I said as the truck departed.

"But he admires you so. He likes your determined spirit."

"He doesn't know anything about me." I slid into wickedness. "Anyway, wasn't he supposed to die by now?"

"Michael! You're awful. The melanoma went into remission. I told you that."

"His days are numbered," I teased. "Maybe the next realtor will sell the house, at least."

She was beginning to laugh. "I do wonder sometimes how he makes a living."

"Suckers like you."

"Ain't that the truth."

"Or maybe the Lord pays his salary."

Dangerous ground to ridicule, this. I sneaked a glance at her, and her eyes grew huge, as though I'd suggested a real possibility. "Wouldn't it be lovely if He made a big deposit in my bank account, too?"

"But, Mom," I said, "you have your *plans*."

My mother's visions of cold, hard cash slapping her palm were not wholly dependent upon the land. Far from it. She was cooking up schemes on a daily basis to keep us afloat. In spite of her complaints, she took to worrying about money with real gusto; it opened the floodgates of her imagination. The atrium was going to become a café where townspeople could meet for an elegant lunch. She'd sell antiques from her home. A device to keep pets out of potted plants, marketed through mail order catalogues, was just the ticket for plant and animal lovers. She discussed with me at length the guaranteed return of pyramid schemes. For weeks she talked of nothing but the National Park Service; they'd plant pine seedlings on your property and you only paid a fraction of the cost. In fifteen years we could harvest them for timber and make a bundle.

My mother did not consider the possibility of failure. We might move houses, change schools, shed fathers like old, dead skin, but what remained constant was her faith, not only in God but in the future. The iron strength of her faith anchored us, and though I did not share the extent of her belief in God, I believed in her will. Too, I was often skeptical and frustrated. I counseled her against the riskier propositions, especially those that required even the smallest investment; it was unthinkable to part with any of our scant resources, I argued. If we were really so desperate for money, then why didn't she just get a job like other people? Emmett's dissent was broadcast at a much more piercing frequency than mine, however, and the message was unvarying—*you are absolutely out of your mind.* In his voice I heard that of every other man who had tried to impose his will upon her, and so more often than not I threw my loyalty alongside even her most outrageous ideas. She was undeterred by Emmett anyway. "I'm not married to him," she told me in private, "so I don't have to listen to what he says."

She carried her plans to various stages of completion. The atrium did not become a dining establishment, nor did the antiques we'd hauled from Houston like a flock of albatrosses descend from their cobwebbed stacks in the room we'd closed off for storage. A man arrived on a bulldozer to assess the cost of excavating the pond and ravine, but after he'd given his estimate I didn't see him again. My mother labored over the design of her petproofing invention for potted plants, then hired a professional draftsman to prepare the drawings, but no mail order company picked it up. One afternoon, when I returned home from school, the fields had an odd, sown appearance. I stopped the car to look more closely. Row after row of three-inch pine seedlings had been planted over the entire property. As I drove on toward the house, I envisioned the great wooded expanse that would transform our lives into arboreal ones in only several years time, but soon after, we headed into a month-long drought. Not one of the pine seedlings survived.

These failures bounced right off my mother. From whatever mysterious coffers she possessed she managed to pay our bills in the meantime, as had always been the case, and undaunted, she was carefully turning over several new plans in the incubator. Late one night, I discovered a light burning in the kitchen. My mother sat hunched over a large sheet of paper, furiously sketching the outlines of a structure.

"Do you like it?" she asked. "It's our new house."

"Our *new* house? Mom, no."

She turned to me, her eyes fiery. "Howard Vole and I were talking today, and we were thinking that this house would be perfect for a corporate headquarters. It could easily be converted to use for company conferences and getaways. The location is ideal, close to Houston but with the privacy and expansiveness of the country. So, if we sold this house and the back pasture along with it, I could clear my debt and make enough to build another."

"Where might that be?" I said coldly.

"Right across the creek. The trees would shield the two houses from each other. And look." She directed me to her sketch. She'd incorporated the elements she loved from this house—the atrium, the Mexican tile—gotten rid of others, added several from her own imaginings. It was unrealistic, and immensely beautiful. My resistance was no match for her enthusiasm, and soon I was suggesting new elements to the design. Swayed by her plans, her hope, as I had been before and would be many times again, I let her usher me into the gilded future.

25

My father sat comfortably low in an armchair, one leg slung over the other, with a drink balanced on his knee. "I ran into an ex-policeman friend of mine," he was saying, "and he told me that nine times out of ten, if some guy holds you up at gunpoint, you can reach into the pocket of your jacket, like you're reaching for your wallet"—he pantomimed this action, then took aim on me with his hand—"and nine times out of ten, you can pull your own gun out and shoot him before he shoots you." He took a gulp of his drink. "Nine times out of ten."

My stepmother burst out with a laugh. She took a drag from her cigarette, regarding him with deep but not unloving amusement.

"You got to take care of yourself in this world," my father said. "Everyone else is out to fuck you over." He tinkled the ice in his empty tumbler until my stepmother retrieved it and went to the bar to pour a refill. At my father's house, the topic of armed robbery was an inexhaustible one. Nearly all of the houses on his block had been burglarized in the previous year, his next-door neighbor had been paralyzed by a housebreaker's bullet, and he felt certain that his home was similarly targeted for invasion. The subject had come up now because I was on my way out for the evening, and he'd begun drilling me on my technique for hiding the spare key. He eyed me with a smile that was not unlike the one his wife had leveled upon him, appreciative but without hope of understanding the being he was faced with. "So you're going out tomcatting," he said.

"I'm going to see a movie."

"I didn't ask you to tell me what you're doing. You've got to learn to keep your hand close." My stepmother held a fresh whiskey before him. "But son," he said, "how many times have I told you not to leave the house with wet hair? You'll catch cold."

"Dad, don't be ridiculous."

"There's a blow dryer right next to the shower. Just turn it on and dry your hair in five minutes."

"Get serious."

"I am serious. Go on upstairs and dry it."

I moved toward the door. "Dad, I'm late."

"Dry your goddamn hair before you leave this house." His shout redirected my steps, spinning me around and impelling me furiously up the stairs, and yet I was unable to prevent a smile from creeping across my face. The frequent fights I had with my father—their inanity, their simple resolution, the purity of our anger—had begun to seem wonderfully normal to me, even liberating; they might be what passed between any regular father and teenage son.

At sixteen, I was getting to know my father for the first time. All my life he'd remained a figure in the distance, a formidable, frightening quantity with whom I'd dreaded having contact on the two or three instances a year it was unavoidable. Since my mother now lived in the country nearly forty miles from my school, and my father lived less than a mile from it, he'd invited me to spend several nights a week at his house to avoid the commute. Whenever I arrived there, usually in the early evening, my stepmother Helen greeted me. She leaned against the kitchen counter holding a lighted cigarette near her mouth, as though she'd been waiting for the sound of the spare key in the lock. I leafed through the newspaper while she prepared dinner, and we discussed current events, school, her three children, or, most often, the eccentricities of my father's character, which without fail made her shake her head and even laugh outright. She was my doorway to him, and I was so grateful for the information, since he offered so little himself, that only rarely was I struck by Helen's own self-effacement. I knew virtually nothing about her except what I could see, an elegant, pragmatic housewife. Every so often I willed myself to remember that this was the woman who had brought my parents' marriage to an end, but the thought escaped my mind as quickly as an eel glimpsed in murk.

Around dinnertime we heard a car in the garage, the backdoor banged, and Helen and I fell silent. My father was a big man, loud, and he filled the room. "Hello, sweetheart," he boomed, and gave his wife a kiss. Parading before us, he asked, "How do you like my new suit?" We complimented it. He dressed impeccably, in suits he designed himself and had tailor made.

Then he left us and returned in more casual clothes with a drink in his hand. The rest of the family filtered in for dinner. My father traded barbs with my stepbrother Howie and pulled the youngest, Lauren, into his lap. Though Beth and I still passed in the halls at school without exchanging a word, we took this opportunity to conjecture about our classmates. Helen served us our plates while we joked and interrupted one another. Dinnertime was my father's only talkative hour; it was when I felt most welcomed into his house, but also the most foreign. He and his new family addressed each other with nicknames—Papa Bear, Mama Bear, Sister—interacting as easily as any Americans in their home, and I was the student from abroad, smiling and nodding as if in fluent understanding of their language.

After the meal, my father retired to the den, where he fixed another drink. I often found myself following him into that room, taking a seat nearby, and while the television played, listening to him gossip with my stepmother about other people in their social circle, who was making deals with whom, who was getting cheated, who was making money hand over fist. He spoke at length of the stock market, naming companies I never recognized; there was always a deal, a big one, on the verge of coming through for him.

"What deal is that?" I hazarded.

My father smiled and looked at the television. "Something I'm cooking up with Mr. Phelps."

I learned that any direct line of questioning met a wall; he answered obliquely or in monosyllables. Before long I simply waited, silently, patiently, as a filter feeder waits on the ocean floor for passing detritus, and from the stray bits of information about his life he let slip I pieced together a patchwork knowledge. He feared thieves, he loved stocks.

For his living, he worked as the regional head of a New York brokerage firm. But he rankled at taking orders, so on the side he cooked up deals, and this, I came to believe, was how he learned the strategies he used in his personal life as well: secrecy, dodging and feinting, the telling of half-truths, trusting no one. I supposed my father was rich. At least, he lived as though he were; he owned a home in the millionaire part of town, sent me to a private school, drove expensive cars. But he cried poverty as frequently as did my mother. Appearance, he claimed—the clothes, the cars, the house—was worth sacrifice. He never mentioned the things I was most interested in: his rural Alabama childhood, his feelings about my brothers and sister. Nor did he ask me questions about myself.

Talking of money through the evening, my father downed enough scotch to send him at last into silent, glassy-eyed contemplation of the television screen. By then, I'd left him alone and gone upstairs to the bedroom I used. This was John's room—John, my lost brother, who was now at college in Austin. In the three years since Hank had forced John out of my mother's house, I'd rarely seen him, as though he'd defected to a different country, adapted to distant, foreign customs without regret. Late at night, I pored over the few belongings my brother had left in that room—some record albums, a drawer full of socks, a handbook on colleges—but it was not much to know him by.

The barrenness of John's room reflected the greater barrenness of the house. There was no room in which I felt comfortable. I liked my mother's way of living. Any house she inhabited was textured, organic; it breathed life. My mother's new house was like a doorway to her character: the exotic flowers and foliage of the atrium, the sketches splayed upon her desk, stacks of magazines marked for design and business ideas, the Bible open on her bedside table. There were no secrets there. My father's house was a sterile place, full of tasteful furnishings, muted colors, magazines in ordered stacks. Nothing beyond a certain degree of formality could be inferred about its inhabitants, and there did not exist wholly conclusive evidence even for that. To speak at all was to ignore the intuition that one's voice should not rise above a whisper.

When I found myself alone, impelled to penetrate the polished surface of that house, I snooped. Going through drawers and cabinets, stealthily entering my father's bedroom to rifle through his closet, examining the stubs of my stepmother's checkbook, I felt that I might like to become an archeologist; the heart-stopping moment of discovery was more intense than any other pleasure. In drawers throughout the house I found loaded pistols, in my father's dresser a packet of letters written by me and my older brothers from summer camp a decade earlier. I passed hours with my ear to the safe in my stepmother's closet, aching to hear the tumblers fall into place as I slowly turned the knob. One night I cracked open a carved wooden box on a shelf in the den, an arm's length from where my father sat nightly, and discovered the most shocking cache of all: a collection of pictures of my mother—in her wedding dress; holding Nick as a newborn; sitting beside my father at a bar, her hair halfway down her back, he with a cowboy hat perched atop his head, the two of them looking so alike they could have passed for brother and sister. I stuffed them back into the box and stormed. By what right did he keep these pictures? Did Helen know about them? The few memories I possessed of my parents living together were nightmarish—harsh, drunken shouting, the sound of a slap that ever since had echoed in my head—but what child of separated parents does not dream of their reunion, even in the most unlikely circumstances? I spent stores of jealousy on Nick and John, old enough to remember our family sitting at dinner together the way I witnessed my father's new family having dinner now. To staunch these dreams and jealousies, to understand them as unreasonable, even ridiculous, I forced myself to keep in mind the violent decisiveness of our parents' divorce, my father's affair with Helen, and the finality of their subsequent marriage. I could not forgive him for holding on to the pictures.

It was always with relief that I left my father's house and hit the westbound freeway headed for my mother's, though it was no brief flight. I spent nearly four hours a day in my car, inching along miles of freeway amid swarms of other commuters, many of them black-taggers, what we called the nomads with black Michigan license plates and others from the industrial East who'd come to booming Houston in search of jobs. The hours on the road took their toll. Leaving my mother's house at six in the morning, I had to turn the radio to its highest volume in order to keep myself awake; and following an episode in which I fell asleep at the wheel and woke to find my car gliding into the next lane, missing a collision with a pickup truck by a matter of inches, each afternoon I swallowed two caffeine pills before my commute.

Soon enough, I'd return to my father's house for a break. My mother took the opportunity of my shuttling between their houses to relay messages to my father. The messages were pleas for money, since he owed her thousands of dollars in back child support. As I left for school at dawn, my mother handed me a sealed envelope, and this I dropped on my father's desk with the rest of his mail. The envelope remained there unopened for several days until I carried it to him personally and requested him, if he would do nothing more, simply to read the note inside. He gave me a thunderous look as he opened the envelope, glanced at the card, and dropped it on the nearest table or countertop without comment. Then I read the note. These cards were always humorous, cajoling reminders that she needed that monthly child support check and not to forget. Regardless, he paid her sporadically, when the whim took him. In his view, she was just another creditor to evade.

When her gentle approach failed, my mother became desperate. "Please," she begged me, "tell him I have to have that money. He has to understand I can't survive without that money."

In answer, he barked, "Tell your mother I don't have any money to give her."

So began an escalation of hostilities.

"Tell your father I'll start court proceedings if I have to."

"Tell your mother she'll never get a dime from me that way."

"Tell your father I can have him put in jail."

"Tell your mother she will seriously live to regret it." Then, in that surprising way he had, he broke into a smile and shook his head. "Your mother," he said, almost fondly, and looked at me with conspiracy in his eyes. For me, this was the most painful moment of these interchanges. In spite of my discomfort in his house, I liked my father; I liked that he enjoyed having me stay with him, I liked our growing attachment to each other. I did not want this attachment jeopardized. But to align with him as he was asking me to do now was to disavow my mother, and that was unthinkable. He must have sensed something turn hard in me, because the smile left his face. "Tell her I'll pay her, for God's sake," he said, brushing me off. "Anyway, I know she's bluffing."

Then I did return his smile, because he was right. She had all the evidence necessary to have him jailed for not paying the child support, but she would never act on it. Throughout the years of my father's absence, his gruff and often disapproving treatment of us his children, his inability to express even the most simple words of love, my mother continued to perpetrate the notion that he was capable of metamorphosis, that any day he would begin to make himself active in our lives, supportive through difficult times. She believed in this possibility of transformation so deeply that her hope became instilled in all of us; I never doubted it until I lived with him.

One night as I was doing homework, I heard a gun blast outside the bedroom window. My stepmother screamed my father's name, and I rushed downstairs. They stood on the back patio, a silver revolver finding easy residence in my father's hand.

"What's going on?" I cried.

My father gazed into the branches of a mimosa tree. "I saw a rat up there."

Helen stared at his face for a long time, as if at inscrutable tea leaves. "You saw no such thing," she said, then left us.

"You were shooting at a rat?" I said.

He pointed with the gun into the tree. "It was running right along that branch."

"I guess you killed it with a sonic boom."

"It'll be back," he said seriously, and took a seat in one of the patio chairs, holding the gun across his lap. "Sit with me for a little while, Mikey." I nearly protested—my homework lay unfinished—then bent to sit beside him, but he stopped me with a raised hand. "Wait, bring me a drink first."

After fixing him a scotch, a skill I'd polished to a fine art, we sat together in silence. I never knew at these moments if he shared my discomfort or if it were a source of enjoyment for him to sit in my presence without the bothersome need for chatter. The night was warm, humid, and full of the songs of insects, and my mind began to drift away from him.

"What have you thought about college?" my father asked abruptly.

"College?"

"That's what I said. Don't you listen?"

"Well," I began, then stalled. To speak to him about something on which I pinned all my hopes—hopes for freedom, happiness, a life of my own—felt dangerous. "It seems like a good idea to go someplace different."

"Different from what?"

"From here. For the experience."

"Goddamn it, son. That's your mother talking. Be decisive. What do *you* want?"

I tried to speak offhandedly, but I almost whispered, fearing he would hear how badly I wanted it. "Stanford's supposed to be a good school."

"Here's how I see it," he said. "You'll apply to Stanford, and Yale, and University of Texas if you think you need some kind of backup. But you don't need to worry. Your SATs are high, and your grades will get you into any school you want to go to." He polished off his scotch. "You won't apply to Harvard. They're all assholes at Harvard."

Silence bound us once again. Even his pride in me abraded. Recently, my college counselor had called a meeting and requested the attendance of both my parents. I arrived first, then my mother, and at last my father, sweeping into the office in a beautiful dark suit as though paying us a regal visitation. But the princely clothes could not hide his rough, bumpkin origins any more than the ragamuffin getup my mother wore, the bell-bottom jeans and t-shirt, could obscure her natural gentleness and grace. My parents sat opposite each other in the tiny office, their knees almost touching, and though they directed their attention and comments solely to the counselor, the fierceness they focused on each other was beyond anything I'd known. They had been married for fifteen years. I wondered if any two human beings on earth had ever been so unsuitably matched.

"Hey," my father said. "You haven't heard any noises, have you, coming from the closet?"

"What closet?"

"Upstairs, in John's room."

"What kind of noises?"

"Squeaks, rustlings."

I shook my head. "Nothing like that."

"I think a squirrel has made a nest in there. Gotten in through the roof somehow, had some babies. Check it out, would you?"

"Okay."

"And take care of it. I hate those damn things."

For once, I allowed my silence to speak for me; he'd interpret it as acquiescence, and I thought it would buy me time. He meant, of course, for me to kill them.

"So you want to go to California. Take part in some revolutions." My father laughed affectionately. "There are bullet holes in the buildings at Stanford. From the sixties. Did you know that? Are you ready to take that on?"

"Sure," I said. "Maybe I'll make some bullet holes myself."

"You're adventurous, aren't you, Mikey? John thought about Stanford too, but he isn't adventurous enough. Nick, off in Germany, well, maybe he's too adventurous. I think Stanford is a good choice for you." He kept looking at me with a pleased grin, then he stared into his empty tumbler. When he next spoke, it was with a raised voice, as if he were orating to an audience gathered in his backyard. "Independence of thought is the greatest gift a man can give himself." He paused, chuckled. "I just made that up, but it sounds good. You've got to make peace with the vicissitudes of life." He gazed into the distance, or perhaps he was looking once again for the rat in the tree, and I had no earthly idea how to respond. My heart was clouded, confused. Whatever interior life my father possessed—a dense braid of money concerns and xenophobia—would be forever incomprehensible to me, no matter how much time I might spend with him.

"Vicissitudes," he repeated. "That's a word, isn't it?"

"I think so."

"Go look it up."

I quickly left him, and in the dictionary upstairs confirmed that *vicissitude* was indeed a word. "It means *change*," I yelled down to him from the landing.

"I knew that," he shouted back. When he did not call me down, I returned to John's room and my schoolwork.

My stepmother knocked on the door an hour or so later. "Have you seen your father?" she asked. "His car is gone."

I shook my head.

"He didn't tell you where he was going?"

I shook my head again. By the time I went to bed he still hadn't returned. Their fighting woke me in the middle of the night.

"Where the hell have you been? It's four in the morning. I didn't even know you'd gone."

"Leave it alone. A man's got to wander sometimes."

"You can wander all night for all I care. Just do me the courtesy of telling me you're going out."

The pillow I pulled over my head could not block out her strident tones, his grumbling defense. If some part of me longed for my parents never to have divorced, then living at my father's house had finally revealed what that would have held for me: my father's mercurial temperament, his belligerent, willful secrecy, his constant drunkenness. I'd gotten off lucky.

I was already awake, watching the room lighten with morning, when I heard a noise nearby like claws on wood. I opened the closet door and out of the dimness two black eyes stared into mine. The squirrel leapt to the rear of the closet, made for a hidden exit, and scrambled across the roof outside, but my eye was fixed on a hole in the cardboard file box from which it had emerged. Inside the box, upon a nest of shredded files, lay three fuschia, newborn squirrels. I carefully replaced the lid, shut tight the closet door, and shut tight my mouth. I made no mention of the squirrels at breakfast.

After school, I drove with my friend Lucinda to a parking lot that overlooked the St. John's playing fields, and from beneath the low-hanging branches of oaks we watched spring practice of the track and softball teams and smoked a joint. Lucinda expressed unmodulated disdain for the cliquishness of our classmates, so I felt flattered that she'd chosen me as her friend, and aspired to the same strength of character. She'd arrived the previous year from Idaho, which may as well have been Borneo as far as I was concerned, but in a striking coincidence, she now lived in Brookshire not two miles from my mother's house with a secretive, hard-drinking, wheeling-dealing father, a replica of my own.

Spotting several faces on the softball field, I realized that I naturally gravitated toward a certain kind of friend: Gloria, whose mother had been married and divorced eight times; Lucinda, who'd been driven from Idaho by her violent stepfather; and Belle, whose mother, on leaving her family of six children, cleaned all the furniture out of the house. Belle still slept on a mattress on the bare floor. "Parents are so weird," I said vehemently. Lucinda nodded, and I felt absolutely understood. My friends knew what I knew: the pressure exerted by a parent on either side, the conflicting loyalties and love. So often in my parents' presence I felt I might explode from keeping silent, but now, with Lucinda, I began to speak.

"My father wants me to exterminate some squirrels in his closet," I said. Lucinda smiled, shook her head. "He hates things getting into his house. The other night he started yelling for me to get downstairs, and I found him in the middle of the room pointing at a houseplant with a wild look on his face. 'There's something alive in there,' he told me, so I picked up the plant and took it outside. When I was really little, we had a pet squirrel named Mr. Stubbs. I rescued it from our dog's mouth. It was a baby that had fallen from a nest in the yard, and we raised it on milk from a bottle. I must have been about five because my parents were still married. I remember sitting on the kitchen floor in the morning and feeding almonds to Mr. Stubbs while my mom fixed breakfast. She wore blue slippers that had little roses on the top. Then my brothers came in, and then my dad, all dressed up for work, with a briefcase, and we had breakfast together." I stopped, because I did not know if this last part were true or fabricated. "At least, I think we did. Then Mr. Stubbs bit my sister, and we had to let him go."

Outside, dark clouds had gathered, and Lucinda was contemplating the drop or two of rain that had fallen upon the windshield. "I finally figured something out," she said.

"What about?"

"When I first mentioned you to my dad, you know, when I first said your name, he asked me a lot of questions about you and your father. Then you told me your dad had been curious about me too, and kind of strange about it."

"But he's strange about everything."

"So it hit me that our dads know each other."

"Probably," I said. "They're two of a kind."

"Do you know anything about the scandal?" she asked.

I shook my head. "Scandal?"

"It's why my mother moved to Idaho in the first place. I was born here. My older brother and sister even went to St. John's."

"They did?" I was suddenly, momentarily frightened. "What happened?"

"Our names were in the paper every day. My mother took us away because we were getting death threats."

"Because of the scandal."

"It was some major financial blowup here in Houston. Several banks were involved. To this day my father says he was set up. It wasn't just embezzling, something much more complicated."

"Much more clever," I said.

"My father went to prison for five years. When I was little, I used to get dressed up and fly to Kansas to visit my dad in the pen."

"Wow. I didn't know that."

"I don't tell everybody." We laughed.

It was not the effect of the marijuana alone that diluted any surprise I might have felt at Lucinda's revelation. Our fathers were beings in a distant galaxy; other gravities governed their behavior. We monitored their movements through telescopes.

When I returned to my father's house that afternoon, the marijuana did grant me a calm fluidity of motion. I stuffed a shoe box with toilet paper and gently placed the three newborn squirrels on their interim nest. Then I threw the file box into the garbage can outside, where I left it protruding from the lid so that my father, on his return from work, would see that I had killed the invaders. With the shoe box in the passenger seat, I drove beneath a ruffled, blue-black blanket of clouds to my mother's house.

I unlocked the gate she'd installed over the door to protect us from rural bandits, and entering the kitchen, home at last, I felt my entire body loosen and relax. My mother was speaking on the phone and she grazed my arm as I went past. From the linen closet I extracted a heating pad, then returned to the kitchen where I'd set the shoe box of squirrels. "Yes, I understand," my mother was saying; to me she mouthed my stepfather's name, rolling her eyes. After more than a year of bitter battling their divorce had been finalized, but they still communicated several times a month to arrange Henry's visits, at which time Hank lectured her on how she mismanaged their child's parenting. I transferred the baby squirrels to the heating pad while my mother made faces for my benefit. She stuck out her tongue, frowned in exaggerated concern, and held the phone at arm's length from her ear, both of us stifling our laughter. At last she hung up. "That was your lovely ex-stepfather," she said, kissing my forehead, "telling me once again what a terrible mother I am. Honestly, sometimes my entire marriage to him seems like a dream. When I think of being married, it's to your father."

"Look what I have," I said, grinning. "They were in a nest at Dad's house." I folded back the heating pad and watched her face, which sparked with surprise and delight, just as I knew it would. "Mr. Stubblets."

She checked her watch. "It's almost five," she said in a rush. "We'll have to run right now to the vet. They're so tiny, I'm not sure they'll make it, but we can try." She was already gathering up her purse and keys.

Speeding up the highway, I told my mother how I'd been ordered to kill the squirrels but had secretly taken them away. This prompted her to recount another episode: my father had once taken a stray dog I'd brought home and dropped it off miles away, confessing to the abduction only after the dog showed up at our door several days later. He didn't try it again; he admired the dog's spunk. While we sat in the waiting room at the veterinarian's office, I broached the subject of the scandal.

"To be honest," my mother said, "I don't know much about it. He would never tell me." She spoke as if it were not a particularly important event in their life together, by no means the worst deception.

"Did you know Lucinda's father went to prison for it?"

She shook her head. "There were several men involved, but only one or two masterminds. Your father was just starting out at the time. He said that he knew absolutely nothing about what they were doing." She smiled with a distant look, as though the picture in her mind were more vivid than what lay before her eyes. "As bad as it gets, I'll always come out smelling like a rose," she said in perfect imitation of him, her face glowering. Then her features dissolved back to their true form. "And you know, he always does."

I didn't pursue the subject further. Regarding my father, I was always maddened by how a question could remain unanswered and at the same time be answered too fully. The vet handed us a can of powdered formula, several eyedroppers, and a pamphlet on raising wild animals in the home, which I leafed through on the drive back to our house. The illustrations of baby raccoons and skunks sent my thoughts ahead to three tame squirrels scampering across the kitchen floor each morning, taking almonds from my hand. But my mother's mind was still focused on the past. "I don't know if you remember my friend Mary Stewart," she asked, "Jimmy Baker's first wife?"

"You've told me about her. She died of cancer, right?"

My mother nodded. "And when she knew she was dying, she wrote a letter to their four boys. This was around the time Celeste was born, and Mary Stewart and I had just talked because I was sure I was going to have another boy, a fourth, just like her, but at last I had a girl. She read me the letter. She asked her boys to do one thing for her, and that was that they grow up to be like their father, to become men as honorable, kind, and generous as he. I realized then that I didn't want my children to grow up to be anything like their father. That's when I knew my marriage was over."

The clouds had broken up while we'd been at the vet's, and the sky was beautiful and dramatic, with deep, iron clouds scattered above us like dark gnarls of regret, yellow rays of evening sunlight, and in the distance, lightning flashes of a storm. We turned off the road and headed down the red gravel driveway. I was impatient, both with my mother's talk and with wanting to begin my project of raising the squirrels. When we'd returned to the kitchen, she mixed the baby formula and handed me the eyedropper, then moved to the sink to wash her hands. I touched the heating pad where I'd left the squirrels and quickly drew back my hand from the hot fabric. I'd turned the dial to far too high a setting. Unpeeling the cloth, I found the three baby squirrels motionless, their scarlet skin filigreed with burst capillaries. For a moment I was overcome. I could not speak. Then I raised my head to tell my mother that I had killed the squirrels.

Her hands had dropped to the counter, and she stood gazing through the burglar bars at the storm miles away. "If I were a more forgiving person," she said lightly, a smile curling the corners of her mouth, "I'd probably still be married to your father."

26

or a couple of weeks after school let out for the summer, I steered clear of my father's house, slept eight hours a night in my own bed, and worked on projects for my mother. We'd lived in Brookshire for over a year, and the garage was still full of boxes we had yet to unpack. I was content with what I saw as my reward—sleep, solitude, one remaining year of high school—but one morning my mother surprised me. She held up two plane tickets, grinning at her own pluck, and said, "I told you we'd go to Mexico."

We flew in over the jungled mainland at a low enough altitude to see Mayan ruins guarding ocean cliffs, then our shadow skittered over the fifty-mile channel that separated the coast from the island of Cozumel, where a suite at the Hotel Presidente awaited us. A handsome dark-skinned man of short stature and indigenous features led us to our room. My mother ran her hand along the limestone counter in the bathroom, imprinted with antediluvian shells, and when I stepped onto our private deck, a three-foot iguana ambled away from the doorstep. Together we strolled beneath palm trees, skirting the cove on which the hotel was built, and to the end of a stone jetty. A calm evening was settling into night. Mainland Mexico lay invisible across the water, but we could imagine that the wind carried to us the perfumed tropicality of Tulum, Uxmal, and Chichén Itzá. Beneath the Caribbean sea at my feet, fish swam suspended over the coral reef like a whorling galaxy of stars. I felt as though

I'd slipped into my true skin at last. My life in Texas was a false one, a shadow life; I belonged here.

After showers, we caught a cab into town. The tourist pamphlet in our hotel room guided us to Pepe's for dinner, and in the waiting area we ran into a pair of honeymooners we'd met earlier on the shuttle from the airport, playing with a monkey on a chain. Like us, Glen and Cindy had come from Houston on a five-day package, and in the wonderfully open spirit of travelers, we decided to have dinner together. Cindy possessed a long face and gangly build, with shoulder-length platinum hair. Her husband's sincere, pleasant manner transformed his ordinary features into handsomeness. Their arms were in constant, entwining motion, like octopus limbs. As if the Mexican air were acting upon us like an intoxicant, we laughed continuously and hilariously throughout dinner, and very soon we'd grown intimate.

"We met in the office," Cindy admitted. "But he wasn't my boss."

"We work in different departments," Glen said.

"I had to flirt with him for months before he asked me out on a date."

"I was shy."

"Then one thing led to another."

"That was the easy part," Glen said. "We kept it secret at work for a while. I'm not even sure why anymore."

"Once we spent our whole lunch hour kissing in the supply room. Finally we took the plunge."

"Yesterday."

My mother gazed at them almost as lovingly as they gazed at each other. "That's wonderful," she said, with genuine feeling.

My mother and I both drew close to the glow of our newfound friends' happiness, warming ourselves, but as the evening progressed I understood an important difference between the two of us. We stood on opposite sides of this story of fiery romance. My mother had passed through it herself and emerged with burns that were taking years to heal, and I longed to throw myself into those flames.

Talk moved on to more practical matters—jobs, home owning, my school and plans for college. My mother described our house in Brookshire, how it was abandoned when we moved in and now, a year later, it was gorgeous. "It's a work of art," I said, beaming at my mother, the artist.

"But I couldn't have done it without Michael's help. He has slaved away for me."

"So now we're here to celebrate."

"But Brookshire," Cindy said, "is really out in the sticks, isn't it? I think I drove by it once."

"Oh, it is," my mother said with a vigorous nod. "But I had to get out of Houston. The divorce from my second husband was one of the most awful experiences of my life. Brookshire was perfect for me, even though, I know, it's been a real hardship for Michael."

These words silenced me as effectively as a sock stuffed into my mouth. Of course, this was precisely how I'd explained her motivations to myself, but she'd never breathed a word aloud of it, her emotional life as private as her religious one, talking instead of money, investments, and property as the reasons for our move. Now, to open up to complete strangers!

Glen leaned toward me as if to make a confession. "I traveled to Europe with my mother when I was your age. For six weeks. We had a great time."

"So do we," I said distractedly. "We always have. And we're good diving partners."

The next morning this assertion was sorely tested. Motoring out to a nearby reef in a hired boat, we discovered how atrophied our scuba diving skills had become in the two years since our class. The equipment baffled us, appeared wholly unfamiliar, and our clumsiness threatened to overturn the boat. Finally, when we were moored at the reef, the boatman's impassive stare exerted the disciplinary influence we needed to pull our wits together. Arrayed in our gear we somersaulted over the boat's side, and the disorienting plunge recalled to me the naturalness of underwater being. I spun around to take in everything at once, and I saw that this was unlike submersion in any YMCA pool. Silvery shapes glided through a blue expanse flickering with sunlight, and down below, the colors of the reef did not remain static but moved and shifted like the relentless biology of my own body. I righted myself, made eye contact with my mother, and we set our sights on the reef thirty feet below.

I drifted downward with steady beats of my fins, my ears pressurizing with a high shriek, but when I looked back I saw my mother still at the surface, her arms stretched before her like a superheroine's, suspended in place. Seal-like, I reversed direction and returned to her. Treading water, she spat out her regulator. "I forgot my weight belt," she said. "I float."

"But I don't have one, either," I said. "I sink."

"That's one difference between us. I've got some extra padding."

"Let's try," I said. "Kick hard." I attempted to pull her down by the hand, but her body resisted the descent with fierce buoyancy. Both of us kicked with as powerful strokes as we could muster, making infinitesimal progress toward the coral reef below, which seemed to recede ever distantly like a mirage in the desert. At last we swam within several feet of the reef, subjected to sights of breathtaking beauty but with little concentration to attend to them. We kept laughing at the absurdity of it, losing air in big bursts, until at last we gave up our strenuous kicking altogether and shot upward to the atmosphere, racing the silver bubbles of air we'd just expelled.

We had better luck after lunch careering around the island in a rented jeep. The dusty, desolate highway hugged the coast to the southern tip of Cozumel, where we crawled on our hands and knees through dark tunnels of ruins, the stones etched with spiraling, caracolic designs. Emerging, we discovered a sugar white beach, on which crashed tremendous turquoise waves. There too lay a sight that disturbed us both, piles upon piles of the carapaces of slaughtered sea turtles.

That night at La Langosta we ran into Glen and Cindy again. They waved from their table, and as I moved toward them my mother firmly took hold of my arm. She waved hello, graciously declined their invitation to join them for a second dinner, then directed us to our own table.

"But they're fun," I protested.

"They're also on their honeymoon," she said.

"So?"

"We don't need to intrude."

Was she embarrassed to be with me, I suddenly wondered, her gawky seventeen-year-old a great sidekick but no substitute for a spouse? Or perhaps the situation seemed cruel to her, running into the newlyweds again and again when her divorce was still so freshly painful. To dull my inquiring senses, she allowed me one tropical drink with dinner. Though I'd been secretly experimenting with alcohol and believed myself proficient in handling its effects, the piña colada made me clumsily drunk. I became talkative, swiped at a fly and knocked over a full glass of water I'd been advised not to drink. As we walked back to the Jeep, my mother gently lifted the keys from my hand.

After two more practice dives, to a sunken plane and again to the shallow reef in front of the hotel, we felt in better shape, ready for the big dive we'd come for: Palancar Reef. This was a world-famous barrier reef at the northeast corner of the island, the home of a rare black glassy coral found only hundreds of feet deep. The boat picked us up at the hotel dock and we began the forty-five minute journey, accompanied by a couple from San Antonio, two couples from California, and Paula, a young woman from Houston with whom, I would discover several days later, back home, I inadvertently exchanged one rigid, black swimming fin.

From where we anchored in the open water, the coast of Cozumel was visible as two horizontal lines of color, green upon white. By now, my mother could ably handle her scuba equipment alone, but after we suited up I ran my eye over her gear just to check. Following our guide into the water, the group of us began our descent to the reef sixty feet below, our moves slow and balletic. I kept rolling over to look above me, where aqua water met silver air, like a pane of mercury covering the world.

But soon enough I was transfixed by what lay right before my nose. Upon the mountainous terrain of the reef, sea fans and gorgonias waved in the current like scarlet scarves, and fish danced about sea sponges as big as urns. Splitting open a sea urchin, the guide brought on an orgy of fish fighting over the meat. My body was activated by an electric sense of wonder. I followed what caught my eye, swam this way and that, in downward chase after two black and yellow French angels the size of dinner plates. A hand grabbed my ankle. Paula, indicating ninety feet on her depth gauge, warned me of the lure of the abyss.

The boat ferried us to a cove for lunch: barracuda, conch, and grilled pineapple. The legs of our table and chairs were washed by the surf. During a second dive in the afternoon, my regulator developed a leaking stream of bubbles, and after twenty minutes I was nearly out of air. More out of play than necessity, I motioned to my mother; I tapped my air pressure gauge, cut a line across my neck, then immediately understood my mistake: this was no joking matter. She took control, firmly gripping the frame of my scuba tank with one hand, drawing me close to her. She took two breaths from her regulator, then removed it from her mouth and placed it in mine, performing careful, measured actions, just as we had been taught years earlier. I took two breaths and passed the regulator back to her. With synchronous, ascendant scissoring of our fins, we buddy-breathed to the surface.

"You're such a wonderful traveling companion," my mother said. "I've loved having this time with you." On our last afternoon, we sat with our feet upon the stone parapet of the hotel overlooking the ocean, sumptuously tired from our dives. Below us lay the swimming pool, and below that the private beach. We'd only been here four days, but I felt so complete, and so completely at home, it seemed to me like an entire lifetime.

Surrounding the pool on chaise longues lay a crowd of sun worshipers, honeymooners like Glen and Cindy, several families with small children. "Look at those two men," my mother said, her voice strangely smug. She motioned toward a large group of people, but I knew immediately which ones she meant. The men walked through the throng of lazily laughing couples, wearing tight Speedo bathing suits, their skin pasty white. "I think they're gay," she said behind her cupped hand.

Every so often, my mother shocked me with statements of blatant prejudice or ignorance. Scientists had proved that black people had smaller brains than whites. Everything wrong with our country would not have occurred if we'd only won the war; and I ticked off wars in my head until I reached the one she meant: the Civil War. I would upbraid her, make certain she understood these statements to be offensive or misinformed, but in this case she was right. These men didn't belong here.

I looked past them to the beach, where several boys surrounded a pretty teenage girl. Following my gaze, my mother said, "You should meet some people your own age if you want to. You don't have to keep company with your ancient mother all the time."

"But I like keeping company with my ancient mother."

She laughed. "We do have fun, don't we?"

"So where are we going on our next trip?"

We tossed out various possibilities: Baja, Grand Cayman, Australia, the moon. Then we faced the sun again. I closed my eyes to slits, but kept watch through my lashes on the two men my mother had pointed out. They lay on their backs on adjacent chaise longues, and though nothing in their actions registered the other's presence, the lines that connected them were as visible to me as taut cables.

"Emmett has asked me to marry him," my mother said.

I sat up. She watched my surprise and laughed as though she'd been pulling my leg. "You're kidding."

"No, I'm not," she said. "You don't like Emmett very much, do you?"

"That's not true!"

"Then why do you disappear into your room every time he comes over?"

"I don't know."

"You intimidate him."

"I do not." I was too inarticulate on this matter to explain adequately. "It's not that I don't like him," I began. I did like him, I was glad that he was around, but I just couldn't involve myself.

"Of course I told him I couldn't marry him. I mean, I *love* Emmett . . ." She let her statement hang incomplete. "Anyway, could you imagine if he were here now? What a pain in the rear he'd be." My mother laughed and reached for my hand. "Why do I never meet a man I like as much as my own children?"

Exhausted from the long flight, we bickered in the car on the way home from the airport. She told me I was driving too fast. I told her I would take responsibility for my own driving. She was still my mother, she said, the question was not up for debate. Slow down, smartypants, or else.

We gathered the children from their fathers, where they'd been staying during our sojourn, and resumed country life in Brookshire. One afternoon, Celeste stepped out of the house and noticed two small rubber sandals afloat on the surface of the pool. Then she saw Henry motionless on the bottom, his skin anoxically blue. At the sound of her scream, my mother came running. She dove into the water and brought him up, resuscitating him with CPR at the pool's edge. An ambulance took them to the hospital, and over the course of the night a battery of tests confirmed that Henry had suffered no permanent physical injury. Though, the doctor said, if he had been found even a minute later he would have drowned.

The close call electrified us. I'd been in Houston and returned the moment my mother telephoned me. I understood that I'd been wrong to believe in a romantic life for myself galavanting in Mexico. Now that my mother and I had created a home, surely my place was in it, protecting my family. If I left, *when* I left, what was to distinguish me from all the men who had left before?

27

Senior year in high school I hit a snag. No matter which way I tugged and pulled, I could not loose myself from a deeply hidden shoal. My sadness flummoxed me. Listening to melancholy music late at night, I penned short stories in which all reason was lost, people became untethered. Middle-aged women with no previous history of depression put guns to their temples. Trucks flew out of the night to maim innocent boys. No story felt true to life that did not include the deaths or paralyzings of all major characters. While chatting with my stepmother before dinner, I clipped from the newspaper any articles that dealt with mental illness. Cheryl Ladd caught my eye from the cover of *Good Housekeeping*, smiling over the headline: "Are you suffering from depression? Test inside." I filched the magazine. Ranking on a scale of one to ten the severity of my appetite and sleep problems, my feelings of worthlessness and suicide, and my desire to escape gave me exactly what I craved: quantification. In late autumn a boy in my class discovered his father in their attic with his head blown to pieces, his hand still gripping the shotgun, and for weeks I watched him in the halls at school with a kind of envy.

I experienced outbursts of anger that left me horrified. Leaving for school in the morning I often found our goat on the roof of my car, where it liked to spend the night, and on some instances the sight of the goat leaping from the hood quickened every molecule of rage I possessed and impelled me to attack, flailing my fists and chasing the goat into the field with wild, swinging kicks. Once, during a fit of obstinacy on Scotty's part that appeared to have no limits, I found my hands gripping his shoulders, shaking him with such force that his head swung back and forth like a rag doll's. Another evening, I entered my mother's room to say good night, sat on the edge of her bed, and heard a strange monologue escape my lips.

There was an abandoned house that my cousin Hayley and I had found near her farm, I told her, when we were children. "It had at least a hundred window panes, and we spent hours breaking them all. We threw stones at each one, singing songs we made up, 'a spoonful of rocks makes the window go crash.' " My mother said nothing, simply watched me with a steady smile. "The glass was so perfectly smooth and breakable. Sometimes I feel as though I want to break glass. It's like I'm hungry. I'm hungry to break glass." I spoke humorously, as though I were joking, yet behind my mother's smile I knew what she was thinking: *what sort of monster have I created?*

Not long after, Scotty went on a rampage with a pellet gun. He shot out everything around the house that was made of glass: the exterior light fixtures, my old fifty-gallon aquarium, the mirror and windshield of my car. At the time, he was still seeing the child psychiatrist, and I wondered if I should make a visit to one as well, but I could not picture myself lying on a psychiatrist's couch without laughing out loud at the sheer melodrama of it. To bring my sadness to my mother's attention I also found inconceivable. Any sort of focus on myself, any want or desire, was somehow a betrayal of her; it could only cause harm to the fragile balance she'd attained. So I stuffed my glass-breaking impulses down into a hard kernel deeply hidden at my core, where they could do no damage. The kernel was already there to accept them, the receptacle of other lurking wants and visceral longings I had understood at once to be too dangerous to acknowledge. I had to blind myself to them, at any cost. This was my secret.

On the depression test, my desire to escape had scored in the highest percentile. For some time, my sights had been set on college, Stanford in particular, as the destination of my flight. In late autumn my mother entered my room as I sat puttering over college catalogues and forms. These applications I handled like delicate parchments; they were my ticket out, the only way to break the iron grip of sadness. My mother was going through a sad time of her own; over the previous months her father had been repeatedly hospitalized. More than once she had taken out of storage a dark blue velvet case and shown me his decorations for valorous military service and the gold medals he'd won in international competition for rope climbing. She spoke of my grandfather's physical decline with a sorrow that seemed to carry its own gravitational force, bearing her body earthward. He'd fought on both the Atlantic and Pacific fronts during World War II, rising to the rank of admiral, but he'd borne no sons to carry on the navy tradition, and this loss my mother felt keenly for him.

"How are those going?" she asked, indicating the applications.

"I can't seem to get started."

"I'm sure you'll get into Stanford. They'd be crazy not to take you." She took a breath, set her gaze on the floor, and said, "I was wondering if you'd consider applying to Annapolis."

It was rare for her to make this kind of request; she never pressed her ideas for my future upon me, only encouraged my own. This was not one of my own. I pictured men in uniforms ordering me around, shouting at me, treating me roughly; the image alone filled me with rage. "No way," I said.

My mother's face crumpled. "I just thought I'd ask," she said quietly, then left the room.

Alone in Brookshire on a Saturday night. My mother had gone to stay at Emmett's, where she'd once pointedly shown me her separate bedroom; Celeste and Scotty were with friends, and Henry with his father. I mixed a pitcher of vodka and orange juice and, just as I had when I was a child, settled in for an evening of television. The highlight for me on Saturdays was *The Love Boat.* During the course of a four-day voyage, translated into an hour of television viewing time, passengers on a cruise ship found love "exciting and new," just as the theme song promised. A maritime blaze of romance could always be counted on to mend years-long family rifts, breathe new life into ailing loves, and forge lifelong partnerships from the most incompatible of couples. I could not prevent myself from being cheered.

Saturday night in Houston. I mixed up a batch of piña coladas in Gloria's kitchen. Her mother was never home; in fact, when Gloria was fifteen, her mother had married, moved to the ranch of her new husband, and left Gloria living alone for a year, until she divorced again and moved back. After getting good and drunk on the piña coladas, we went out dancing until the clubs closed, then drove aimlessly around the city, singing to her tapes. *Am I wrong to believe in the city of gold that lies in the deep distance?* Her mother had refused to buy a Christmas tree because after all these years she'd come to realize they were simply too messy, so around four in the morning, fortified by a couple of blasts of rum from the bottle I kept under the seat of my car, we drove up to the Christmas tree lot at the local Weingarten's, tossed one into the trunk, and screeched off. We stayed up until dawn decorating the tree with ornaments and lights Gloria found in the attic.

It was a particularly promising holiday season; we stood at the threshold of a new decade. In 1980, we would finish high school and flee, and both Gloria and I were chomping at the bit. Though I had evolved into a fairly successful and busy social being in a way I would not have believed possible when I first entered St. John's, I spent most of my free time with Gloria. She was my best friend, but we were not in love. Throughout high school, my heart had been like a lazy Susan, offering me a rapidly spinning array of crushes, but I'd never had a girlfriend. I dreamed of a great, soul-melding love. On the drive to school each morning, I popped eight-track cartridges into my stereo and gave myself over to the music. *It happens all the time, this crazy love of mine.* I loved cheap sentiment; it promised me that out there in the greater world my longing would someday find an object to which it could passionately attach.

I stared at the college applications in a pile on my desk. I was procrastinating. I'd completed filling out all the strictly factual information, but I had yet to attack the meat of the applications, the personal essays. I had neither analyzed a social problem in my local community nor chosen an adjective to describe myself. Furthermore, a mouse or other small creature had recently died in some undetectable quarter of my room, and the odor made it difficult to concentrate. I left the applications where they were and entered the house, where I found Celeste, Scotty, and Henry on the couch watching television. Nick was there also, home for the holidays, but he'd been getting on my nerves. Whenever he visited from college, he immediately rolled up his sleeves and set to work cleaning out the refrigerator or reorganizing the garage, then lectured me on how I needed to help more around the house. I glared at him stonily, swallowing my acid anger. He was no different from any other man who wanted to swoop in and impose his version of order upon my mother's life, then leave.

I joined them on the couch, where Henry, whose fourth birthday we had recently celebrated, nestled against me. I found him to be an immensely handsome, loving, funny child; my pride could rival any father's. I had always been determined that if anything happened to my mother I would fight Hank for custody of Henry, but each time I looked at my college applications I knew that I was making a choice, myself over my family. Nick whispered to me, "Mom's on the phone to Montgomery," but I avoided the meaning in his look and watched the television screen, where J. R. and Sue Ellen were fighting on the patio of their ranch house beneath a wide Texas sky. My mother appeared in the atrium, moving inexorably toward us, five of her six children. She knelt beside the couch and said very gently, "Grandaddy died this evening."

Tears made her eyes bright. Her cheeks were ruddy, warmly alive. I couldn't help but notice that she was extraordinarily beautiful at this moment; her grief transported her. From the television, the *Dallas* theme song began to play. Henry left my side and put his hand on my mother's knee. "Who shot him?" he asked.

She laughed softly and drew Henry close. "Nobody shot him, honey. He was sick for a long time, and now he's in heaven."

Henry tugged on her dress, near tears himself. "But who *shot* him?"

The rest of us were quiet as she tried to explain that there were other ways to die. I did not know what I felt. After a while, I returned to my room and stood beneath a hot, forceful shower, trying to melt the coldness that was creeping into every part of me.

My mother insisted on going alone to Alabama for the funeral. She was gone a day only and came home on Christmas Eve, silent and intent. She tried to rally her spirits, but our Christmas was a solemn one, and late in the day she entered the bedroom where I was talking to John. On the occasions he visited us, such as Christmas, I shadowed him.

She sat beside John on the bed and looked at the bundle she carried in her arms, an American flag folded into a triangle. "This is the flag from his funeral," she told him. "I have something else to give you. He wanted you to have his Annapolis ring." Then she lay on John's chest, and he put his arms around her while she cried.

I wanted to shout, But aren't I the rightful heir to the ring? Hadn't John left us? Hadn't I been asked to apply to Annapolis? But then, I had rejected her offer. She hadn't come to me now for comfort but to John, and when at last she wiped her eyes and stood, she left the room still carrying the flag like her bundled, private grief.

While she'd been away at her father's funeral, I had at last faced the college essays. On none did I have such ease and fluency as the essay at the heart of Stanford's application, for which I was to write about the person who had most influenced my life. "*Sorry to be such a cliché,*" I began, "*but of course I must write about my mother.*" I wrote energetically, without having to think. In the history I provided of her life, I held nothing back: her two marriages that had both ended in divorce, having a child at the age of forty, the single-handed raising of her six children, her tireless efforts to provide financial stability for her family. Throughout my life, I wrote, I had witnessed my mother endure these and other hardships, never ceasing to embrace the world with deeply felt goodwill, with innate trust in the goodness of others. By her example, she had taught me to live with compassion, imagination, and humor. I knew that everything I valued in myself, any special qualities I possessed, and the strengths by which I would survive, had all come from her. She had taught me faith.

In May, a fat envelope arrived from Stanford offering me acceptance into the class of 1984, and my mother and I jumped up and down in the kitchen, baying jubilantly. She might have described the letter as a life raft thrown me by the Lord, but I knew that I'd done it myself. With her help. She was the bow that shot me into the world.

After school let out, my mother told me that Howard Vole wanted to give me a graduation present because he admired me so much. I begged her to tell him not to.

But when the moment arrived, I was not strong enough to resist. At the truck stop on the edge of town, I had just filled up my car with gasoline and was walking inside to pay when I ran into Howard Vole. He stood beside a rack of potato chips with his wallet already out. I stared, wide-eyed, as he peeled off five twenty-dollar bills; my hand closed over them like a Venus flytrap.

I planned to drive to California with a high school friend also on the way to Stanford, and on the day he arrived to collect me, my family gathered to watch me pack a few belongings into his car. The rest my mother would ship later. I was excited and hurried, and I did not linger over my good-byes. After I'd kissed Henry and set him down, he latched onto my leg. "You're my *brother*," he cried. My mother looked deeply into my eyes, as if to burn me into her memory, and a question sprang into my mind as I gazed back at her. *What do you want in your life? Now that you are free, now that you've created a home of your own, what do you want to create with your life?*

I turned to Celeste and Scotty. They were so fully themselves, such independent beings, I did not feel they needed me any longer. Celeste had just turned thirteen, the age I'd been when I became the oldest child at home, and as I hugged her I thought, *Now it's your turn.*

For five days I drove west at ninety miles an hour, across arid, haunting landscape, through West Texas, New Mexico, Arizona, the desert wheeling at me. When the dry, golden hills of California came into view, I felt that I had never seen anything so beautiful and strange. At Stanford, a letter was already waiting for me. *After you left, I lay on my bed and sobbed for hours,* my mother wrote. *I miss you already, but I guess I'll have to get used to it. You've given so much to me, my special love.*

EXPLORER

28

Homesickness was not a state I ever mapped. As I drove up Stanford's palm-lined entrance, my melancholy shed away like the skin of an immature self, and a new, take-charge personality emerged. I found myself natural and confident in groups of absolute strangers, at home in the easy fellowship of dormitory life, and eager to speak to new faces that might yield literate, exciting minds. Among the new minds I discovered were Sophie, whose mother had divorced a violent, manic-depressive husband when Sophie was an infant; Linda, whose father had died of cancer during her adolescence; Carlos, whose mother had spent much of his childhood hospitalized for depression after the death of his little sister; Gabriel, whose schizophrenic father had killed himself with a shotgun; Tam, whose mother had also committed suicide before her family emigrated from Korea; and Hannah, whose father had pursued a series of affairs with young women similar in physical appearance to his daughter. Though the histories of our families were not fully confided until later, after we'd come to know and trust one another, we quickly recognized a special kinship, one which, in spite of the traumas on which it was based, translated easily into laughter. Our academics took second place to nightly gatherings in dorm hallways, where we drank beer until two or three in the morning, played cribbage and spin-the-bottle, recited absurdist proofs for God's existence, and debated Carter's handling of the hostages in Iran. I regaled my new friends with stories of Yolanda the pig, of Emmett the man and Emmett the turkey, and from them I heard similar tales; the episodes that had once confused and pained us were now the source of our communion.

One of us was different from the rest. The least worldly of my friends and the most compelling, Rose had dark, curly hair that fell to her shoulders and pouting, curvaceous lips. She had just turned seventeen and naively wore her pinstripe oxford shirts tight enough to strain the buttons. And her parents were still married. As Rose revealed more about her family, we listened with the rapt silence of children hearing stories at bedtime. She was the oldest of six kids; the youngest was less than a year old. Her parents, she said, had met in a perfume shop in Paris while studying abroad, he from the East Coast, she from the West, when they were only sixteen. After years of long-distance courting, as full of perils and mishaps as of rendezvous beneath full moons, they'd wed and settled in Oregon. Her loving descriptions of her parents and five siblings—their closeness and loyalty, the esteem and warmth with which they regarded one another—were as fantastic to me as any fairy tale.

At Thanksgiving, eight of us rented a van as big as a covered wagon and hit the Oregon trail to Rose's home, where at last I met her wry, energetic mother, her hospitable, joke-cracking father, her two brothers and three sisters. I dandled her baby brother on my knee. This was a family most at home in large groups; the table easily seated fifteen. Its centerpiece for dinner was the wizened branch of an apple tree, complete with leaves, lichens, flowers, and ripe apples still hanging from their stems. On my first Thanksgiving away from home, I entertained some disloyal thoughts. Holidays at my mother's house, though full of noise and bodies, rarely escaped an edge of solemnity. Our eyes were on the empty seats. Like a family in wartime, we were mindful of those who weren't able to join us and those who had been lost, but this was hardly the case at Rose's house. After the meal, her father led the entire brood in harmonized songs at the table, and I felt that I'd been transported into the pages of a book, or perhaps into a parallel universe. Being with this family, I saw a door opening onto my own future, where greater riches than I'd ever imagined were suddenly brought into the realm of the possible.

Back at school, I fell into spending much of my free time with Rose.

We stayed awake all night flexing our newly discovered ironic tendencies, in discussions of the free offer from our bank for Wells Fargo belt buckles, the agenda-setting function of the press, and the imp and the perverse. How could an omniscient, omnipotent, all-good God allow evil and suffering in the world? Free will, of course.

As we got to know each other, I understood my great fortune in finding such a friend, whose mind was so alive and investigative and funny, and who helped me spark into life my own mind, where, I began to understand, in its previously unexamined territory I would find my salvation. Her wit and intellect, her insistent grappling to understand what was meaningful, were constant sources of delight to me, but I did not fall in love with her. My energies were young, diffuse, too exuberantly wild to focus upon one person. On weekends Rose and I and our friends explored our new home: Big Sur, Yosemite, Disneyland. In San Francisco we ate sourdough bread and cheese on the wharf, with Alcatraz as our backdrop. I gazed at these characters; in such a short time they had materialized from hope, become utterly real, as though at last I'd been born into my true family.

In May I received an urgent phone call from my mother. "I just wanted to let you know," she said breathlessly, "that we're all okay."

"What do you mean? What happened?"

"Haven't you heard about the tornados? It's been all over the news. We've had them for three days." Our house had sustained only minor damage to the roof, she told me, but the aviary had been spirited away completely. She'd found pieces of it hundreds of yards out in the fields. In town, a wing of the elementary school had been destroyed while the children huddled inside, Scotty among them, but no one was hurt. My heart thumped as my mother gave this report; we'd escaped by a hair's breadth. "But," she added gravely, "Emmett was killed."

I thought I could not possibly have heard her correctly. "Did you say Emmett?"

"The turkey. He was in the chicken coop. At least I think he's dead. All we found was a pile of feathers."

We talked for a long while, and by the end of our conversation I felt grateful that school was nearly over so that I could return to Texas. My mother painted a vivid scene of green skies and debris whipping through the air, laughing as she spoke with the relief of narrow escape. She'd been alone in the house, the children all at school, and had actually witnessed the tornados moving high over the fields, their funnels touching down every so often like the long, delicate necks of birds. Then she interrupted herself. "Oh, and I think I finally have a buyer for the house. I've decided this time we'll move to Austin. Probably this summer. You'll be home just in time to help."

She sold the house a week later, with no thanks to Howard Vole. She struck the deal herself. But she wanted to give him a commission anyway; he'd worked so hard, and for so long.

It was with a sense of homecoming that I took on the project of packing up my mother's house. I liked the work itself, which was solitary, methodical, and I felt a pleasurable pride when at the end of the day my mother expressed her surprise and gratitude at how much I'd accomplished. She was busy also, traveling to Austin several times a week on house-hunting expeditions and working out the complicated conditions of the sale of our Brookshire property, for which there were two buyers. She alone was financing the sale. This did not offer her enough protection, in my opinion, but she was impatient, even slightly offended, by my concern. Nobody had believed she could pull it off, she said, but she was flush at last, she never had to worry about money again. The buyer of the front pasture was going to build a factory to manufacture oil-drilling machinery; the other buyer believed in my mother's vision of a waterside community enough to take on the development himself. A large sign appeared on the side of the highway advertising lots at Lakeview Estates.

Though I rustled up some odd jobs for money, such as landscaping more of Emmett's houses, I felt as though I had two full-time occupations: helping my mother move to Austin and corresponding with my friends. After a day of packing and cleaning, I wrote letters late into the night, keeping Rose and the others up to date on the state of my mind and heart, including photographs I'd taken of the view from my room: the flat fields seen through the bars on my window. When my mother returned from her own doings, she knocked lightly on my door. "Don't you want to come have a glass of wine with me?"

"Not tonight. Maybe another time."

"You're always writing," she said as she pulled the door closed.

Midway through the summer I could bear the separation from my friends no longer. I began to take trips to their home territories: Kansas City, New York, Tucson, Boston, Mexico City, New Orleans. Before my eighteenth birthday I had rarely strayed outside the borders of Texas, but now I felt born to become a continental explorer.

While I was away on one of my trips, my mother signed the deal on a new house in Austin, which stood on a steep hillside west of the city overlooking green, brambly hills. The name of the street—The High Road—we took as a good omen. To my great relief, she hired a moving company to transport our possessions, and as the Brookshire house was emptied I dug every plant out of the atrium. I was not sorry to leave that house; in spite of the energy my mother and I had put into it, for both of us it had been a stepping stone, and for both of us, too, a place of hardship and loneliness. We were pushing forward to greener fields than these.

Traveling from Brookshire to Austin was a move from rural isolation back to civilization, back to the country of man, and my mother was quickly at no loss for suitors. The postman began bringing our mail to the door several times a week; sometimes we found him waiting on the steps when we drove up the driveway, and he asked himself in for a glass of water. The hottest summer in recent memory, he explained. On opening the mailbox one morning, I found it full of miniature boxes of Fab laundry detergent. Other days, small packets of shampoo or hand lotion tumbled out to the dust at my feet; the mailbox had been stuffed to overflowing. He courted her with free samples.

The end of Emmett the turkey appeared to herald the end of Emmett the man as well. Austin was nearly a three-hour drive from Brookshire. As my mother had answered each time he'd proposed over the last several years, she told him firmly for the last time that she couldn't become his wife. Even so, Emmett showed up at our door in Austin without warning, holding his weekend duffel bag and kicking sheepishly at the dirt. In late August he took us all water-skiing, my mother and I, Celeste, Scotty, and Henry. It was a blazing, beautiful Texas summer day, and the lake was cool and mirror smooth, reflecting cumulus cities in the sky. As the boat skimmed across the water's surface, I was immersed in pure sensation, in the roar of the wind and the hot, blasting air. I saw the look on Emmett's face, configured by sadness and longing, and I understood that this would probably be the last time I'd see him, a gentleman who for years had loved my mother faithfully, who had been more constant to my younger brothers and sister than their own fathers. But I was powerful with the discovery of my friends in college, to whom I was soon returning, and I felt inured to loss, as gloriously immune to it as to growing old or to nuclear war. Emmett fixed his gaze upon my mother, and I turned away from them both to catch the full heat of the sun on my face.

29

Reeling drunk in New Orleans. Two or three hours past midnight, and crowds still thronged Bourbon Street, jazz bars blared, a revolution of lights and noise. The thick, humid summer night had laid a sheen of sweat upon my skin. It felt good. Some time had passed since I'd seen my friends.

Pushing through the swinging doors of a bar I'd spotted earlier in the night, I fell blind into smoky, tangy darkness. The alcohol in me pursued a violent course, killing thought, freeing sensation. I began to discern shapes circling through the room, one standing beside me that after a while I reached toward, touched a face with my hand, found the wet mouth, kissed with a lifetime of want. Led outside, into a car, I was traveling across the city, zigzagging through an unfamiliar quarter. Through the door of an apartment, where we stripped, tumbled to the bed. I had never before touched the life and heat of flesh, but I needed no map to explore the body that lay beneath me.

Abruptly, near dawn, fear reclaimed me. I leapt away from the bed, from the body, began pulling on my clothes. "Take me back," I said.

"Hey, it's okay, calm down."

"You said you'd take me back."

"Alright, just take it easy. It's alright."

Driving once again across town, a hand clasped mine, reassured me. "Can I see you again?"

Unthinkable. "I'm leaving tomorrow," I said. "I'm going home."

"Really? Where's that?"

"Oregon."

"You told me earlier that you lived here."

"No, I didn't."

"You lied to me." He wrested his hand from mine, and I felt a knife digging out my heart. In the French Quarter, the car pulled up to the curb and spat me out. The sidewalk was wet, hosed down from the night. Heading for the hotel where my friends lay sleeping, I broke into a run. I held something in a fist: my socks. The air was cool on my ankles as I sprinted through the empty streets.

30

During the winter of my junior year in college, my stepmother Helen was diagnosed with lung cancer, which advanced with such brutal regularity she was able to predict the month of her death in the spring. Helen's disease, and the lucid dignity with which she faced it, sunk me into a deep, isolated well of contemplation. Over the phone, my mother said, "I've been walking around like a zombie ever since I found out," and I understood precisely how she felt, encrusted in ice.

My close friends remarked on my changed spirits, but for a reason I couldn't explain I shrugged off their inquiries, unable to confide in any of them except Rose. I tried to explain how my stepmother stood in such ambiguous relation to me. My father had divorced my mother to marry her, but she'd always been kind to me; she was the door by which I'd gained access to his life. There was a gentleness in his voice when he told me of her diagnosis that I had never heard before; I knew that he would be lost without her. Why did Helen's dying force me back into the powerful claim of my family? Especially now, just as I was beginning to make my own life? Rose had no answers; she simply listened.

I was slowly beginning to realize, several years into college, that I had come to a dead end. My friends had begun experimenting with romance and sex, but I could not. In Rose I had come to believe I'd found a life partner. I was giddy with the idea: a life partner! Together we would create a family—she would show me how, she'd learned from her parents—and somehow that would reconnect all the fragments of my own history. But I could not make this vision real. My friendship with Rose was profound, even romantic, but we had hardly touched each other, had never once kissed. She began her first love affair with another man, and I did nothing more than watch from the sidelines. Then I would go home to my mother's house, and only there, working alongside her, would I feel myself again. I understood my place.

Rose, Sophie, and others had rented a house for the summer, and they entreated me to stay in California, but I couldn't. After Helen's death I longed to return home, so I packed up my Volkswagen van and drove eastward, buffeted by desert winds. In Austin I got a job in a Mexican restaurant and registered for a summer class at the university, but I instantly resumed the role of my mother's worker bee. In the two years she'd lived on The High Road, she had installed costly solar heating panels on the roof, added new wooden stairs and a deck to the front entrance, and purchased custom-designed electric awnings that with the push of a button extended over the most brutally sunlit sides of the house, and still taped to the refrigerator was a list of projects twenty items long. She felt particularly pressed to accomplish these because, she informed me not long after I arrived, she'd decided to sell the house. She didn't have a choice; it was a matter of money.

The bottom had fallen out of the Houston boom, seemingly overnight. Failed housing developments across the city were reverting to the banks that had put up the loans, and in turn, these banks were going bankrupt and reverting to larger banks on the East Coast. Houston was becoming a ghost town. One of the bankrupted victims of the city's collapse was the developer who'd bought our Brookshire property, and because of the arrangements of the sale, made much to my mother's disadvantage, she was bilked of $400,000.

I was dumbfounded, but my mother handled this financial catastrophe with quiet resignation, countering it with a new scheme that took on locomotive momentum. Before putting The High Road house on the market, she was determined to get it looking just right. She'd discovered that the original blueprints called for a terraced hillside garden with restraining walls of rough yellow limestone descending from the pool, and construction of these walls had already begun. The house was built on a hilltop, with a driveway that approached in steep, direct ascent. She was also determined to jackhammer the asphalt and reroute the driveway in a lazy spiral around the hill, converting the steep approach into a limestone staircase that would wind among ten-foot-square planters filled with flowering trees. The limestone plan was more than visionary; it was prohibitively expensive. I cautioned restraint, but my mother was deaf to reason. She had her own logic; in such a tight market, the limestone improvements were necessary to sell the house for a profit. Attacking the plan with monomaniacal fury, she fulfilled her vision in a year's time, to the tune of $50,000.

In spite of her restlessness and misfortunes with money, Austin suited my mother. Set in the arid hills of Central Texas, among lakes and winding rivers, the region had a Wild West flair and rugged casualness that aligned with her own. She was more sure of herself, her will had sharpened, and she was less lonely than she'd been in Brookshire. I felt confident that in Austin she'd at last found her home, and perhaps not far behind was a man who would deliver her from worry, who would take care of her at long last. Before leaving Stanford for the summer, I'd received a letter from my grandmother, who, on a recent visit to Austin, had made the acquaintance of Milt, my mother's latest admirer. She sent the following report: "tall and lean, steel gray hair, flat tummy." My hopes were high.

Not long after I arrived, I spent a long, rainy afternoon in Milt's presence with a smile plastered to my face. Installed in my mother's living room for the duration of the storm, he told an interminable series of Polish jokes, proving himself a member of the later, nerdy period of my mother's boyfriends. This was evident in the cut of his steel gray hair, and in the cut of his tan, gallon-pocketed leisure jacket.

After he left, I turned to my mother. "What bargain rack did he come off of?"

"He's funny sometimes," she said. "Don't be such a snob."

She was right. I was being a snob, but not for the reasons she assumed. It wasn't only Milt's stupid jokes or his unfashionable jacket. How could I tell her that ever since my childhood I'd secretly nurtured an idea of the perfect man for her, and that Milt was so far from that ideal it broke my heart? Or perhaps, I thought the next day as I lugged limestone blocks up the driveway, I was unwilling to examine what lay beneath my childish wish, that I wanted a man to take responsibility for her so that I could get myself unstuck and move on with my own life. But still even more difficult to admit was this: I had never stopped craving a father for myself, who might be open, loving, and warm, a man I respected and looked up to; I wanted her to find someone quickly before I grew too old to benefit. Over the course of the summer, I could not hide the depth of my relief on Milt's less and less frequent appearances, and finally on his disappearance altogether.

In August, Houston was hit by hurricane Alicia. Downtown streets were left knee-deep in shattered glass from skyscraper windows, and in my father's neighborhood hundreds of old oak trees were felled, crashing into homes and blocking the roads. Electricity was knocked out in much of the city. Not long before my stepmother's diagnosis with lung cancer, my father had formed his own stock brokerage firm, and he'd been struggling in the months since her death not to lose everything. He'd put up his house for sale, but the hurricane hastened his departure. When I called to say I was coming for a visit, he told me he was staying with a friend for the time being, and I jotted down the new address.

Arriving in Houston, I found that my father's new place of tenancy, a small, nondescript house, lay ensconced in a development only half a mile from where I'd grown up, built upon land cleared of the woods I explored as a child. I was buzzed in through a security gate, and the front door opened as I came up the walk to reveal my father standing behind a woman. I thought: *so soon.* At the same time, I knew that he needed someone to take care of him; he couldn't even cook a meal for himself. "Son," my father said, "this is Violet Woolfe." The woman offered me her hand so that I had to reach forward, nearly bowing, to take it. "Hello, dear," she said, with a syrupy Louisiana bayou of an accent. She gave the impression of beauty, enhancing a resemblance to Elizabeth Taylor with a dramatically swept back hairstyle. At her neck sparkled a large pendant in the shape of the letter V made entirely of diamonds. Unquestionably, I was faced with a formidable personage, and yet her gingham puff-sleeved dress seemed calculated to make her appearance ridiculous.

At Violet's invitation, I stepped into the baroque interior of her house, which, done in lime green and lemon yellow, bathed me in a citrusy sensation. So many surfaces simultaneously claimed my attention that I found it difficult to focus. A white baby grand piano resided in one corner. Objects jammed every inch of space: intricately carved elephant tusks, curlicue furniture, ceramic chandeliers, glassed cabinets full of crystal and china, paintings and ornamental plates on the walls. Violet must have noticed my darting eyes because she took hold of my arm and said, "Let me show you my collections." She twirled around the room pointing them out. "Here are my ivories, my vases, my Russian boxes. I collect things. I love things." Again she stood before me, and it was I who felt vertiginous after that dance. Her expression, too, was bemusing; I felt certain she regarded me with sly amusement, as if wondering if I were quick enough to get the joke.

Navigating through the things to a back den, we found my father already seated on a leather couch watching television. The couch was familiar; it had come from his house, as had many of the other objects in the room. The walls were covered with the results of taxidermic labors: deer heads, ducks, a javelina, geese, an owl. I spotted a large watercolor of a hunting scene, a marsh at dawn with birds flying overhead, a dog tromping through the water to retrieve a duck, two men aiming shotguns, who on closer inspection proved to be my father and his best friend Jimbo. The likenesses were good ones. On the couch was a collection of pillows, each with a needlepointed maxim. *Nouveau riche is better than no riche at all,* I read, and, *Inner peace through materialism.*

"I was just telling your father," Violet said as she took a seat on the arm of a chair, "that those people working on their house right across the street are friends of mine. They've been renovating for months. First they knocked out all the walls so they could rebuild every room, but they didn't like the way it turned out so they knocked them down all over again." She threw her head back and laughed. "They're so crazy. Then they decided the pool was all wrong too. It was oriented north to south, so they bulldozed it and dug another so that it lined up east to west." She paused. "I love that."

I maintained a poker face, but my father watched Violet with the expression of disbelieving amusement I'd so often seen Helen beam upon him.

I excused myself to take my bag upstairs to the guest room. The bed was hard as a slab, but antique. In the bathroom I attempted to wash my hands. The wallpaper had a psychedelic spiderweb pattern that camouflaged the light switch so efficiently I ended up groping around the sink in pitch darkness until I found the soap.

"And of course he married her for her money," Violet was saying when I returned. "I mean, she's a mute, for God's sake. She's in a wheelchair. Welcome to the circus. It's a horror show."

My father grunted assent. Their conversation reminded me of my high school days when I'd listened to the gossip of my father and stepmother, but then Helen had served as the level-headed foil to my father's monologue, and now it was he who served as Violet's straight man. Her gossip—who had filed bankruptcy, who was on the verge, what deals so-and-so was desperately trying to make to stay afloat—was sometimes outright vicious, occasionally sympathetic, always edged with biting humor. The words *estate auction, foreclosure, Chapter 11* escaped her lips like whispered maledictions. I would soon learn that my father and Violet were themselves immune to the fear and scrambling that had infected so many of their acquaintances, because by the end of the summer he would possess virtually nothing but the clothes on his back, and Violet had an unfathomable fortune, perhaps ten million, perhaps a hundred, left to her by her last husband, an octogenarian oil billionaire who had promptly died after the wedding.

"So, Michael," Violet said, turning to me. "You're finishing up at Stanford?"

"I'll be a senior."

"What are you studying?"

"English," my father harrumphed.

"English and Biology," I said.

"Now that's an interesting combination," Violet said. "You could do all sorts of things with that."

I thought so too. My visions of the future encompassed far more than writing novels in a Greenwich Village garret. I would launch myself into adventure, as a researcher in the Amazon jungles, a conservation biologist in New Guinea, on board the *Calypso* with Jacques

Cousteau. My mother had taught me that through sheer force of will, dreams could be brought to life.

"He thinks he's Indiana Jones," my father said.

"I do not," I cried.

"I think it's wonderful," Violet said. "Follow what you crave. *I* always do."

To prove to my father that my head was not entirely in the clouds, I divulged a plan I'd been nursing since my stepmother's death. "I've thought I might eventually like to work in a medical research lab. I think I would be good at it."

"You could find a cure for cancer," Violet said rousingly.

"Why not?"

My father was shaking his head sadly. "Oh, son, you're talking bullshit again."

I thought I'd been doing so well, maintaining the balance of a trapeze artist in this high-wire act of a house. So I threw at him an intentional blasphemy. "You just don't like the idea because I won't make as much money as you."

"Now you're really talking bullshit!"

But then Violet laid a hand on my father's arm, and he immediately calmed. "Michael, dear," she said, "I'm going down to Galveston tomorrow. Want to come?"

I eyed my father and told her I'd probably be heading back to Austin.

"I feel like buying a beach house. They're so cheap right now, and I bet after this hurricane even cheaper. I'd do something special with it, too. White carpet and full of antiques, what do you think?"

"Sounds a little risky. You know how much tar there is on the beach."

"Oh, you kids are old enough to know not to track sand into the house. I think it will be beautiful."

On the way to their favorite restaurant, we drove past my old neighborhood, where the house my parents had built twenty years earlier still stood. About that house, my father, hardly a sentimentalist, still waxed poetic. Since that time, I thought, the course of their lives had steered them so far from what they must have imagined when they first arrived in Houston, a booming backwater where their grandest dreams would be realized. They had followed what they craved, and look where it had gotten them. Out the window I surveyed the passing scene. Bulldozed were the hills on which my brothers and I had played as children, paved over the bayou, gone the fields. In their places stood office buildings, town houses, and strip malls for sale or rent, some boarded over. Across from the supermarket where eons ago I'd shopped for my family rose Four Leaf Towers, twin thirty-story purplish condominiums built by an Italian developer. Most of the floors were still uninhabited, my father remarked. Someone in Houston, drawing on his knowledge of Italian architecture, had spread a rumor that the towers actually leaned, and no one had wanted to move in. As we drove, I overheard my father say that the average occupancy in Houston office buildings was now sixty percent; many floors and some entire buildings stood empty. Violet and my father continued their discussion of Houston's financial hard times, and I sat in the backseat looking out at the city, searching for landmarks I still recognized.

"Violet Woolfe!" my mother said, clapping her hands. "They're perfect for each other."

"You know her?"

"Houston was a very small town once upon a time. I've known her for twenty years."

"You have?" I'd kept silent until I couldn't bear any longer not reporting the sensational details. But learning that Violet had known my mother, and no doubt Helen as well, gilded her with a newly titillating and unsavory edge.

"Do you remember a man I went on a date with, years ago, before I married Hank, and you threw up all over the backseat of his new Cadillac?"

"Of course I remember my first act of guerrilla warfare."

"That was Violet Woolfe's first husband."

"You're kidding."

"I told you it was a small town. All he talked about on that date was Violet."

"Praise Allah you got out of Houston."

"Allah?" Her eyebrows raised disapprovingly.

"It's just an expression, Mom."

Not only had my mother left Houston behind, she'd wasted no time enmeshing herself in Austin. The limestone project was in full swing, transforming the hillside into a cascade of rock and greenery, and unleashed by the failure of the Brookshire deal, she'd whipped up a handful of schemes. She was selling antiques wholesale out of a warehouse, and had recently bought into a vending machine franchise, traveling each week to three disparate points in the city where her machines provided microwaved popcorn for the needy. "The microwave is *inside* the vending machine," she cried, expecting me to share her wonder, and though the purchase price had been exorbitant and the returns a pittance, I held my own disapproving tongue. In a drawing class she'd discovered a latent, untapped prowess, which she was honing in her spare time so that she could cash it in drawing pastel portraits in the mall. She showed me some of her early attempts, and secretly I marveled: at the vibrance, the detail, the life she'd eked from the pastel crayons; but I should not have been surprised. My mother had a Midas flair, not, as she would have wished, in the traditional, golden way, but one I found tremendously more valuable: whatever her fingertips brushed transmuted into beauty.

At the same time she was losing patience with my father. He had stopped paying child support completely—he owed her over twenty thousand dollars—and she felt that in her current circumstances she couldn't afford to make excuses for him as she'd done in the past. "I know he's having money problems too," she said with a newly acquired hardness. "But he's never had a problem coming up with cash for the things he wants himself." This time she didn't ask me to be the messenger. "I've already contacted an attorney. He really will go to jail if he doesn't pay. I'm not fooling around." She stood at the window of her hilltop home, from which we viewed miles and miles of Texas hill country, and down below in the broken asphalt the stonemason toiled to raise her limestone palace. When she spoke again, her voice had become low, softly regretful. "He won't even return my calls. Not since Helen died. I think he's worried we'll get back together if he lets himself talk to me."

For me, the summer had turned into a festival of lugging. I lugged limestone blocks for my mother while hotly debating with the stonemason the definitions of the words *scatological* and *eschatological.* I lugged plates of Mexican food at work, books to school. From my encounter with Violet and my father I carried a resentment at his world of moneyed, ceremonial excess. In my pocket I carried the letters Rose wrote two and three times a week—to touch them, to recall a specific play of words or sentiment, sent a tincture of joy through my chest. And at night, I carried my desire. In darkness, my body became a vessel for it, brimming with a potent pressure that made me tremble, unable to sleep. Closing my eyes I saw shoulders, hips, chests, curved and muscled lines that I ached to reach for, to touch, to recapture from that single night in New Orleans when for once I had followed what I craved. I reviled this part of me, rising from the depths to which I'd banished it. These images wanted to smash apart the plans I had for my life, and so I waged nightly battle against my own will.

31

From London, my plane touched down in Moscow, New Dehli, and finally Kuala Lumpur, like a stone skipping across the surface of the earth. Dressed for European winter at the start of the flight, I disembarked into a blast of tropical Malaysian heat. My initial wanderings revealed to me a city of eclectic streets, where traditional Malaysian kampongs—wooden houses on stilts—stood adjacent to billboards advertising the latest Sylvester Stallone movie dubbed into three different Asian languages. I ate star fruits and passion fruits and mangosteen and rambutan and durian, the last like a foul-smelling, wrinkled baby mouse. At an open-air restaurant surrounded by stalls advertising "Fish Head Porridge" and "Pork Intestine Noodles," I wrote to Rose while monkeys foraged through the trees above. The familiar voice of Karen Carpenter came crackling over the restaurant's hi-fi, and I incorporated some of the lyrics into my letter:

> *Why do birds suddenly appear, every time you are near? Last night I found myself in a Country-and-Western bar—a recent rage in Kuala Lumpur—listening to a band of Malaysians sing in perfect, sweetly modulated Texas twangs. Closing my eyes, I easily believed I was back in Houston, then I opened them and was instantly transported halfway around the world. Finally the star of the evening burst onto the stage, an Elvis*

> *impersonator of Chinese extraction dressed in a blue sequin suit. He thrust his hips and sang, "I'm a hunk a hunk of burning love," while an immense Indian man with a beautiful dark face encouraged me to chug from his pitcher of beer.*

Everything here is so strange, I wrote, *and at the same time so familiar.*

I arrived in Malaysia on Halloween after having wandered in Europe for four months. The solitary, contemplative rhythm of travel, the constant juxtaposition of the alien and the familiar, and an inundation of memories, primarily of my family, made me long for some kind of anchor. So I carried Rose with me. I spoke to her in my head, and wrote a stream of letters and postcards.

> *Last I saw you, you were handing your boarding pass to a stewardess with one hand and wiping tears with the pillow you carried in your other, on the way to begin your fellowship in Atlanta, and I was just leaving to circumnavigate the globe. We finished college, our friends dispersed. Four months gone already, and now I suppose I'll be in Asia for a while. I miss you.*

In mid-November, I was on a train shuttling across the length of Java. It was my mother's birthday and I should have called her, but there didn't seem to be a phone handy. Through my reflection in the train window, I watched the passing terraced rice paddies and banana plantations, the mountainsides cultivated with coconut trees, corn and pepper and tobacco, with rich, red earth visible beneath. Crisscrossed with rivers and waterfalls streaming over beds of black boulders, the island of Java seemed to burst with vegetation and humanity, people who balanced baskets of rocks, rice, dirt, clothing, fruit, even beds and dining room sets on top of their heads. The previous day, walking around the university town of Yogyakarta, I'd happened upon a bird market. Hundreds of cages were jammed full of strawberry finches, white headed nuns, singing thrushes and bulbuls, tiny owls, and brilliant aqua birds with fiery red beaks. No one on earth could have appreciated that scene with the same bittersweetness I felt—the wonder at their beauty, the despair at their squalid captivity—as could my mother.

Yet each time I'd spoken to her since I left home was like manning a crisis hot line. After I hung up I felt I'd just had a round of chemotherapy. My body ached, I experienced a kind of nausea of the mind. I tried to imagine a life where I never heard again about her money problems or her ex-husbands, the complaints that had washed out my ears all my life. Move on, I wanted to shout, get out of that tired rut.

My impatience with her was of recent vintage, and I didn't have a very firm understanding of it. She'd been so encouraging of my trip and had partially subsidized it, proud of my adventurous spirit as she'd been of every project I'd ever undertaken. Only a year earlier I had pooled my hard-earned wages from a college catering job to buy a ticket to New York, where Nick and his wife had planned a celebration for my mother's fiftieth birthday. The three of them flew from Texas for the weekend, and I arranged secretly to show up as a surprise at her birthday dinner. The plan worked beautifully. At the designated hour, I lurked in a recessed doorway on West Sixty-seventh Street, watching for their taxi to pull up to the Café des Artistes. When the cab let them out, I had to suppress the twitching of my excited limbs. I waited five minutes more until I couldn't bear it, then rushed across the street and through the doors.

I spotted them sitting at the bar with their backs to me. I approached my mother and said, "Sorry I'm late. Happy Birthday," then bent to kiss her cheek. Her mouth fell open, and she gripped my arm tightly, trying several times to speak before she could get any words out, while we cheered and whooped. At that moment I truly believed our lives had turned a corner. The careworn furrows in my mother's brow were smoothed away, and she appeared at least fifteen years younger than the fifty we were officially celebrating. As for me, I had recently won a cash prize for a short story I'd written, and this seemed to bode well for my future. At my side, my brother and his wife Olivia were such a natural, loving pair that I could not easily maintain my belief in a family legacy of joyless marriages.

But there was a fifth wheel at that dinner. Across the table from me sat a round-faced man with deep, frowning creases on his forehead and big goldfish eyes. I hadn't met him before, but I knew who he was—Buddy, perhaps the first man ever to have fallen in love with my mother. They'd gone to high school together in Alabama, where he was her best friend and confidante, but he'd also harbored a secret, burning love. Unfortunately for him, my mother's eyes were fixed upon the boys of the track team, and Buddy was a poet. They had graduated, attended different colleges, married other people, and over the years, in the way people do, slowly lost touch. On a whim my mother had gone to their thirtieth high school reunion, where Buddy found her unchanged from the girl he first loved, and he'd been visiting Austin on a regular basis ever since. She was grateful to regain the dear friend but, unfortunately for him still, remained as uninterested in romance as she had in her girlhood.

Dinner lasted for hours, and we drank several bottles of wine. We made toasts to my mother, and Buddy praised her beauty repeatedly. Near the end of the meal, he leaned across the table and whispered to me, "Your mother is so beautiful. She hasn't aged a day. I love her still." He paused, then said slowly, "She showed me some of your stories. I hope you don't mind. I love your stories. And I love you, because of your stories." He spoke so softly and liltingly I wasn't sure I'd heard him correctly, but my body knew. I gripped the edge of the table and clenched my jaw with such force my teeth were put in jeopardy. Here was the chance I'd been hoping for all my life, a cultured man who wanted not only my mother but me as well, the son he'd never had, and I was pressed right up against the falseness of my wish. Maybe if I'd been able to embrace him as my daddy we both would have been much happier, but by that point I'd had too many daddies already.

In the bus station of Banyuwangi, Java, at five in the morning, I felt a tug at my elbow. Beside me stood an Indonesian boy about ten years old, with a serious, earnest face. He wanted to practice his English, he said, and asked me to look over a recent homework assignment.

Please check which of the following are universal truths.

(1) Goat and cow eat grass.	Yes ☐	No ☐
(2) Snake fly.	Yes ☐	No ☐
(3) Snake live in a house.	Yes ☐	No ☐

His teacher had marked the answer to number three as yes; it was a universal truth that snake live in a house. The homework, I soon discovered, was a ruse. My friend proceeded to drill me about the United States, though he already knew what Texas was like, he said, from watching *Dallas*. "What religions are there in America?" he asked. I'd become quite a patriot in my travels, and I answered proudly that America was founded on freedom of religion, and so there were all religions there.

"Then there are many mosques in Texas?"

I laughed out loud and had to concede that no, mosques did not exactly dot the landscape of the Lone Star State.

I boarded the bus toward Bali, but I was thinking of home. I'd spent my first eighteen years in the Lone Star State, and ever since I left, I'd run back every chance I had, like a two-year-old exploring the world then rushing back to Mommy. I wondered if the rest of my days would be spent bouncing back and forth between my own life and hers. She'd visited me in California the first time during my sophomore year, bringing Celeste and Scotty and Henry. For five days I paraded them around Stanford and San Francisco, so excited to show her my new life that I wanted to dash from place to place, but for some reason she wore a pair of skyscraper heels that virtually crippled her; she walked about as quickly as a goat and cow eating grass. Henry, five years old and fearless, took off running every time we came to the crest of a steep hill in San Francisco, flying down the slope so fast he could barely stop himself from running into the street at the bottom. Before I noticed, he'd be halfway down the hill, letting out a scream from the thrill and the speed, and then I'd go after him, chasing him down and bringing him back to our slowpoke mom. For five days I ran from my mother to Henry to my mother to Henry. Then he'd run off again, flying away from us. And I was jealous of him.

I knew my letters to Rose must have mystified her, because I never explained with what memories or thoughts I'd brought myself to such a nostalgic and declarative state of mind.

> *Do you remember writing me this in a letter before I left?*
>
> > *It has occurred to me fairly often that I don't tell you nearly enough just how much I appreciate*

> *you, how much I love being with you. I wish I could tell you how un-alone you make me feel. In many ways, Michael, you make all the difference. And not just now, you have for a long time. Do you ever think that there are very few things that really* last? *But once they do, they get more and more interesting and complicated and satisfying.*

I don't have it memorized, in case you're wondering. I brought it with me. I picture you now, your fellowship in Atlanta over, finding an apartment and job in San Francisco, going about the business of creating your life. When I am done with these peregrinations, I think I will join you there. In college I kept going home to Texas out of responsibility to my mother, but each time I returned to California I felt that I was returning to you.

Sometime in January I was traveling into the interior of Borneo on the Rajang River. I'd gone first by an all-night cargo boat from Kuching to Sarekei that boiled up a phosphorescent wake, then by speedy passenger boats to Sibu and Kapit, and onward into the forest toward my final destination: an Iban Indian longhouse. Lined with thick, mountainous jungle, the river was the color of frothy coffee. On the bow of the boat lay a heap of animals I was hard pressed to identify, a couple of jungle deer or antelope and what looked like a prehistoric fish seven feet long. That there were any animals at all surprised me because everything I'd read of the disappearing rain forest was true; large swaths were cut through the trees, and acres of logs crowded the shore awaiting transport. The air inside the boat was chilled to about fifty degrees, and I shivered watching the television at the fore continually playing kung fu movies with a sound track of grunts and groans. Across from me sat a woman with a dark, broad Indian face, smoking a cheroot. Her earlobes dangled in long loops, and in the folds of her sarong she carried her baby, a little boy wearing a Superman t-shirt who looked at me every so often and burst into tears.

I'd grown used to a land without blond folks. Shop girls occasionally barreled out into the street to gawk as I passed, others had run after me waving and smiling. In contrast, the Iban were very shy, though their hands and faces were marked with swirling, spiky tattoos. My guidebook informed me that until recently they'd been headhunters. Once they cut jugulars, now they cut logs. Apparently the Iban were so hospitable that I had only to present myself at their door to be welcomed for as long as I wanted to stay. Or so said my guidebook. My part of the bargain was to bring gifts of food and toys, and never, not ever, even consider stopping at a longhouse that displayed a white flag, a signal that the community was in mourning. Every few miles, the boat passed a longhouse on the riverbank—long, wooden structures on stilts with many apartments—each of which had a television antenna rising high above the forest canopy.

> *What shows are they watching, do you think?* The Brady Bunch? Gilligan's Island? *I have arrived here in search of the rarest, the strangest the world has to offer, the most distant from everything I have previously known, and yet just this morning, in a market along the river, I discovered a rack of* Star Trek *postcards.*

Longhouse after longhouse passed, and finally I marshalled my courage and asked the boat driver to let me out. I scrambled up the muddy river bank, removed my shoes, then up the rickety wooden ladder and through the longhouse entrance I went. Leaving the bright equatorial daylight, I stood and blinked in the dim longhouse unable to see, but then I began to discern a group of figures, five or six men, sitting in a circle around me, smoking. They were just silhouettes, and when I sat with them, they appeared not even to acknowledge my presence. I dug around in my bag for the canned tuna and bead necklaces I'd brought as gifts, and from my guidebook I read my request to stay the night: "*Malam ini mungkin saya minta tinggal di rumah?*"

Did I perceive a slight nodding of their heads, a whispering murmur of acceptance, or was that only wishful thinking? I repeated my question, enunciating more clearly, and again they seemed to nod, but I wasn't certain. I looked to the man beside me. He leaned close and said into my ear, as soft as a lullaby, "I just called to say I love you."

Then he leapt up and motioned me to follow the length of the longhouse, and in better light I could see that he was only a teenager.

Adults sat in small groups going about their daily business, weaving fishing nets and baskets, carving wood, sharpening knives. A band of children tagged along in my wake. They each wore a small red packet on a string around their necks, which I later learned contained their umbilical cords ground to a powder, to be used in a concoction whenever they became sick. One of the children, Jemat, a boy of eight or nine, kept touching my hair in wonder at its light color, then would suddenly grab my hand and smile up at me. I thought that maybe they had seen me on a *National Geographic Special*, just as I had seen them, and here I was in the flesh.

Dinner that night was provided by the Tuah Ramah, the longhouse leader: pork, rice, corn, and some greens picked right from the river's edge. On the walls were posters of the Six Million Dollar Man and Heather Locklear. Was there some place more removed than this? I asked Rose in my head. Had I to go to Papua New Guinea, the Congo? As I lay down to go to sleep with the Tuah Ramah's family and others—a kind of slumber party with the alien—Jemat sat up watching me, as though he would never grow bored.

> *With Jemat nearby, I thought of your little brother Curt, and last year when I visited your family again for Thanksgiving. There was one night—do you remember?—when you and Curt and I were driving around, doing some errands for your mother, not talking, just listening to music, I think it was Joni Mitchell. You drove, and Curt was sitting in my lap with his hand resting very trustfully in mine, and I thought:* our little family.

The last morning of my stay I stepped outside the longhouse to stretch. The sun was already blazing, a flock of tiny birds flew low over the river, and then, to my dismay, I viewed a great, billowing white flag on the roof. I stepped gingerly back inside expecting to receive the admonishing stares my disrespect deserved. Instead, the Tuah Ramah led me onto a verandah overlooking the river, where I sat with ten or twelve men on a rug woven with an intricate design of skeletons and severed heads. Others crowded around us. I noticed a small, grunting pig trussed in the corner, and several bowls were set out in a circle, each filled with roots or grain. A bottle was passed around, and I drank, propelled into drunkenness by the clear, scorching liquid. Plates were passed next, from which I ate an extremely bitter root. I swallowed more fiery liquid. A bowl was placed into my hands, and as I spooned beaten eggs onto the ground, a man waved a chicken over my head and chanted. He waved the chicken over the pig, then chopped off its head, dipping feathers into the blood and stirring the bowl of beaten eggs with the quills. The pig served as the next sacrificial victim. It screamed as its head was sawn off, and then the boy who'd called to say he loved me clambered up the longhouse roof and threw the pig's head over the peak.

Drums were beating. An old man with drooping earlobes and tattoos on his throat danced around me, waving a machete in one hand and a bamboo stick in the other. I gulped my ritualistic drink. With each drum beat he thwacked the bamboo with the machete inches from my face. He danced until a big plate of steaming meat was placed at the center of the circle. All eyes were on me as I took the first taste. I popped a piece into my mouth—fresh pig liver—and everyone erupted in cheers. Soon, we were all drinking and eating pig liver and dancing together.

> *If that was a funeral, it was certainly the way to go. I was still light headed from the alcohol as I waited on the tiny dock for the afternoon boat, the denizens of the longhouse waving to me from the verandah. On the riverbank a group of children were jumping into the water and splashing each other, Jemat among them, and impulsively I decided to follow their example. I stripped off my clothes and dove into the river. The water was wonderfully cool, and the current so strong it carried me twenty feet before I reacted. I splashed crazily, drunkenly back and hauled myself onto the dock, breathless, elated, feeling as though my life had been saved.*
>
> *Now, as I write, I'm on the boat, headed home. Not long before we graduated, Sophie said to me, "We all know that you have always loved Rose. She knows it, you know it, and all your friends can see it." I wanted to*

tell her that she'd gotten it wrong. The truth is this: I wish I could tell you how un-alone you make me feel. *It seems to me that only a membrane separates us; you and* I know *each other. So much of my life has been broken up and splintered, and I didn't know how it felt to be whole until I met you.*

I've said nothing to you all this time because, to be honest, I'm terrified to attach myself to another human being. That's why I've had to travel halfway around the world to tell you that I love you.

32

e're a funny little sexless triple, aren't we?" Sophie said. We were driving home from Santa Cruz after spending the day at the beach, and my skin tingled from the sun. Rose nodded in agreement.

"No, we're not," I said forcefully, then turned it into a joke. "Anyway, it's quadruple, please." I indicated the life-sized inflatable skeleton strapped into the backseat beside me. "You'll hurt Mr. Bones's feelings."

Since I'd returned to San Francisco six months earlier, the three of us spent nearly all of our free time together. Sophie had recently broken up with her boyfriend, and Rose's of five years had moved to Arizona. A couple of years out of college, many of our peers were taking part in the mid-eighties scramble for cash, but our friends had become nomads, wandering out across the country and the world; Rose and Sophie set up housekeeping together in a part of San Francisco guidebooks advised tourists to steer clear of, and my own apartment was not far away. Sophie's job in a bookstore downtown introduced her to the spectrum of city life, from which she arrived home every evening with stories of crazy urban personalities. Rose worked at a women's health clinic, where giving presentations on birth control and running a panel of teenage mothers for students in Oakland schools had earned her the nickname Sex Lady. She too returned from work with tales of a world previously foreign to us, of poverty, drug abuse, and gritty hardship and endurance. I was hired to write environmental protection guidelines for a federal research lab, where I attended seminars on espionage and the Strategic Defense Initiative, strange words to my ears. After a day's labor the three of us convened, bringing back news from the front, then set out to explore our adopted city. Finding first jobs, first apartments, learning together how to pass as adults, we gave texture to one another's lives.

Late in college Rose had decided to become a doctor, and around her work schedule she was still finishing up her medical school requirements. I was in awe of her energy and the passion and generosity of spirit she brought to her job. She was a live wire. Since I'd returned from Asia, during the bustle of job hunting and marauding through San Francisco, I'd managed to evade any direct confrontation with her. On the other side of the world my heart had felt so clear, and now, when I was seeing Rose daily, it was once again clouded, timorous. Most of the time, busy herself, she allowed me to pretend I had never written her a single love letter, but on occasion I found her watching me with curious frustration, as if I were a logic problem she couldn't quite make sense of.

By the time we reached home from Santa Cruz, we were already late for a party; one of our college friends was leaving the next day for the Peace Corps. There was no time to go to my own apartment, so I rustled up some clothes out of Sophie's closet. We dressed hurriedly, chose a blue Laura Ashley dress for Mr. Bones, and headed across town.

We'd driven a few blocks before our clothes began to strike me as comically inappropriate for public display. Rose and Sophie had thrown on identical sundresses, one blue and one red, and they each wore a white jacket. Looking at myself, I found that I was wearing a ruffly Mexican shirt and baggy, high-water seersucker pants that were too tight to button at the waist. "I look like a fool," I said.

Sophie glanced at me, then looked from Rose to herself. "We're buffoons," she cried, and we choked on our giddy laughter. Even at the party, as we chatted among others, Mr. Bones's inflatable arm slung across my shoulders like a comrade's, the powerful ties connecting the three of us stretched and bent like elastic bands. I did not know a happiness more piercing than this.

"I first met your mother when she was fifteen," Buddy told me over dinner at Vanessi's. Since my mother's fiftieth birthday in New York, he'd continued to visit her in Austin, but I hadn't seen him again until this evening nearly two years later. He called out of the blue. He was in San Francisco on business, he said, and wanted to treat me to a fancy meal. "I remember a night on the beach, she told me everything she hoped for from her life. Marriage, children. She was as fresh and lovely as a flower, and so full of hope, so full of hope." Buddy, I discovered, had lived nearly all his life in the South and was prone to lyricism.

"I got a girl pregnant when I was your age," he said, after we were well into our second bottle of wine. "We weren't in love, but abortion wasn't a consideration then. We got married. The baby was born dead. The married lasted two years."

As he told me these stories, the gently Southern cadence of his voice seemed to sing his words, as though they formed part of an ancient epic. I wanted to resist them; he was an intrusion into my life here, which I had created separate from my mother, an emissary, a call to me, and I did not want to return. But he opened up a world from which I'd always felt excluded—the Alabama life of my parents before they'd moved to Houston, the early years of their marriage—and I listened greedily. I was also flattered by his interest in me, even if at the same time I judged him unsuitable for my mother.

"Are you still writing?" Buddy asked. "You know I always loved your stories."

I told him I was applying to a graduate writing program for the following fall, at Columbia.

His goldfish eyes lit up. "New York!" He leaned forward. "I lived in New York. I was going to be a writer too." A dreamy smile crept across Buddy's face. The risk and uncertainty of the writer's life had proved too much for him, he admitted, so he'd gone back home to Alabama and built a career in the hotel industry. "But don't you ever give up. Do it for me."

After dinner we retired to the bar of his hotel and he launched once again into long, labyrinthine stories—most of them with my mother as the subject—of disintegrating marriages, alcoholism, and undying love, until I felt queasy. As he grew drunker he became more heated, repeatedly citing the brutishness of my father's character. "Your mother sure knows how to pick them," Buddy said loudly enough to draw the attention of other patrons in the bar. "Why couldn't she choose the faithful, not the faithless?" I was ready to stick my fingers in my ears so as not to hear that Southern voice any longer. "A toast to your beautiful mother," he shouted, raising his glass of cognac high, attempting to stand. "She is a goddess."

Buddy fell back into his seat, where he gazed glassy eyed into the distance, perhaps viewing there the life he'd possessed only at night, in dreams: my mother on his arm, their artistic children. I understood now that what entranced Buddy was the glamorous dinners in New York, the jet-setting, the rediscovery of my mother after so many years of separation, the mist of romance. He didn't want her as a wife, or me as a son, or the life of a writer in New York in any real, daily sense at all; we never could have lived up to his perfect vision of the life he might have had. When I bid good night to Buddy, he barely looked up, still lost in the contemplation of his forty-years-long dream.

At a Halloween party Rose danced the dance of the forty veils. I'd dyed my hair black, freeing myself to make raspy, lecherous comments throughout the evening. Our life together I had pictured in perfect detail—the house on an Oregon riverbank, built strong to withstand storm and flood, our four children—but in forty years would it still be only that, a beautiful, static picture? After seeing Buddy, I was determined to speak.

Leaving the party we drove to my apartment in silence, my mind whirring: *On three I will say it, something, anything, one, two, three . . . Okay, when we cross the intersection of Valencia and Twenty-fourth, here it comes. . . .* I parked beside her car and did not grasp Rose's arm to prevent her from getting out. Loyally I stood beside her as she fished around in her purse for her keys, and then I knew that I could never do it. I had deluded myself as thoroughly and eternally as Buddy had.

Keys in hand, Rose faced me. "Well, that was fun."

"Wait," I said. She was wearing a doctor's white coat with a stethoscope around her neck. Had she applied it to my chest, my heartbeat would have deafened her.

"Is something wrong?"

"The letters I wrote," I mumbled.

"What letters?"

"You know what I mean. The ones I wrote from Asia."

Rose considered this for a moment. "They were pretty letters."

"I wanted to. . .," I began, but I didn't know what I wanted. My tongue seemed to have fallen asleep. "Maybe we could talk about it."

"Oh, Michael. I'm tired of words."

She stood rigid; she might have been very angry. I said, "I've always cared for you a great deal."

"You've waited long enough to say anything."

"I was shy, or scared, or something. But it's not like it's a surprise. I never hid how I felt."

"That's not true," she cried. "I never knew what you were thinking or what you wanted. You wrote those crazy letters whenever you went away, and every time you saw me again you kept me at arm's length. I didn't have any idea what you felt. You make me crazy. You're exasperating."

"Are we having a fight?"

"Yes, we are. We are having a fight."

"Our first."

We stared at each other. Rose made a sudden motion; I thought she was reaching for the car door, but instead she threw down her bag on the hood and stepped toward me. I received the kiss she planted on my mouth as immovably as a chunk of cement, but then, warming, followed her example. My lips softened. Rose drew back, and now she appeared frightened of what she'd initiated.

"After all this time," I said, moving toward her, "is that all?" We kissed again. Then she broke away, got the car door between us, and drove off.

After that night there were further kisses, but we were full of trepidation. Though we were intimate with each other's mind, our bodies were wholly foreign; for two months we made cautious preliminary forays, kissing and touching like teenagers. We lay in bed embracing for hours, moving toward sexual congress at a pace any outside observer would have described as glacial, but which I felt carried me along at a gallop. I had never before lain all night beside the radiating heat of another person; the sensation kept me awake until dawn; I did not want to sleep. Running my hand down the length of Rose's arm, across her breasts and throat, filled me with exploratory wonder, and when at last we made love, it was with the gentleness and care of long acquaintance, yet physically exultant. Afterwards we lay together and made plans; we'd travel the South American continent, live for a year in Cuzco, practice medicine, write books. I believed that our plans for the future could bind me to real and lasting happiness.

"I'm at a crossroads," Rose called down to me from the loft in my apartment, six months after Halloween. She'd recently been accepted to medical school in Cleveland, and I to Columbia; the imminence of leaving bore down on us. I sat at my desk below where I couldn't see her, paying bills.

"What kind of crossroads?"

"About you," she said. "About falling in love with you."

I wrote a check slowly, inserted it into an envelope. "Is it a choice?"

"Right now I think it is."

"Then it would probably be wiser not to."

She didn't respond, and that night in bed we were shy with each other. It was the friend, not the lover, who cautioned her not to open her heart to me. Loving me was dangerous; I harbored a bomb. When Rose and I made love I often could not look her in the eye, afraid she'd see what I had always kept banished to darkness. Yet my longing was like a lighthouse beacon, a beam forever revolving back, sweeping toward me, then the blinding flash of desire for physical and emotional closeness with a man. The long history of our friendship and the new exhilaration of sex had not prevented this beam from relaying the urgent message I'd heard since adolescence: *you must contend with me.* The community of friends I'd found in college and my relationship with Rose had given me a belief in myself wholly apart from my family, and it was this strength I would have to marshal to explore my own heart, though I thought it might kill me to do so. What I could not tell Rose was that I longed to leave. I wanted to go alone to New York so that the most dangerous exploration of my life would harm no one I loved.

Rose and I traveled in Europe for the summer. We hiked Pyrenean peaks, picnicked in Spanish meadows, ate octopus and snails in southern France, walked the streets of Paris arm in arm. We made grateful, tender love every night, and made plans to visit our new Eastern cities in the fall and to live together the following summer. In the shadow of our departure, we had never loved each other so well.

CHAOS

33

In August, my mother's garage maintained a constant temperature of ninety-nine degrees Fahrenheit. It was a new garage—while I'd been in Europe she'd completed her limestone monolith, sold the house for a marginal profit, and moved off The High Road to a modest suburban neighborhood with streets named after birds—but it shared with her previous garages the appearance of having suffered a tornado's wrath. Upon arriving, I viewed a maelstrom of half-unpacked boxes, furniture of both the intact and broken varieties, birdcages, various antique-looking rusted artifacts, a stationary bicycle, deflated air mattresses hanging upon the scene like Dalí timepieces, cans of paint, and other buried items not immediately discernible. I set to work with ritualistic thoroughness. I cleared a workspace, erected shelves, categorized the items. My blood alive, I harnessed the whirling chaos of my mother's universe: this was the work I'd been born to.

I was home for a week only before packing up my pickup truck and moving to New York. In Spain we had boarded different aircraft, Rose to Cleveland to find an apartment, and I to Texas, crowded against the window by an immense Ugandan intent on spying the Atlantic. While I organized paint cans and brushes, a telephone lay nestled nearby in a beanbag chair the color and shape of an avocado, and on it I received updates from Rose about her first medical school classes. I checked in, too, with my older brothers. Nick and Olivia awaited my arrival in New York, where they'd moved a year earlier; and in June, John and his wife had had a baby girl. I hoped to visit them in Oklahoma on my drive to the Northeast, but on the phone John admitted he wasn't feeling well. I attributed his exhaustion to the baby, yet I couldn't picture him—pacing in the deep of the night, a screaming colicky newborn in his arms—without laughing in delight: my brother, a father!

During my week in the garage, I saw Scotty and Henry on two instances a day, the first as they passed on their way to school and the second when they arrived home, each time giving me the sympathetic, condescending look they might have reserved for the village idiot. I recognized this look. It was the same I'd directed at Nick ten years earlier when he'd come home from college for the sole purpose of cleaning out my mother's refrigerator.

My younger brothers' faces were the only ones I saw. Celeste was at college in Colorado, and my mother was out of the house all day long. With a man. I'd returned from Europe to find her schoolgirlishly happy. "He's hideous," she admitted, "but if I close my eyes and put my hand out to touch him, and know that I love this man, what difference do looks make?" She'd met Louie early in the summer in a tennis class. I was pleased for her, I told myself, I really was, but then why did I quail at her use of the word *love?*

Her step was clearly springier than I'd witnessed in quite some time, not only because of her children—John's baby, Nick's and my prospects in New York—who had always provided the backbone of her happiness, but at long last for her own reasons. And yet I didn't buy it. Perhaps I was hesitant to accept her changed fortune because of Louie's startling, horrific life, which she related to me within an hour of my arrival. During the Korean War he'd been an ace navy pilot, whose plane was shot down over enemy territory. He survived the crash only to be captured and imprisoned, where he was mercilessly tortured, beaten until the bones of his face fractured, his leg broken and never set, his teeth drilled one by one from his mouth. Starvation was just one more element in this campaign of terror. Over a period of months he witnessed the executions of his fellow prisoners until, realizing his own life was to be taken next, Louie killed a guard with his bare hands and escaped from the prison camp. Traveling through the jungle at night, he ate insects and scavenged from the trash piles of villages. In eight days he covered the hundred miles to the coast. When he arrived at the ocean he continued without pause into the surf and began swimming; he knew that American warships patrolled these waters. A few miles out, one picked him up. He was the only American prisoner of war during the Korean conflict to escape and survive, he told my mother.

His story certainly stretched the limits of credibility, I had to admit, but my mother's past was not unlittered with heroes; I still recalled Robert the journalist, pegged by a sniper's bullet, with great fondness. Besides, my mother and I shared an unshakeable trait: we trusted people. We did not believe they would lie. Twist the truth, perhaps, but not outright, boldfacedly lie. Any doubts I had were dispelled immediately when I met Louie. His scarred, misshapen physiognomy, as if reconstructed with wire and putty, bore hideous corroboration. His mouth bulged with dentures, and an ill-fitting toupee perched upon his scalp. He limped. His adoration of my mother was displayed like a medal pinned to his barrel chest. Scruffy, rather short, with a heavy Louisiana accent, Louie was a model of eagerness to please.

He whipped up a cauldron of gumbo one night and directed every line of conversation into a story about the war. ("You driving up to New York? That reminds me of shipping out of Korea . . .") During the meal Scotty and Henry responded to his jokes and familiarities like co-conspirators, and my mother obviously delighted in Louie's attention. I alone felt a visceral sense of unease, like the segmented legs of insects scurrying over my skin. After dinner, we watched a movie on the VCR, a Grace Kelly film I'd chosen because she reminded me of Monaco, where I'd just been with Rose. My mother sat holding Louie's hand on the couch, and I took refuge in a local armchair.

Five minutes into the movie, Louie brayed, "What a terrible actress!"

"Hush," my mother admonished with a giggle.

"No, really, she's awful, she's really awful."

I beamed a command through his knobby skull: *shut up*.

"I never knew she was such a terrible actress. Beautiful of course, but look at her; she can't act to save her life."

Judging from my mother's reaction, Louie wielded the wit of a brilliant humorist. She failed to stifle a cascade of giggles every time he erupted into patter, an occurrence of military regularity throughout the movie, but it took no more than half an hour for me to truly, deeply despise him. Louie was hideous, a gasbag, a liar; my mother had thrown her judgment to the wind.

After the movie I corralled Henry and Scotty around a box of old wigs and hairpieces I'd come across in the garage that afternoon, and the three of us put on a wig show. My mother doubled over laughing as we paraded around in the wigs, then clapped a hand over her mouth, but Louie didn't muster a smile.

The day before I was to leave I backed my pickup into the spotless garage, loaded the bed with my computer, books, and the furniture my mother had given me, and was tying a blue tarp over the sum of my possessions when the phone rang. I picked it up from the beanbag chair a moment after my mother had answered somewhere else in the house, recognizing the voice of John's wife on the other end as I returned the phone to the cradle. About an hour later Louie's car pulled up to the curb, where he lurked until my mother came out of the house, rushing by without acknowledging me.

Nor did she return for dinner. Angrily reheating the gumbo, I did not ask Scotty and Henry if this were newly typical behavior for her. After they'd gone to bed I waited up, reading a novel on the couch, the house dark but for the single lamp beside me. The hands of my watch reached eleven o'clock before I finally heard the door opening. My mother strode quickly across the room and stood before me, and it was only then that I viewed what I had not allowed myself to see earlier as she'd fled the house, the ravaged, rent appearance of her face. She knelt at my feet like a supplicant. "They've taken John to the hospital," she said. "They flew him in a helicopter to Dallas." My mother lay her head on my lap and began to sob, an animal sound, her body convulsing. "They think he has leukemia." I could not absorb her words. My hand smoothed her hair, over and over. I felt myself beginning to detach from everything I'd previously known or believed or wanted, merging with what I heard in her voice: a filament of horror. "I knew I could always take anything that happened to me," she whispered, "but not to my children."

34

I felt a little pinch as the phlebotomist tightened a rubber thong around my arm. The four vials he'd set in a row were to be filled with my blood, then shipped on ice to Texas, where John's doctors would determine if I could serve as a bone marrow donor. On this day, each member of my family was doing the same, in another doctor's office in another city: Celeste in Boulder, Scotty and Henry and my mother in Austin, my father in Houston, Nick and I in New York. Henry's and my parents' blood tests were for informational purposes only; the donor would necessarily be one of John's full siblings. One of us would have to match, or else there could be no marrow transplant. Without the transplant, John would die.

The phlebotomist had pulled his chair near mine, our knees intercalating. I watched the lines of intent on his face as he readied a syringe over my arm, tapped the vein, so close to me I could feel the beats of his breath upon my skin. The sleeve of his white coat was rolled tightly over his own muscular forearm, the skin a molten brown. One vein stood prominent on his broad forehead, and his voice was threaded with an African musicality. "Do you mind watching me do this," he asked, "or shall I tell you when to turn away? It won't hurt, but some people don't like to watch."

"I want to see it," I said.

Knowing the reason for my visit, he treated me with extraordinary gentleness. He explained each step as he slid the syringe beneath my skin, then attached the first vacuum-sealed vial. Blood spurted from my arm into the glass cylinder, a beautiful dark, velvety red, which in John had taken fierce, mutated form. I was mesmerized by the blood quickly filling the first vial, then a second, third, fourth. *Let it be me,* I thought. *Let me be of help.*

"Are you feeling alright?" the phlebotomist asked. My eyes moved slowly from the blood to his concerned face. I realized that my head had fallen back against the wall, and as he removed the needle from my arm, a tight knot of nausea unraveled like a snake in my gut. Black particles descended into my vision, crackling and popping. "Put your head between your knees," he ordered, and the blackness halted, hovering over me as I maintained a thin grip on consciousness. His hand, big and warm on my back, helped me to the examination table, where I still lay when he ushered Nick into the room.

Nick cracked jokes throughout his own bloodletting, but not once did his glance alight on his arm or the syringe or the blood. By the time his four vials were full, I was able to walk unassisted. We packed the blood in ice and headed across town to Federal Express.

It wasn't me. It wasn't Nick, or Celeste. In our bone marrow sweepstakes, only Scotty held the winning card. Scotty, who since his birth had been ignored, worried over, berated, was going to save our brother's life.

I felt frozen. I wanted to freeze time, freeze belief. I wandered the streets of New York, which were full of poor people and shouting people, a child dancing on a broken fire hydrant, random agents without cause, until I battened down, locked up my grief, banished self-pity. If I were to be of any use, I knew I'd have to forge myself anew of steel and iron. Near the end of the day I invariably found myself climbing the stairwell to Nick and Olivia's apartment; on the massive slab of this city we huddled together like refugees.

My heart and mind were in Dallas with John. Celeste had moved there from Colorado to help care for the baby, and Scotty was in Dallas as well, enduring a series of his own tests as the marrow donor. I felt envy at their usefulness, and anger that I could do nothing but pretend to carry on with my own affairs. Beside the gravity of what was happening to John, my own life had gossamer weight. I wanted to shirk life. Classes at Columbia, fixing up my apartment, even talking with Rose on the phone felt airily untenable; only the details emerging from Dallas carried meaning. My mother called with daily reports. John's leukemia had progressed into blast stage, the doctors determined, the cancerous marrow cells reproducing at such a spectacular rate they'd built up painful pressure inside the bone. In order to shock the cancer into remission, they'd begun John on a course of chemotherapy as soon as he'd been admitted into the hospital, but only a bone marrow transplant could rid his body entirely of the leukemia. I skipped my classes to sit on the steps of Low Library and read the medical articles sent by John's wife, to learn what I could about bone marrow matches, the Philadelphia chromosome, chronic myelogenous leukemia. As a child I'd been an idolator of nature, and in college a student of biological science. In nature it was the predominance of order that made life possible, a perfection that I found to be a kind of beauty, but in John's body genes had taken unregulated, chaotic form. Reading the articles, I was not certain I could believe that order, once lost, would ever prevail again, and because of that, I did not contact John. I knew that if we spoke he would hear the hopelessness in my voice.

My mother was spending most of each week at John's hospital bedside, and when we talked on the phone, I felt bound to her as if to a lifeline. When the course of the chemotherapy reached its end, she reported, John was too susceptible to infection, and too weak, to receive visitors. In his presence, she had to wear a mask and gloves at all times. John's spirits were high, but each day was a battle with raw pain and boredom and fear. Weeks would have to pass before the doctors could determine whether the chemotherapy had succeeded, though in the meantime they were moving ahead with plans for the marrow transplant. In early October, she called with good news. The leukemia had gone into remission. The doctors had never seen a patient quite like John, she said—her voice not untinged with a mother's pride—who maintained such good humor and a tireless will to live. All month she'd remained bright and tirelessly faithful herself, but there were moments, such as when she spoke to me of the night John had fainted in the shower and she'd thought he'd died, that allowed me to glimpse the fragility beneath the brightness, like the flickering of a light. "When they do the transplant he'll have to have more chemo," she told me. "They might have to give him radiation therapy too, but they're trying not to, because it would probably damage his lungs. Then he wouldn't be able to play all the sports he loves so much. But he could still go fishing. He could go fly fishing in the mountains. He always loved fishing so much. God wouldn't take that away from him."

I felt that I was talking with a delusional woman. Given the information we had, John's death was more probable than his survival, and I was furious that she chose to turn from the truth, taking refuge instead in the blind faith, as she had throughout my childhood, that at the last minute we would be whisked to safety by an omnipotent being. We would *not* be saved, I wanted to shout. But after I got off the phone, I began to understand she knew John's chances as clearly as I did, that she was neither ignorant nor deluded, but that she willed herself to believe in life over death. To me, this was an act of courage greater than facing the statistical truth, courage I did not possess. So I called her the next day, and the next, nursing on her faith as I had all my life.

Three days a week I took an elevator to the seventh floor of the American Museum of Natural History and drifted down the length of a palatial green hallway, where doors opened onto wispy-haired scientists tinkering over trays of fossils, then climbed a spiral staircase to the top floor. There I worked on a study of depth perception in the Israeli spiny mouse, a desert rodent with acute vision and extraordinarily developed leaping abilities. The spines were purely figurative, suggested by the mouse's spiky pelt. Each of twenty spiny mice I set upon a ten-inch-high stand in a small chamber, the floor of which was either solid gray, allowing the mouse to gauge distance, or checkered black and white, a pattern that disrupted its visual ability. Then I observed the mouse's behavior. A pencil slash in a box marked every forward or lateral motion, a stance upon hind feet, the state of the mouse's alertness or fear, and whether or not it produced one of its famous leaps from the stand to the checkered floor, to fall an unknowable distance. Afterwards, at a desk overlooking the red-gold autumn foliage of Central Park, I tallied my results. My gaze often drifted to the park, and I wondered: how to quantify fear and uncertainty, to understand the checkered nature of my faith? How to leap and believe I would land upon solid earth?

35

Through the fall, I sent Rose the stories I was writing for my classes at Columbia, stories in which people were set adrift in lives of violence and disorder, but that was the extent of my ability to communicate with her. Whenever we spoke on the phone, I heard the torpid monotone of my voice. What I offered in place of feeling was information about John and the clinical details of his treatment. In October, I visited him for a weekend, reporting back to her the shock of his appearance: his bloated face, the gray pallor of his skin, the few remaining wisps of hair. He'd been let out of the hospital for only a week before the marrow transplant, for which he'd been given a fifty percent chance of surviving, but he was as irrepressible as a schoolboy on vacation. He gave me a tour of his house, played with his daughter, and joked, as if to make fun of my own gravity, about the different cities he might be buried in. He showed me the catheter set permanently into a vein beneath his collarbone, through which Scotty's marrow would be dripped, and I stared at it in grim fascination.

In the first week of November he received a second course of chemotherapy. Through two incisions in Scotty's back, thick soupy marrow was excavated from his pelvis, then introduced into John's bloodstream, where the immigrant cells would have to elude his immune system and find their way to bone. Isolated in the bone marrow unit of the hospital, where his wife Grace and my mother were the only visitors allowed, John began an endurance contest with pain. The chemotherapy killed every type of rapidly reproducing cell in his body; the lining of his mouth, stomach, and intestines all shredded and ulcerated, the way our skin had sloughed in ragged chunks after childhood sunburns. But his spirits remained high, my mother told me, and so did hers.

After I exhausted the latest news of my brother, Rose consoled me with tidbits from her own growing medical knowledge, but over the weeks I became ever more recalcitrant and she more uncertain how to respond. Often we sat in silence for minutes at a time. I felt I had nothing to give her, not even words, and wanted only to shut myself away until the danger passed, to be free of all responsibility to another person. But even the frustration I felt at my inability to speak was as distant as a memory of emotion. I was anaesthetized, while Rose smoldered. The controlled evenness of her tone was like a cage upon her feeling; behind it prowled love and anger clamoring to be set loose. If writing stories was my attempt to still the confusion inside me, then Rose threw her energy into ordering the outside world, as she had always done—in college, in her work with Oakland teenagers, and now in medicine—and from this order believed she could make sense of life; but this put us at odds. I no longer believed there was sense to be made; to try was an act of foolishness.

At Thanksgiving she came to New York, and we fought. "I don't want to know about John anymore," she said. "I want to know about *you*. It's as though you've given up. Don't keep shutting me out."

I eyed her silently, clamped inside a polished sphere.

"Say something," she cried.

"You want me to reassure you, and I can't."

"I want to know if you're sad, or if you miss me. I want you to take comfort in the fact that I love you."

I didn't answer.

"Do you want to break up? Do you want to say one word? You don't give me anything to go on."

"I can't. I'm just trying to hold it together."

"For as long as I've known you, you've been warm and caring and funny. Now you're like ice."

In the abandoned, rubble-strewn lot beside my apartment building, I witnessed a group of rats romping through the first snowfall of winter. The softness of the snow soon turned to sooty slush, revealing once again the harsh outlines of the city. A jittery man on the street demanded money, then punched me in the neck when I told him I had none to give. A woman on the sidewalk ahead collapsed to the pavement and went into violent convulsions, pieces of her shattered teeth marking a circle around her face. Even these daily brutalities I preferred to the necrosis inside me.

Leaving the Columbia campus one afternoon I was joined by Seth, a classmate of lanky stature and lanky brown hair, whose long, thin face possessed some of the more agreeable qualities of a spiny mouse's. Walking alongside me, he covered a variety of subjects in a short time—the outrageous cost of Columbia, an essay he'd published in *Harper's* magazine, a tricky part of the novel he was working on—speaking torrentially in the gesticulating, nervous manner I'd come to associate with natives of the East Coast. Though I was only half listening, a rare sense of peacefulness settled over me. When I turned from Broadway onto 112th Street, I was grateful that Seth followed. Halfway down the block his chatter ceased, and out of the corner of my eye I found him watching me. He lifted his hand and ran it along the back of my head.

I jumped, as if I'd tread upon an electric eel.

"Sorry."

Against the atmosphere's bracing cold, I could feel the prickly outline of my skin. "Don't," I said, then shut my mouth. I had been about to say, Don't worry about it.

"I just felt like touching you."

We continued up the street in silence, a yard or so now between us. Beyond the vacant lot where I'd seen the rats in the snow, I started up the steps of my building, and Seth continued on. I called after him. "You want to come in for some coffee or something?"

He turned. "Coffee?"

I stood holding the door open. He followed me up the steps.

Inside my studio apartment, we divested ourselves of winter coats and scarves and gloves. The only two chairs in the room faced each other from opposite corners. He looked around. "You sure have a lot of stuff."

We both took in the tiny apartment, which was crammed with furniture my mother had given me, all that I'd loaded into my pickup and hauled to New York: wooden chests, tables, a Persian rug, bookshelves, a rocking chair Emmett had brought from Costa Rica, which Seth now occupied. Then our eyes met. "So," he said. "Here I am. I don't really want any coffee."

I could not return the directness of his gaze. During the course of John's hospitalization I'd passed through my classes in a trance, forgetting why I'd come to New York at all. But Seth recalled to me the reason: I'd come to do just this, to invite a man into my house. Yet that was absurd. I no longer had the willingness or interest to explore dark territories in myself, not while John was sick, perhaps dying. "I'm sorry," I said. "I think I made a mistake."

"Excuse me?"

"It might be better if you left."

Seth gathered his things without argument. I crossed my arms over my chest as I watched him go.

On Broadway several weeks later, lost in thought, I looked up to see Seth beside me once again, this time walking a bicycle. He smiled to show that there were no hard feelings, and I told him my good news. The transplanted marrow had begun establishing itself. There were no signs of rejection. As I spoke, I spotted Nick half a block ahead, approaching me with a huge grin, flapping his arms like a chicken. "Did you hear?" he cried. "They say John is cured!" My brother grabbed hold of my arms, and we hooted and hopped in front of a Korean market. By the time I remembered to notice Seth, he'd already gone. I thought I saw his head bobbing down the street as he bicycled away.

"The new marrow has definitely taken," my mother told me over the phone, and I was amazed that the extremities of relief and joy and exhaustion in her voice did not confound the fiber-optic lines. "The old marrow is definitely dead. They can't find any evidence of cancerous cells. The doctors say John's a miracle."

John was alive, cured, news that shocked me nearly as much as his initial diagnosis, but the release of joy I heard from my mother was not immediately available to me. Rose was right. I was ice. Strangely, now that John was out of the woods, I was no longer convinced he'd ever been in real danger. While he'd been so sick, I wasn't able to admit hope, and now I couldn't admit my fear. I could pretend I'd believed all along in his recovery, even to myself.

36

"We have to wait five years to be sure," my mother said over Christmas dinner. "They say that after five years there's very little chance the cancer will come back." Her caution was ill fitting, hardly able to obscure the vitality of her actual thoughts: *thank the Lord my son's alive*. John was in Dallas with his wife's family, broken free of his hospital prison. Scotty displayed the scars on his back, and with a new confidence described the transplant procedure, how afterwards he felt he'd been kicked by a horse. A streak of tropical winter weather conspired with our hearts. The days after Christmas were so sunlit and warm we went swimming at the natural springs in the park, my mother content to sit on the grassy bank watching her children splash and play.

Louie invited the family over to his house for dinner. Frankly, it surprised me that he was still hanging around; my mother hadn't mentioned him in the months since August. But Louie was drinking a glass of wine in her house the night I arrived from New York, and I saw that Scotty and especially Henry enjoyed with him a bantering affection: during my absence, a rat had gotten into the pantry. "He's been such a constant help and support," my mother told me, and admitted she'd been a support to him as well, helping him recover from his own deep emotional wounds. After he'd reenlisted in the navy to fight in Vietnam, Louie's wife had left him; simply put, she'd believed he was a lunatic.

"He reenlisted?" I asked, forming a silent alliance with his ex-wife.

He'd been so traumatized in Korea, my mother explained, that he hadn't been able to acclimatize to civilian life. Louie fled back to the military as if to the security of his true home, though his experiences in Vietnam turned out to be even more scarring than those in Korea. He was still haunted by the faces of the people he'd killed.

Louie so pervaded her conversation that I suspected he'd asked my mother to marry him and that she had not banished from her mind the possibility of accepting. Of course she was a sucker for a military man, I realized; she'd come from navy stock, had worshiped her admiral father. My mind became haunted as well, by a picture of Louie waking in the middle of the night and planting an ax in my mother's forehead.

This was the suspicion I carried with me, like a chancre in my gum, when we arrived at Louie's house for dinner. My practiced mien of polite distance was momentarily disrupted by the interior of his house, which displayed a catalogue of military paraphernalia—rifles and knives, photographs of bombers and warships, a small decorative cannon beside the couch—and terrible, hideous art. A huge oil painting of a boy in clown makeup, a tear rolling from one oversized eye, hung over the mantel, and at the sight of it I whipped my head toward my mother—she who had taught me that a room such as this was an expression of the most unimaginative, fascistically ignorant mind—hoping to catch her attention. Wouldn't she roll her eyes for my benefit, confirm that we shared the same judgment? But no, she averted her gaze, pretending not to see what I saw. Or worse, perhaps she'd grown used to it.

"Michael, you're so skinny!" she proclaimed as I stood at the kitchen counter preparing a salad. "Aren't you eating anything in New York?"

"I eat," I said.

"Then you have to eat more."

"It's true I've lost a little weight."

"More than a little."

"Your mother's right," Louie added. "Looks like a whole nigger family moved out of your pants."

His laughter was like the grunt of a hog. I stared at him, unable to respond. Surely my mother would react to this vast, blatant ugliness, but if so, she kept her reaction suppressed. She swatted Louie's arm, glancing at me nervously, and I left them alone in the kitchen.

After a meal monopolized by Louie's war stories, he produced his Christmas presents. Each of us received a check for five dollars, except my mother, on whose lap he set two boxes, one big, one little. The large oblong one contained an electronic piano keyboard, which Henry immediately set upon. Pushing buttons, he discovered a salsa beat that impelled Nick and my mother to dance the merengue until Louie held her arm, calling attention to the second present, a tiny box that had fallen between the cushions of the couch.

From the second box my mother mined a pair of diamond earrings, shockingly, laughably, multifacetedly huge. "Oh, Louie, they're beautiful," she cried, in a tone whose sincerity I no longer had the power to divine. She demurely replaced the earrings in the box and shut the lid. "But I can't accept these."

"You most certainly can."

"I really can't."

"Are they real?" I said.

"Of course they are." Louie beamed. "They're insured for five thousand dollars."

The day after Christmas, John paid a visit to his doctor, worried by a dull pain in his legs. The transplanted marrow continued to take on vigorous life, the doctor said, but John's bones still held the memory of pain and would release it slowly, over time. In the following days the pain grew more acute, and a second checkup found his white blood cell count skyrocketing. John was immediately readmitted into the hospital. All along, the leukemia had been in hiding, covert as a guerrilla force, and had surged once again into blast stage, furiously reproducing. There would have to be another course of chemotherapy, another marrow transplant. It was starting all over again.

My mother flew immediately to Dallas, accompanied by Celeste and Scotty, but I did not leave the house. I wandered the rooms, stared for an hour at the garage I had organized, stood at my mother's dresser tumbling the unopened earring box in my fingers. By the time she returned two days later for a change of clothes, I had set up habitation on the couch. "You haven't even tried to contact him," she said. I stirred from my paralysis enough to nod. "Call him," my mother pleaded. "He thinks he's dying."

37

John lay back in the hospital bed with his daughter Christina upon his chest. He cooed baby talk, held her aloft, and she stared back at him without emitting a sound. His physical appearance had worsened since I'd seen him in October, but he bore the same clear, ingenuous smile that had been his signature since boyhood. While John played with the baby, his wife Grace, my father, and I bantered about New York and Oklahoma, debated the pleasures of small town and big city life, and discussed the trials of parenthood with voluble, forced heartiness.

"Come here, Dad," John said. "Why don't you hold your granddaughter?" My father obeyed, but he removed Christina from John's outstretched arms with panic in his eyes.

"What do you want her to call you when she starts talking?" Grace asked.

"Hell, I don't know." His glance darted around the room and lit upon me; Christina was unloaded onto my lap with breathtaking speed.

"Well, you better think of something quick," Grace teased. "My sister's baby girl has just started calling my father Boppy. You don't want to get stuck with something like Boppy, do you?"

"Boppy sounds good to me," I said.

"We can't have two Boppies," Grace said.

"How about Floppy?" I said.

"How about Gramps?" John suggested.

My father did not comment on these proceedings. His

lips formed a whitened cicatrix. Compared to my mother's strength, his fragility in the face of John's illness was striking, and it made the gulf of her absence from this hospital room even more enormous. We needed her faith.

My arms had locked over my niece, the warmth of her small back pressed to my abdomen. Instinct smelled our common blood and sparked in me an instant territorial love, bewildering in its intensity. Christina stared at her mother, then turned, watchful, to the window, then to John in his bed. Like me, she was an observer. The hospital room, the blue sky, the family drama unfolding around her she absorbed with equal fascination and distance. Hope did not affect the slant of her vision.

John and my father had begun talking about the stock market. Though as a child I had spent much of my time aching to be with John, as adults my brother and I had grown into strangers, a subtle schism whose roots I traced back ten years to when John first left my mother's house and went to live with my father. After college, he'd attended business school, then won a job as a financial analyst for an oil company. My father's vocal approval of John was something he denied the rest of us, and it was this alliance that Celeste had referred to when she once said to me, "John's gone to the other side."

Grace took Christina from my arms, hugged and kissed her, breathed her in. "She keeps me going," she said to me quietly by the window. "I'm a little low today. John got so mad at me earlier because I told him I was scared. He just blew up. He can't hear anything right now that's not absolutely positive. But sometimes I need to say that I'm sad too."

Her openness seemed to me a kind of generosity. My ignorance of John's life included Grace; we hardly knew each other. Among my family she had a reputation of meekness, but since John's diagnosis Grace had revealed herself to be ferocious in her devotion to her husband's care, humorous and diplomatic with my father, steady in the daily ordeal of John's hospitalization—energies that, despite what she had just confessed, rarely seemed to flag.

My father wrapped up his financial consultation and bid us farewell. It was nearing Christina's nap time, so Grace walked out with him, promising to return in the morning. Then John and I were alone.

"How does it look?" he asked me. He stood before the mirror in his hospital gown, trying on a cowboy hat he'd received for Christmas.

"Looks good," I said cheerily, and to myself I marveled: how quickly we grow accustomed to horror. His face was swollen, he was virtually bald, and his long confinement had transformed the sturdiness of his frame to flaccidity.

"I'm getting fat," John said, scrutinizing his reflection.

"No, you're not."

"Don't lie to me," he said smiling. "Look at the proof, right before your eyes." He began inching back to his bed, using his IV stand as a support. "When you come into this room, you tell the truth. Every night someone stays here with me, usually Grace or Mom, sometimes Celeste, even Scotty. They sit right where you're sitting now. Doesn't it seem ridiculous not to speak the truth, considering why you're here?"

I did not feel willing to consider why I was here in his hospital room, but I nodded.

"They tell me now that when I was first admitted in August, the chemo almost killed me. I almost died the first day, and Dad stood here and held my hand and said that he loved me."

"He actually said it?"

"I'd never heard him say it before. Celeste told me she's believed all her life I didn't like her. And that she thought I was Dad's favorite."

I was saved from responding by a knock on the door. Every few minutes another stranger entered the room, a nurse to take John's temperature, an intern on his rounds, and now an aide bringing in his lunch. While John ate I gazed out the window at the whiteness blanketing the city. An ice storm had hit the previous night, and just that morning my car had slipped through the slush on the way to the hospital. I had not been to Dallas since John's wedding four years earlier, an event marked by things getting lost, first my mother's car keys, then Celeste's wallet, finally my grandmother, who'd run up to her hotel room to fetch her purse and never returned. After an elevator alarm had jangled for nearly an hour, the doors opened and out spilled my grandmother into the arms of my gathered family.

I turned back from the window; John had finished the meal and lain back on a bank of pillows, his half-shut eyelids twitching, his breath even. When I swiveled the tray away from the bed, his eyes snapped open. "Sorry," he said. "Sometimes I just drift asleep for a minute. It's the morphine. When I get out of here I'm going to be a morphine addict."

"No you won't," I said, unable to joke.

"Could you get me some water? It's so dry in here, I have to drink about a gallon a day so I don't die of dehydration."

In the bathroom I filled up his plastic cup, thirst-buster sized with the motto "Proud to be Texan" printed on the side, then returned to the armchair that would later fold out into my bed. "Have you met Mom's boyfriend?" I asked. "Louie?"

"No. She's told me a little about him."

"The navy-hero, prisoner-of-war saga?"

He nodded.

"Has she mentioned that he's psychotic?" Then I checked myself; I wanted to speak the truth. "He says he was tortured and maybe he really was, because he's very strange. Mom doesn't see it. She lets men blind her."

"She wants to be taken care of," John said.

"She does and she doesn't. It wasn't just that she married jerks. She could never practice what she preached about the woman obeying the man. She's too strong." I could hear my mother's voice whisper: *I always knew I could take anything that happened to me, but not to my children.* "I wish she had more faith in herself. She puts it all in God. What about you? Do you believe in God?"

John eyed me suspiciously. "Don't you? Or were you in California too long?"

"I don't know what I believe."

"Faith in God has helped me live this long. And even if I don't make it, even if I have to leave Grace and Christina behind, knowing that I'm going somewhere better, where they'll join me, eases that."

"You believe in heaven, then? In an afterlife?"

"Of course I do."

"I believe in life." The statement snapped clear of me, so sharp I felt it to be cruel. I changed the subject. "Grace reminds me of Mom a little, gentle and tough as nails at the same time."

"There have been times when I really wanted to stop fighting, but she wouldn't let me. She's fought to keep me alive as hard as I have. I have loved so much being married. It's hard to believe now how scared I was to do it."

"Scared because of our family?"

"Yes."

"It's hard to believe in the stability of anything, because of that," I said. "But I want to be married too. I'd like building a life with someone. I think of it like a house, a place you build that's strong and solid, that you live inside of, that lasts."

"How's Rose?"

"We're not doing so well, to be honest."

"Then do something about it. You'd be a fool to lose her." He stood up from the bed as though he were going to come beat sense into me, as an older brother should.

"I know," I said. "I don't want to lose her."

"Enough said." John moved slowly across the room toward the bathroom door. "I may be a while in here," he joked. "The drugs I'm on give me the worst constipation in the world."

I left him then, following a yellow line on the hospital floor from his room to the cafeteria, where I gummed a stale hamburger and watched a man wearily tear a styrofoam cup into ever smaller bits. On the return trip to John's room I lost the yellow line and darted with the anxiety of a spiny mouse into several dead-end hallways. In one of them I leaned against the wall and closed my eyes. We were not so unalike after all, John and I. He had done what I found impossible for myself—established a career, married, bought a house, had a child—but this was his response to the same flux and change that had made me peripatetic.

When I returned, I said to my brother, "Celeste's not completely off base to say that you're the only one Dad approves of."

"That's crazy."

"You're the only one who can even talk to him. He doesn't get impatient with you. You lived with him."

"So did you."

"No, I didn't. I stayed at his house when I had to. I slept in your bed. I never was comfortable there."

"I wasn't, either," he said. "Dad and Helen fought all the time. It never felt like my home."

"Then why did you stay?"

"I didn't have a choice. I wouldn't clean those fucking bricks on the front porch, so Hank kicked me out of the house."

Years had passed since either of us had set eyes on our stepfather, but the mere mention of his name evoked a palpable dread. "That was just a threat," I said. "You didn't have to leave."

"He loved everyone else—you and Kiki; he was such a joker with Nick; but he hounded me all the time. I couldn't do anything right. He hated me and I never knew why. He made it impossible to live in that house. He would have just kept hounding me and hounding me."

"After you left, that's what he did to me."

"He did?" Surprise altered John's features, smoothed the furious creases on his forehead.

"He did it to everyone, to Mom, you, me, his own kids. It was his nature to grind down anyone in his path."

"But no, it was just me. I thought that he saw something in *me* that he hated."

"After you moved out of Mom's house, I couldn't really believe you'd gone. I rummaged through your room, but all I found was a pair of shoes you hadn't taken. They didn't fit me but I wore them sometimes in secret, walking circles in my room. I wanted to feel the lift in the one heel, to remind me of you. Polio always seemed like an exotic thing to me because it made your feet different sizes, because it made you special."

"I hated it," John said with real bitterness. "It made me feel like a freak."

"You're a very special person." I began laughing and couldn't stop.

"What's so funny?"

"That was a book I had when I was a kid. About freaks. *Very Special People.*" Then I grew quiet. *There is a freakishness in me as well,* I wanted to say, but that was a truth I could not pry out of myself, not even here. To speak the truth would give it control over the course of my life, and I had other plans. "Do you remember," I said, "when we were little, how I used to follow you everywhere? I sat like a little dog at your feet when you did your homework, even followed you into the bathroom. I actually woke up at five o'clock on Sunday mornings to help with your newspaper route, just so I could be with you."

"You did come in handy sometimes."

"I worshiped you."

A knock announced the resident on his afternoon rounds. He looked about John's age but didn't allow this coincidence to produce any warmth or familiarity with his patient. I half listened as he discussed the results of John's most recent blood test, speaking in a brisk, factual tone that did not comfort, but neither did it telegraph danger. After the resident had gone, though, John sat forward, his head bowed. "They found a cancer cell in my blood," he said quietly. "They've never found one in the blood before." His voice broke, and I realized that he was crying, almost silently. I sat on the bed beside him, my hand on his broad, bent back. "They only give me a one percent chance of surviving this," he said. "Did you know that? Sometimes it's too hard to keep believing. I can't beat it. I just want to give up."

I helped my brother lean back against the pillows. He was physically ravaged, but his appearance, I knew, was a lie. He was too lucid, too strong, for me to believe he was dying. I wanted to cry out: *You show me what it means to be alive. You diagram a beauty so brilliant I must look at you through my fingers.* The religious timbre of these thoughts was not lost on me. Perhaps this was what separated me at last from my mother: I saw the divine not in God but in the human, in my brother, lying here before me.

"Could you get me some water?" John asked. "This hospital's so fucking dry I have to drink a gallon a day so I don't dehydrate."

I winced at the repetition; was he beginning to lose his mind as well? But I realized that the afternoon of talk had exhausted him, and went to fill his cup. I noticed in the bathroom mirror that the aridity of the hospital atmosphere had affected me also. My lips had gone white and cracked, lined with dark striations of blood. I handed John his water, but after he took a sip his eyes fluttered closed and he wandered off into a morphine sleep. The cup began to tip, and I reached to take it from his loosening fingers before it spilled. His eyes opened, close to mine.

I kneeled, my ribs pressed against the mattress. "I don't think I ever forgave you," I said, "for leaving Mom's house."

Closing his eyes again John offered a drugged smile, but I was uncertain whether he had even heard me.

As I drove south toward Austin, my mother and Scotty were passing overhead on their flight to Dallas. Over the next few days, the chemotherapy began, and marrow was again harvested from Scotty's still aching ilia. I slipped away to Houston to visit friends overnight, and though I did not inform my father I was there, in the morning, as if guided by sorcery, the telephone rang. My friend handed it to me. A heavy, viscous dread was already spreading through my veins as I took the phone. "Hey, Dad."

"Son, have you heard the bad news?"

I coughed a laugh at this; he would provide no cushion for the blow. "No. Tell me." *Tell me John died.*

"Your mother's house burned down."

38

I'd believed myself beyond the reaches of further astonishment, but as the landscape blurred past on my way back to Austin, I felt the alien logic of shock twist its tendrils into my mind. If we were to lose John, I reasoned, then it made sense we were also to lose everything material. My father had not been able to tell me the extent of the damage; Nick reported only that no one was hurt. I began to hope that my mother's house had been consumed by fire, that it had burned clean to the ground, leaving no more than a silky layer of ash. Better not to be led into the temptation of believing we could ever be again as we once had been.

By the time I turned onto my mother's street, this logic had grown exhaustingly baroque, and once I wound my way on foot around lumbering vehicles—a fire truck, a moving van—what I saw relieved me: the house was still standing. Sections of the roof had burned off, revealing charred and blackened beams; windows were broken; the garage was a cataclysm of ashes; but we had not lost everything. Nick stood beside the front steps shouting orders and directing a swarm of workers carting furniture out the door, firemen, curious neighbors tromping through the yard, a phalanx of kids on bicycles.

Out of this crowd, Olivia materialized and took my arm. I had known my brother's wife for ten years—a woman who had left home at sixteen, supported herself through college, and forged an independent life out of spirited self-reliance—but I gazed at her now with dazed, idiot eyes.

Beside us, firemen rolled up hoses and loaded them into the truck. "They just got the fire out," she told me. "After eight hours."

"The fire's out?"

"It started in the garage, then swept across the roof. There's a lot of damage from smoke and water, but almost nothing in the house burned."

"Nothing burned?"

"Not really, no."

"Does Mom know?"

"I called her. She said, 'It's only things.' "

A woman wearing a pink sweat suit lunged at us. "Did I tell you my house burned down too?" she asked. "Years ago, but I know how you feel." She looked back at my mother's house and shook her head. "It's a nine-eleven life. Emergency!"

"A neighbor," Olivia told me after the woman rejoined the mass of gapers. "She let me use her phone at six o'clock this morning."

She went to speak with the departing firemen, and I advanced up the front steps, nearly barrelled over by a couch emerging from the door like a battering ram. I stepped into the dim interior of my mother's house, where an aromatic, tangy haze of smoke and dampness thickened the air; the walls were stained black, and the sky shone through the rafters. The sodden carpet tracked the indentations of my footprints, as though of a ghost walking upon sand. Some rooms I found virtually undamaged, while others lay buried beneath three feet of collapsed ceiling. Two women conversing in Spanish wrapped up dishes in the kitchen, and in my mother's closet a strange man with streaked hair packed her clothes into a tall box. "Do I know you?" I asked, because I felt it truly possible that he was familiar to me but, in my altered state, unrecognizable. He toted the box past me without answering.

By heat alone the garage had been reorganized more dramatically than I'd been capable, into a gray sludgy mass free of any salvageable object. A large terra-cotta pot provided a dash of color, and absently I lifted the silver trash can lid someone had placed on top. Inside the pot I viewed a gray coil, similar to an electrical cord, twisting and encircling a larger mass that beneath my stare slowly resolved into the charred remains of our cat. I replaced the lid.

Parked outside the garage, my mother's station wagon had been enveloped by the fire. Viewing the shattered windows, the rusted and pitted metal, the melted tires, the burned interior, I smiled to myself, reminded of the abandoned car Howard Vole had once brought to my mother as an offering of love. I sensed a body approach and stand close by my side, but it did not speak until I looked up. "I was in a plane like this once," Louie said. "During the war."

"Really."

"Except that it was still on fire."

"What did you do?"

"Put it out."

"But how?'

"Flew it into the ocean."

I didn't know how to respond, and after he told me one more story, about a cat who had jumped from an airplane and survived, I left him.

I joined Nick and Olivia in the front yard, where a man in a dark suit and rubber boots stood with them in insistent, sycophantic conference. Like ants on a carcass, the river of people continued to crawl from the house carrying furniture and boxes.

"Where is it going?" I asked.

"Vandals," the insurance agent replied. "Weather. You have to protect it. It's covered."

"They're taking everything to a warehouse," Nick told me.

"All those people packing and moving," I said. "That's not free, is it?"

"It's covered," the agent said, thrusting a sheaf of papers at Nick's chest. "I need for you to sign here. And here. And here. Here. Here. And here. Thank you." Nick's signatures acted like repellent. The agent buzzed off.

"We didn't even call them," Olivia said. "They showed up right after the firemen. They must have been listening to the nine-eleven channel."

"Maybe they smelled the exploded cat in the garage," I said.

Louie paced into sight from around the corner, panning a video camera across the house and zooming in on the station wagon.

"He's sending the tape to Dallas," Nick said, "so Mom can see the damage."

For a while we drifted into a mutual reverie, watching the scene of movers, neighbors, and my mother's limping, video-bearing boyfriend as we prepared to gather our forces. Louie joined us and didn't speak, seeming to respect this moment of silence.

"Does anyone know how it started?" I asked eventually.

Nick pointed to three men congregated in a corner of the garage, prying at the brick wall. "Those are fire inspectors from the insurance company. They think a gas leak caused it. If they can prove the water heater had a faulty gas line, they plan to sue the water heater company and recoup the payment they make to Mom."

"It's all about money, isn't it?" I said.

"Just calm down," Louie screamed at the top of his lungs. "Everything is under control." A wild look took possession of his face, then he stalked away.

We hardly dared to speak.

Nick said, "Someone needs to put him back in that prison camp."

Henry was in his pyjamas next door watching the neighbor's television. Of my family, he alone had been in the house when the fire broke out, accompanied by a friend and the baby-sitter; Nick and Olivia were staying with friends, and my mother, Celeste, and Scotty were still in Dallas. Henry didn't see me enter the room, and I hesitated to call his attention, because I liked watching his face, unguarded as a person's is only when he believes himself in solitude. This was how I'd gazed at him years ago while he slept in his crib, but he was no longer a newborn baby, nor the toddler I had felt to be, by right, my own child. In the seven years since I'd left home, he'd grown into a precociously lusty, yet pious, boy of twelve. At his age I was building my first aviaries, and he, my mother reported, was sweet-talking girls into spin-the-bottle parties, then walking up the street on Sunday morning to attend church services alone.

When I sat beside him, Henry clung to me and spoke in a rush. He'd woken at five in the morning to a loud banging, like shotgun blasts. From the kitchen window he witnessed orange flames leaping from the garage, engulfing the station wagon, and as calmly as he was able, he went to wake the baby-sitter. She panicked and ran outside. Henry then returned to his room, where his friend still lay sleeping, and they made their escape from the house, already filling with smoke, by climbing the back fence into the neighbor's yard. Henry called the fire department, but by the time they arrived the entire roof was ablaze.

For several days we camped out at the neighbor's, where Henry and I shared an air mattress that leaked most of its cushion over the course of the night. In his sleep Henry whimpered and mewed. He leapt and jumped and scratched, knocking his head against mine, but he was not wakened by these midnight gymnastics. I held my brother's body still with my arms until he calmed, and then I too could sleep, but near dawn he smacked my eyes open again with his fists, like a thrashing, feral thing.

We worked sixteen hours a day to salvage what we could, to perform an emergency move. Picking through rubble with a rake, I found myself unable to quit laughing—I couldn't hold in the hysteria, couldn't breathe—but every so often I was rewarded with the discovery of household treasure: a ceramic espresso cup, a cordless telephone, a photograph in a frame. The smell of smoke and wet ash took on the taint of organic decay. Two cats more fortunate than the one in the garage shot wildly out from beneath a bed buried by plaster and insulation. Their burned rubber: a ragged scratch on Henry's neck. Arduous labor was a relief, absorbing me, allowing me not to think about John; at last I was able to take action to beat back catastrophe. At night I sat exhausted at a restaurant with Nick and Olivia and Henry, smelling of smoke and decay, our faces streaked with ash. We ate without a word.

We toured rental houses to find a temporary residence for my mother, all of them depressingly dark or small or plain, until at last we entered one with airy light and a floor of Mexican tile. We cheered, knowing we'd done well for her, and signed on the dotted line. Neighbors responded quickly with donations of blue jeans, pink mattresses, clock radios, a lime green refrigerator. Nick, Olivia, and I drove from house to house loading these donations into our truck with speedy, cartoonish motions, pretending to be suburban bandits, singing antic melodies. We hypothesized about the true cause of the fire: Louie had set it, using the pyrotechnic knowledge he'd learned during *the war,* in order to force my mother out of her house. Vulnerable, she would succumb to his proposal of marriage and hand over the insurance money, which he would use for his own dastardly ends. We elaborated this theory nightly, and when the fire inspectors determined that the water heater had not suffered a gas leak after all, that they were stumped as to the cause of the fire, no doubt remained in our minds of Louie's guilt. In the rented house, I stayed up past midnight in the furniture-free living room with an expanse of carpeted floor as my bed and flipped the channels of the donated television. I wanted to watch something light and utterly vacuous, something that might buoy my spirits with fake TV families or cheap romance, but I couldn't find one show with *love* in the title.

An invitation was tendered by the insurance company to visit the warehouse, where we found my mother's furniture, paintings, and electronics displayed as if at a sale, though judging by the quality of the merchandise, thrift rather than retail. Duane the insurance agent had traded in his rubber boots for tasseled loafers and presented us with an estimate of $30,000 for the restoration of my mother's fire-damaged belongings. Only when pressed by Olivia did he admit that we'd already accumulated an $11,000 debt simply for moving and storage, which he had claimed on the day of the fire to be covered by the policy. Olivia, whose job in New York was to negotiate contracts for movie locations, took hold of Duane in her teeth. Over the next hour he cajoled and bargained, pleading the efficacy of laboratory-formulated polishes and ozone processes for destabilizing carbon residue, but by the end of their session Olivia had convinced him to halve the $11,000 debt and to deliver all of my mother's possessions to the rental house the following day. We drove home with the ozone machine, no bigger than a portable heater, tucked between my feet.

This moral victory raised our spirits. That night we got drunk and danced in the empty living room, but my mother called with news from Dallas that ended our festivity. John's chemotherapy had been rough on him, and he now lay barely conscious in the bone marrow unit.

The next morning a van unloaded the smoky merchandise, furniture and boxes that overflowed from the garage into the driveway, and the delivery heralded a cold war between us and the insurance company. In order to receive the full amount covered by my mother's policy, we were required to provide proof that her loss exceeded $80,000. In the week that followed I exhumed the contents of each box, making lists of each item's retail cost. If the authorities required me to be picayune, I could be maddeningly exact:

17	assorted spices	@ .50 each	8.50
9	Tupperware containers	@ 2.00 each	18.00
1	box capellini pasta		2.00
1	bunch bananas	@ .69/pound	1.50

After itemizing the kitchen boxes, I moved on to the contents of the garage. Of course I had no physical proof, but since I'd so recently reorganized it, my memory provided quite a lengthy inventory of tools, hardware, and gardening and pet supplies, though perhaps I was overgenerous in my estimated worth of the avocado beanbag chair.

My mother returned from Dallas a week after the fire, and she returned to us changed. Vacant, without vigor, she resided deep within herself. Her voice was as low and whispery as the rustling of leaves, but there was something in her manner that resisted comfort. She'd donned a mineral carapace. Rather than fear, I felt fury; I wanted the powers of a conjurer to transmute her grief into a living beast and wrestle with it myself, to the death of it or me.

Curiosity did not immediately lead my mother to view the burned shell of her house—she'd seen it already, she said, on Louie's video—but Duane stopped by three times the day after she arrived to insist on a tour together. He needed her signature to start rebuilding. I taxied her over, and when she caught sight of the house she drew in her breath and said, "My word," as if viewing one of the seven natural wonders. Duane was already waiting for us, the rubber boots restored to his feet, his amiable, helpful personality restored as well, though not to me.

Inside, Duane emitted a stream of talk neither my mother nor I listened to, and she emitted a squeak of what sounded like amusement each time she stepped into a doorway and saw another rubble-strewn room. I remained silent as a child. As the three of us toured the house, I received tantalizing echoes from the past, from the ancient days of traveling through Houston with my mother, my eye beaded upon civil servants and retail salesclerks in order to catch a man for her. Here at last was the manifestation of the threesome I had so ardently dreamed of: man, mother, and child, looking at a home together. Other echoes, too, bombarded me from that time: the firm protectiveness I felt for my mother, a yearning to be protected myself, the awareness of her charm and beauty in the presence of a man, the desire of that man to impress her. But that was years and years ago. We'd traveled worlds since then. The truth was this: my mother had no wish to charm this man; he was trying to manipulate her; I was an adult; the house was burned.

"Well," my mother said as we stood in the front yard taking in the sight, "obviously it's destroyed."

"On the contrary," Duane said.

"But that's alright. We'll tear it down and build another. I never liked it all that much anyway."

"That won't be necessary," Duane said brightly. "I believe we can rebuild the house exactly the way it was. You won't even know the difference. All I need is for you to sign right here, and we can begin today."

My mother faced Duane directly for the first time. "No," she said. "That's not what I want."

The expression on his face underwent a shift, to the hardened, brittle smile he'd used at the warehouse, which would have been subtle had I not had so much practice with my stepfather. "It's our policy to rebuild when we can."

"Rebuild?" my mother said. "Look at that beam. The entire house is supported by that beam. It's burned halfway through."

"I can promise you the integrity of the beam is not damaged. An engineer has already been out here to examine it."

"You expect me to live in a house with damaged roof beams?"

"I can promise you they're not damaged."

"With scorched, burned beams? Do you live in a house with burned beams?"

"Well, no."

"And I'm not asking you to."

"But that's not the point. We're not asking you to live in an unsafe house. Some of the same beams, even if slightly burned, might be used to rebuild, but the house will be safe. Trust me."

"Trust a man who tried to charge me thirty thousand dollars to polish my furniture?" She spoke without raising her voice, calmly immoveable. "My insurance policy covers sixty thousand dollars' worth of damage on the structure of my house. The structure is destroyed. You won't have to rebuild a thing. I'll take the sixty thousand and build a new house myself."

"But I can't authorize giving you that money. It's our policy."

"And it's my policy to expect what I deserve." My mother's attention was caught by something at the side of the house, and she scooted away, out of disinterest, it appeared, rather than ire.

Duane caught my eye and shrugged; I had just become his one potential ally. "How are the clothes coming?" he asked. "Is the smoke smell washing out?"

"Not completely," I admitted.

"You might want to try a dash of Murphy's wood soap." He took a last look at my mother and retreated to his car, all in a day's work. I joined her beside the garage, where she was looking over some potted plants. The exchange with Duane seemed to have enlivened her, retrieved her from a faraway confinement. Here we were again, the two of us together. My mother's gaze lighted upon the ruination of the station wagon, and she smiled at me for the first time in weeks. "God sure has a funny way of telling me I need a new car."

Pages upon pages I filled with lists, of destroyed salt shakers and paperback biographies and silk blouses and *Star Wars* coffee mugs, climbing toward the $80,000 summit, while my mother dressed for battle. A contractor she hired declared the house unsalvageable, so she stood her ground against the insurance company, resistant to compromise. Duane agreed to allow her to rebuild if he maintained control of the finances; she said absolutely not. He would allow her to have control if he first agreed upon the blueprints; she said no. She insisted on payment without conditions, and at last Duane relented; she would receive the $60,000 to use for whatever purposes she wished.

My mother was so consumed with the insurance company that for days after her return she had no time to see Louie. A phone had not yet been connected in the rental house, and at night she sat solitarily with a glass of wine, staring into the empty living room or sketching lackadaisical designs for the house she planned to build. When the phone was at last hooked up, she called Louie to apologize, but he was so brimming with complaints he wouldn't let her talk. She received a full catalogue of the ways in which she'd disappointed him. After she hung up, she said, "Why did I even listen to that? That was like talking to a child. No, that's not true. No child of mine was ever that bad."

We received daily, noncommittal reports from Dallas about John's condition, but more often the ringing phone announced Louie. He accused my mother of ignoring his needs, pleaded for more of her attention, and charged that we, her children, were plotting to keep her away from him. These calls left my mother more visibly shaken than those from either Dallas or the insurance company, and after five days of them she told Louie that perhaps she shouldn't see him for a while, not until she was settled again, until John was better. She admitted to me that he'd been pressing her to marry him, to use the insurance money to build a house, not for her but for the two of them together.

Louie stopped complaining over the phone, but rather than surrender altogether he launched a second campaign along new tactical lines. He began leaving gifts on my mother's doorstep. He called to say that he'd been driving by our house at two in the morning and had noticed a light on; was everything alright? Olivia spotted him parked at an intersection up the street with an inflatable woman strapped into the seat beside him, by which, we conjectured, he hoped to fan the flames of jealousy in my mother's heart. Another morning I caught him as I was leaving the house. He'd parked around the corner and was getting out of his car with a package in his hands. When he saw me, he nonchalantly climbed back in and drove away at fifty miles an hour. My mother returned the diamond earrings he'd given her for Christmas. The next day he deposited them in her mailbox. At my urging she took them to a jeweler, who recognized them instantly as fakes. "Why would he lie?" she asked me, weighing the earrings in her hand.

"Because he's a liar," I said, unmoved by her loss of this man, the one thing she'd believed solid.

A friend of Louie's contacted her with news: Louie was engaged to be married to a woman who'd already put her house on the market and moved in with him. Everything he had told my mother, said the friend, about the war, about his job, was a lie, because Louie hardly knew the difference between truth and falsehood. In fact, he was calling to ask a favor; only she might be able to convince Louie to seek professional help.

When my mother quietly told Henry she wouldn't be seeing Louie anymore, he became hysterical. "You can't do that," he screamed, running up the stairs to his room. "You don't even think of us." I stared after him in sudden recognition; I had never screamed, never slammed doors. I had never believed it to be my right.

Now that my mother had been secured in the rental house, the insurance settlement proceeding, and the rat driven from the pantry, I could leave. In late January, Nick and I retraced our highway trail back to New York. Olivia planned to remain in Austin for a few extra weeks to help my mother with the insurance company. I visited John once more in the marrow transplant unit, for less than an hour. As I watched my brother, who lay hooked to a battery of machines and monitors, barely conscious of my presence, I felt a moment of penetrating horror: I knew that I would not see him again. Then I whisked the knowledge away. There was nothing else I could do but wait.

By the morning of my departure Henry had regained his self-possession. "Give us a call sometime," he said, shaking my hand with the firm grip of a businessman. "Let us know how you are."

39

On February 13, around eleven o'clock at night, I ducked into a bookstore on Broadway, halfway between my apartment and Nick's. Leafing through a novel, I suddenly tottered and leaned hard against the shelves, thrown there by the power of a physical sensation like air blowing through my body. Then I righted myself. I knew that my brother had died. Late the next night when Nick and I arrived in Austin, we entered a house in near darkness, and around us gathered Henry, Scotty, Celeste, Olivia, and my mother, embracing us, bringing us back into the circle of my family.

Hot, gusting wind made such a racket in the trees that everyone in the black-clothed funeral party was shouting and gabbling like a flock of grackles. Except for the slanting February light, the day was so glaring and humid it might have been plucked from high summer. We'd driven from my mother's house straight to the cemetery in Houston, and after I parked and helped my mother out of the car, the gleaming silver capsule of John's coffin guided us to our final destination. Among the grackles stood my father, unaware of our approach. My mother reached out her hand to touch the coffin, and then at the last second withdrew it, turning to my father. She cried his name, the first word she'd uttered since we had left Austin three hours earlier, and leaned toward him, off balance so that he would be forced to catch her. My father turned at her voice and his hand shot out, yanking me between them. She fell against my chest so lightly my arms went around to prevent her from falling.

I led my mother to a chair and sat beside her, placing a hand on her back. She stiffened at the touch. She didn't want me; she wanted him, my father, the only man who could possibly soothe her agony, if only for an instant. But I could not take my hand away. As the minister spoke, I watched a single oceanic tear fall onto the sleeve of my mother's coat, where it splattered and soaked into the fabric, a dark galaxy of heartbreak. I wanted to swallow those hot stars, absorb the fire into myself, but instead I did what was possible: I kept my eye on the dark stain, my hand on her unreceptive back.

Propelled by the laws of Brownian motion, I moved through the hordes that had descended upon my aunt's house after the funeral, the few recognizable faces drawing me into brief orbits. At each end of the room resided one of my parents, my father at the bar, roaring drunk and surrounded by cronies, and my mother in a recess, sitting docilely on an ottoman, her eyes downcast. Henry stood at her back, massaging her shoulders and neck, and like a guard dog he leapt out to intercept anyone who approached, shaking hands and introducing himself, undaunted by the adult towering over him.

"He was really a wonderful man," a childhood friend of John's was telling me. "He was so good, and true, and smart. There was no one like him. Probably never will be again."

I nodded to these words of eulogy, but a perverse part of me nearly shouted: Do you really think John was such a saint? Did you know he once tried to suffocate me as a kid? I did not want to accept bland comforts; I wanted my brother's death to make necessary the unfurling of truth, the end of falsehood. But I did not feel capable of carrying on what John himself had begun, what he had helped me to begin in his hospital room. I deferred to good form.

My random motion eventually swept me close to my father, whose arm snagged me and pulled me against his chest. "Mikey," he boomed. A glass of dark, noxious liquid was pushed to my mouth. "Come on, son, drink it down."

"What is it?"

"Metaxa," he roared. "Greek magic. It will set you free."

I swallowed. A fireball shot from my lips to my gut. In the next room, a long table displayed a bounty of food: caviar, cheeses, asparagus laced with vinaigrette. A hand with a knife hacked at a leg of lamb. I had a second dose of Metaxa, a third. My father's arm relaxed and I reeled out into the house, searching, I thought, for a bathroom, then after a while forgetting what I looked for. Behind a closed door I discovered a sitting room, empty, quiet, and dark, its walls lined with old books. I shut the door behind me and fell to the couch, where the Metaxa chugged through my veins, setting me free.

The door cracked open, and Celeste looked into the room where I sat crying. My sister sat on the couch and looked at me with the sleepy, sloe eyes John had also possessed, her long hair the color of fire. She emanated a lovely solemnity, easily ignited into a not-so-lovely temper, which had stirred in me, as she'd grown older, an increasing protectiveness. After a while she began talking softly. She'd dropped out of college and given up her life in Colorado to help in Dallas; she might go back to school, she said, or she might even follow the Grateful Dead around the country for a while. Why not do something fun, away from all this? Then she told me about the night John died.

She had been in his hospital room while he struggled to keep breathing, each rasping breath impossibly followed by another, as my mother stood in the corner with her hands crossed over her chest, staring at the floor. Finally Grace told them both to go home. He died while they were in the car. When they reached the house, my mother had immediately returned to the hospital, and Celeste had sat up alone in the dark living room. "I saw John's face," she told me. "I know it sounds crazy, and now I wonder if I was asleep or something, but I saw his face floating there, and he spoke to me. He said that everything was fine now, that at last he was free. And I knew that it was true."

"He was telling you good-bye," I said. It did sound crazy, but I believed her. In New York, I too had felt the passing of his life, blowing through me like a hot wind.

"Look at this," my mother called from across the garage, where she flipped through the paintings that leaned against one wall, assessing the damage. For the first time since the fire she'd begun to look over her things, contact furniture restorers, visit the site of the burned house to sketch plans. I set down the vase I was cleaning and joined her. She held up her own portrait, painted over twenty years earlier, the one she had never liked, in which Hank had found the likeness of Scarlett O'Hara. The paint had absorbed smoke, blackening the blue sky, blackening her white dress. Her face was as sooty as a charwoman's. "It finally looks like you," I said, and my mother sang out a sound I had not heard in ages. A laugh.

I went back to work. I'd moved beyond the documentation of her lost goods and into the field of restoration. The days after John's funeral hit eighty degrees, and I set up shop outside the garage wearing shorts and a t-shirt, a bucket of soapy water beside me, wiping the soot from the objects I took into my hands. I felt no hurry to return to New York. Most of these objects were books, and many of the books were mine from childhood. I could travel the arc of my life in the titles: *Encyclopedia of the Animal Kingdom, The Chronicles of Narnia, Know Your Mouse, Tropical Marine Aquaria, Very Special People, Parrots of the World.* First I cleaned the covers and spines with a damp rag, then carpeted the utility room with fanned books, letting them soak for an hour in the triatomic atmosphere generated by our ozone machine. Free of the smell of smoke, the books could be packed again into boxes, in wait for the construction of my mother's new house.

I discovered other artifacts as well: photographs of Nick, John, and me as babies; scuba gear; a bridle not used since we owned horses in Brookshire, still caked with green cud. In the wooden chest my grandmother had brought from Guam I found my mother's wedding pictures, the first ones. I cleansed the glass and the silver frames. I stared at my mother's twenty-year-old face brimming with hope. I thought of Buddy describing her at fifteen: *so full of hope, so full of hope.* I thought of Hank and Emmett and Louie, of Bob and Milt, of Howard Vole and all the men in her life fluttering and dancing through the years like a string of paper dolls. We had traveled worlds. And yet I saw now, really for the first time, that I, too, was one of my mother's men, the one who had stayed.

I hope you can forgive me for my absence. As I cleaned and restored, I began this letter in my head to Rose. *I'd like to come live with you in Cleveland, if you still want me. Let us get married. Let us build a house and fill it with children. Let us make something that lasts, you and I, a small pocket of order in the world.*

YOU MUST CHANGE YOUR LIFE

40

Stationed daily at Rose's window, I watched the snowflakes of my first Cleveland winter blur the sky like a plague of silent locusts, whirling and flying and accumulating on the names etched over the porticoes of brick apartment buildings: *The Huguenot, The Palmetto, Hampshire Manor*. Blizzards snuffed out electrical power and buried the neighborhood in snowbanks a child might fall into and not be discovered until the thaw of spring. The snow fell over the big, gutted machinery of Cleveland, on the soot-blackened monument that guarded the tomb of an assassinated president, and on the river that had once erupted in flames. At the beginning of the century, steel mills had bathed this city in the light of molten iron, and the nighttime clouds glowed orange still, as if reflecting the memory of fire.

After finishing my coursework at Columbia, I had left New York to rejoin Rose. During the day I worked part-time at a pediatric hospital, then went home to stare out the window with my unfinished thesis before me. The world was full of event: Eastern Europe was in revolution, Russia had ceased being our enemy, Germany moved toward unification; but in Cleveland I ground to a halt. Two years had passed since John's death, and still I could not let go of the bloated, struggling grief that stuck in me like a pig in an anaconda. My family had become muffled—we never mentioned John—and our silence pushed us away from one another. I sat mesmerized by the falling snow, calculating over and over the date, nearly two years in the future, on which I would begin to live longer than John had lived: October 1, 1991. What had once been a child's wish—to become older than my older brother—fulfilled at last.

In her third year of medical school, working a grueling schedule around the clock, Rose arrived home and fell into exhausted monologue—the invasiveness of medicine was so *disturbing;* to slice open the skin of another person, to probe and touch strangers as intimately as a parent or lover, was so *unsettling*—and then fell into unconsciousness. With murmurs of support I was able to encourage these confessions and to prepare dinner while she slept, but when she woke I was unable to open my heart. John's death was not the reason for my withdrawal, and we both knew it. While I sat alone at the window, I could no longer pretend deafness to the message blaring from within: if I did not confront my desire for men, I would in some way die. Still I refused to listen; I had a vision of my future that would redeem all the fragmentation of my past, and I would not give that up. But in using all my energy to silence the broadcast, I became neutralized.

Rose was patient, but her patience had limits; living with a zombie had few consolations. Though she suspected why I stood fortressed against her, she had her own reasons for deflecting the knowledge. "I'm not trying to invade you," she pleaded. "I just want to understand why you're so shut down."

I made words about the difficulty of moving to Cleveland, how I adapted slowly to transition. I could not voice my true belief: self-deception brought me here.

"You think I'm like your mother," she suggested.

"No, I don't."

"That if you don't guard against me, you'll lose yourself."

"That's not it at all."

Silkily, she asked, "Then should I wear the red wig tonight?"

"That's not funny."

With spring, the snow began to melt, laying bare the community garden up the block. My daily work turned from watching the sky to tending a small plot of soil, where I cultivated a bed of lettuces, collard greens, radishes, tomatoes, and peppers, and there, having grown used to living neutralized, I regained my capacity for envisioning the future.

Plans took shape in my mind and obscured my numbness like slides projected on a blank screen: the home Rose and I would make in Oregon, the river, the garden, the children. These pictures allowed me to speak, at last, words that gave her hope of my recovery. My mouth spoke the words; my mind willed itself to believe them; and my heart, buried deep in snow, did not interfere. In the summer I harvested the vegetables from my garden—succulent and bitter lettuce, tomatoes sweet as candy—and by fall I suggested this plan: after Rose's medical internship, we could live in South America for a year, and on our return get married.

Violent turbulence tossed the plane among storm clouds, while the young girl beside me gave a luxurious yawn, reclined her seat, and said, "I'm just going to enjoy the ride." White knuckled, I arrived in Texas. My mother met my flight at the helm of a cavernous white van, its interior empty but for the front seats and a few slabs of Mexican marble. On the drive home, she elaborated upon her latest business venture. She'd opened up a new shop, she said brightly. For two weeks at a stretch she drove this monster south across the border and deep into the heart of Mexico, traveling mountainous back roads in search of village artisans—wood carvers, coppersmiths, stonemasons, potters, and weavers—whose work she loaded up and hauled back to Austin. Each territory she covered on her Pan-American tour—Puebla, Saltillo, Michoacán, and the silver cities of Taxco, Guanajuato, and San Miguel de Allende—was famous for its own particular craft.

"You want to go by the shop?" she said. "It's on the way."

"Maybe later."

"I'm really proud of it."

"Are you making any money?"

She didn't miss a beat. "Not yet. But that's to be expected. I'm pricing everything very low to lure in the customers, then when I get a good client base, I'll raise them."

"Does that mean you're losing money?"

"I'm not worried about that right now," she said. "I love those trips."

She did have a business partner, my mother added to ease my mind,

Darryl, who put up some of the money and did most of the driving on the buying trips. Darryl was the contractor who'd built her house, which caused me to wonder if he were as shadowy a figure in the business as he'd been in the construction. During the year after the fire, my mother had sent me a series of photographs to keep me posted on the new house's progress; I saw her driving a bulldozer, mixing concrete, hauling lumber, nailing up plasterboard. She told me she was only one in a team of laborers, but no other figures appeared in these photos. What I saw documented was my mother single-handedly erecting her own house.

Entering the neighborhood of avian streets, we approached that house now. The van rumbled down Barn Swallow and Peregrine Falcon, their lengths lined with nubby stone domiciles in varying shades of earth tones, not unattractive but so exactly conforming to a single architectural standard they were interchangeable, and then, at the end of the block, I spotted the house my mother had built, presiding over the neighborhood like a monumental Mediterranean rose.

The red-tiled roof, the salmon pink stucco, the imposing two-storied entrance were like nothing this side of the Riviera. Inside, a floor of burnished Mexican tile warmly invited passage as the ceiling vaulted upward to celestial heights. The far wall, entirely of glass, looked upon a garden and a green, thicketed wood; the house was all greenery and space and light. There was no denying its beauty, but on what did my eye catch? The dining room table lay on its back with crooked, broken legs, like a great, dead insect on the floor. Completed two years earlier, the house stood virtually empty. She'd blown all her insurance money on its construction, in spite of my pleadings for restraint, and hadn't been able to afford replacing the furniture damaged in the fire. An opportunity to safeguard herself financially had presented itself at last, and she'd rejected it, choosing instead to settle back into the same precarious position she'd inhabited her entire unmarried life. The absence of couch and armchairs tore the hardened packet at my core, and out leaked toxic anger. I clamped shut my mouth to prevent it spewing forth, but not quickly enough. "Still no furniture?"

"Soon," she promised. She moved through the house and I followed closely, not satisfied with her answer, but in her bedroom I was distracted by a photograph on the dresser: a man with wind-whipped hair, as beautiful as a movie star, a rifle across his knees as he crouched with four African bushmen beside an antelope he'd felled.

"Who is this?"

"That's Clark," she said. "I met him when he came into the shop. But that picture's from twenty years ago. He hasn't aged so well."

"You're seeing him?"

She nodded. "He's going to take me to Africa this summer."

"Is it serious?"

"I like him," she said. "But, honey, to be honest, I could never get married again. I'm too set in my ways."

I left the room, and this time she followed me out; we performed the tight orbits of a yo-yo trick: loop-the-loop. On one wall of the vacant living room she'd hung the portrait of herself that had been so damaged in the fire, now restored. "That's the funniest thing," she told me. "That painting's been in the closet for a year because I wasn't going to pay any money to have it cleaned up, and then a week ago I happened to look at it again. The smoke stains had just evaporated." She laughed at this minor miracle, and yet I knew her too well not to sense that beneath all this—the new business, the new boyfriend, the house—lay a vast, still reservoir of sadness.

The room, I saw now, was not entirely without adornment. Iron candelabra and rough wood carvings of saints brought back from Mexico stood sentry in the corners. The icons, the spaciousness gave my mother's home the feel of a shrine. "I love this house," she said, hugging herself. "Can I tell you how much I love this house?"

In the following days, paintings had to be hung, the garage cleaned—those time-honored standbys—and a little handcrafted artisanry of my own had to be accomplished. Though I fixed the legs on the dining room table, eight wooden chairs carved by a Mexican dentist still required seats with cushions. My mother had invited my father for Christmas dinner, and he would be joining us on this occasion for the first time in over twenty years. His acceptance was a change from his usual parental policy of ruling in absentia, but an understandable one. Since John's death he had been without job, money, or home. Violet had kicked him out of her thing-crammed abode, and for some time he'd been supported by his sister, living at her bay house, where I'd spent my childhood summers and where he now listened night after night to the wash of nocturnal waves with a whiskey in his hand. The previous autumn, my mother had received news that he'd committed suicide, but more surprising to me than the rumor itself was that it had proved to be false. I did not think he would survive the death of his son.

I was grateful for the task of making the seats for the dining room chairs. Measuring the trapezoidal shapes, cutting the plywood with a jigsaw, wielding the staple gun on foam and fabric gave me solace. The day after I'd come to Texas an unbelievable announcement had been made: John's wife Grace was getting married. My mother must have seen how the news unbalanced me; she took my hand and said, "We have to let her know we think it's great. She shouldn't have to spend the rest of her life alone." I heard the truth of this, and yet I wanted to shout that she must not, on any account, remarry. I believed we should remain at attention forever. But as I worked on the chairs, I allowed myself to travel another motivation for my resistance: Grace's marriage plans revealed the self-deception in my own.

Late Christmas morning, my father arrived wearing a dark suit and a green tie sprinkled with miniature snowmen. His shoes were polished to a fine lustre. While the rest of us crowded at the door to greet him, my mother called hello from the kitchen rather than interrupt her cooking, as though his arrival were the most natural, unextraordinary event in human history. He shook my hand, then gave a hoot of surprise at Scotty's height, now greater than his own; my father had not seen him in three years. Nor Celeste. She hung back until he called her, then rushed up to receive his embrace. He engaged in a brief conversation with Henry, whose spunk had always tickled him, but my father's curiosity was already leading him on a tour of the house. Nick and I followed. In each room he made an appreciative comment or gesture, a nod, a grunt of approval; the single thing he had never withheld from my mother was this appreciation of her eye for beauty. Dogging his steps I was propelled back in time; after their divorce, he'd often shown up out of the blue when my mother was gone in order to parade through the house he'd built and loved, just to admire it, to confirm that it still existed, a monument to his youthful power and success. My father had built his house and then, over the years, lost everything; my mother had lost everything before she could build hers.

Outside her bedroom on the second story, my father took a seat on the deck overlooking the Austin skyline and rolling hill country, still green this far into winter. Nick and I leaned on the railing, the three of us gazing at the landscape like ranchers looking over our spread. Only a Texas winter could produce this kind of day, mild, sunlit, the sky blue and clear, but with a frailty that acknowledged bitter cold already sweeping across the plains, coming to bite up the warmth. After a few silent moments, Nick snapped up as though he'd just remembered he had a casserole in the oven, mumbled an excuse, and made his exit. Watching him go, I felt an urgent need to maim him. I had not spent a moment alone with my father in years.

"So," he said. "Cleveland."

"Yep."

"Cleveland." My father laughed as though I'd pulled a caper that was kind of crazy, beyond his understanding but that he might be willing to respect. "How the hell did you end up there?"

Silence was my answer to this man, he who had taught me the art of secrecy.

"Getting married?"

"No," I said, with such force it stopped the conversation dead.

The members of my family dodged and ducked around one another preparing the meal while my father watched a football game on television, his back to the kitchen. Having pulled off the tricky piece of diplomacy of getting him here, my mother was in high spirits, delighted by her own capacity for mischief. She called out to him every few minutes—would he like a glass of wine or an hors d'oeuvre? how were Ducky and Peep? she hadn't seen them in years—and among his monosyllabic answers he called back compliments on the house. She didn't look quite herself; or rather, she resembled an incarnation from her own past, dressed up as if for a date, her hair curled, wearing lipstick and perfume, but she was so natural with my father I could hardly believe my eyes. They had known each other nearly forty years, had brought five children into the world, stood watch together at the bedside of their dying son, and yet I considered them strangers to each other. I glimpsed now in the hospitality she presented to him, untinged with rancor, and in his tentative gratitude at her kindness, how it was possible for my parents, once upon a time, to have shared a life.

But in the end, our family gathering was a flat disappointment. I had not been immune to hopeful anticipation; just maybe, I thought, coming together three years after John's funeral, our circle might reconnect an ancient circuitry and in that moment illuminate our lives. Then I would know what action I had to take. In actuality, my father sat at the end of the table flanked by Henry and Olivia, the only two not bound to him by paternity or marriage, and so they formed an insulation from the rest of us. Mostly he said nothing, though for a slight variation he returned to the subject of Scotty's height every few minutes. Our conversation turned to lessons in geography: I spoke of Cleveland, Nick and Olivia of New York, my mother of Mexico, and Scotty of London, where he was bound in two weeks' time for a college semester abroad. A desperate, forced cheer clung to our talk. The closest we came to mentioning John was Celeste's announcement that she'd decided to attend nursing school. I felt sure all of our thoughts, not just mine, burned with the questions we longed to ask one another: *Does he come to you in dreams? Do you think sometimes you see him on the street?*

Immediately after the meal my father escaped; he wanted time to enjoy the back roads home. We cleaned up, then settled in my mother's bedroom, where pacing the perimeter, Nick spied the photograph of the Great White Hunter and the four bushmen.

"Mom's new boyfriend," Scotty said.

"Which one?"

"Very funny," my mother said. Then she grew grave. "Your father looks terrible. His eyes were yellow. He's been drinking more."

"He's a drunk," Celeste said. "That's what he does."

"Well, if he doesn't stop, he's going to kill himself." She brought up the possibility of a family intervention—she'd heard on a radio show that it was often effective—and I felt my viscera twist and heat up. "They say it's the only way to get an alcoholic to hear he has a problem."

"If he wants to change his life," I said, "then he has to do it himself. We can't do it for him."

"I still think we should send him the letter John wrote," she said, my brother evoked at last.

"You're crazy," Nick said. "Absolutely not."

"But he wanted it sent. We should respect his wishes. It's the only thing that will get through to your father."

Before he died, John had begun a letter that begged my father to stop drinking, to desire life over alcoholic stupor, and to treat the members of his family with care, with the love John knew he felt. The letter, never finished, now lay in my mother's hands.

"It would kill him," Nick said.

"Maybe it can save him," my mother cried.

"You can't save him!" I cut through my own emotion with sarcasm. "It's evolution at work. We're no different than animals. Unfit individuals shouldn't live. They just take up resources."

She was smiling at me strangely, and for a moment my siblings looked back and forth between us. My outburst had shifted the tone of the room. Somehow we weren't talking about my father any longer. My mother's expression remained fixed, perhaps even angry, until finally she said with a laugh, as though she were joking, "You *Darwinian*."

"Darwinian?" The word was so old-fashioned, just as, I realized, she was. We gazed at each other like strangers. "You do believe in evolution, don't you?"

She continued smiling in that sickening way, refusing to answer.

"You don't! Why didn't I know that? I'm twenty-eight years old before I find out my mother doesn't believe in evolution!"

"Dude," Henry said. "Chill."

Everyone was laughing, and so was I. I laughed as the neutrality burst, filling me with bile and acid. She would always believe in the surpremacy of God over human will; she would always suffer from self-propagated money problems; and even now she would give up everything she'd created in her life for the attention of one man, my father. I'd spent the last twenty years urging her on toward self-sufficient happiness, as a parent holds the hands of a toddler learning to walk. How could I ever make her understand that if she would not evolve to walk alone, then my own life appeared to me a waste?

I had to get out of my mother's house. That night I took the van and barreled aimlessly through the streets of Austin away from her. Of course I could never marry. I had to face who I was, what I felt, what I kept locked up. I had to smash up my life, and Rose's with it.

Near the capitol building I spotted a knot of activity down the corridor of an otherwise deserted street. A distant block was lined with cars. Figures walked the sidewalk, crossed the open pavement. I veered around the corner and passed by. From the parked vehicles men emerged, some singly, others in couples, and stepped through the door of a building tucked behind trees. As the men entered, the door swung open like a heartbeat, releasing a pulse of light and, I imagined, the ecstatic sound of laughter, music, fraternity. More cars parked, killed their headlights, while I circled the block, circled and circled like a raptor.

41

"Something happened when you were in Texas." Rose sat across the room curled up in an armchair as though she were frightened of me. For several nights running she'd returned home from the hospital to find me lying on the couch in front of the television, where antiaircraft fire exploded over Baghdad like fireworks and laser-guided missiles devastated their targets.

"Nothing happened," I said.

"What did you do today?"

"Watched the war."

"That's what you did all day?"

It was enough. I feared the end of the world. "Israel is threatening to make a nuclear strike if it's bombed by Iraq."

"Before you left you were talking about getting married. Now you won't even talk to me."

I glanced at her—at her grim expression—then turned back to the television.

"Not that it's a surprise, of course; you've been like that ever since you moved here. I've known you for ten years and you seem more like a stranger now than on the first day we met. Would you turn off the television, please?" She was crying suddenly, and beyond switching off the television I couldn't make a move, paralyzed by the impossibility of offering her solace.

"I'm sorry."

"I've just had it," she said. "I've always thought you were scared to become attached to me because so many people have left you during your life. If I was just patient, if I showed you how much I loved you, that I wasn't going to leave, I thought you'd finally trust me, and maybe by some miracle be able to love me, too. But it's not working, and frankly, I'm not so patient anymore."

I scrambled for the explanations I'd always given, even to myself. "It's just that I can't seem to get back on my feet."

"I don't think this is about John."

"But it is."

Rose moved to sit beside me on the couch, calmer but resolute. "It's just me," she said, stroking my back. "You don't have to fight me. I think there's something you're not telling me."

"There's not."

"Are you sure?" She held out this glimmering chance; I ached to accept it but fought not to. I lay very still with my cheek pressed into the fabric of the couch; if I were absolutely motionless I might keep both of us intact. "Maybe you're not in love with me anymore," Rose said. She smoothed my hair as I witnessed our life together begin to unravel. "It wouldn't be the end of the world."

"Yes, it would."

"I'm not sure I can keep waiting around for you to figure out what you want, not without encouragement, and you don't give me much encouragement."

"Maybe," I began, "we should live apart for a while."

"Oh, God. Are you saying you want to break up?"

"Maybe I need to find out what I want."

"What does that mean?"

"I'm agreeing with you. I need to figure out what I want."

"Don't fight me."

"I'm not fighting you."

"This feels like a nightmare," she said, her voice strained, near hysteria. I knew what nightmarishness she meant: the irreality of shock, the momentum that seemed to wrest event from our control. I could not delay any longer; what I had never spoken, I must now bring into the light.

She was right, I began haltingly, there was something I wasn't telling her, that was strangling me.

"What?" she said.

I'd felt it all my life, it had torn at me, made me feel freakish, so much so that I had buried it, removed it from conscious thought.

"What is it?"

I had wanted to choose how I would live, I had wanted to choose to be with her, but it was no use.

"*Tell me what you mean.*"

I had to explore this feeling, this longing.

"For *what?*"

"For men," I said.

I braced myself for the explosion. Rose withdrew her hand from my back very calmly and did not respond for a long while. "Somehow that makes sense to me," she finally said. "It explains a lot of things, even though I don't want to believe it's true. You mean sexually, I'm assuming."

"Yes."

"You're attracted to men?" She spoke clinically, as though she were back in the hospital interviewing a patient.

"Yes."

"Are you gay?"

"No," I said. "I don't know."

"Well, do you fantasize about men? You have sexual dreams about them?"

I nodded.

"What percentage?"

"I don't know what you mean."

"How many of your sexual fantasies are about men? For once in your life, tell me the truth."

"Most," I said. "All of them."

"All of them? So you probably fantasize about men when you're having sex with me?" Her anger was like a tempest gathering; I had to batten down, go underground.

"Please."

"And you never told me? How could you not tell me this, in ten years? I am in love with you. I planned to spend my life with you." Explosive, the damage was immense, not survivable. "How long have you known?"

"Since I was fourteen."

"Your whole life!"

"Yes."

"How many times have you had sex with men?"

Three, I told her. During college.

"Maybe you were just experimenting," she said bitterly. "Three times in college could fall into the realm of experimentation."

"It wasn't an experiment. I felt that if I didn't touch a man, I would die."

"Well, that's just great. All this time I thought you were scared of falling in love with me and really you were just desperate to be fucking men. So what was it like? Tell me."

"No."

"The first time. Where was it? How old were you?"

"I'm not going to do that."

"Tell me!"

For hours we raged at each other, and at last I told her what she asked: the dark bar in the French Quarter, the drunken kiss, my body knotted with the body of another man. With these images from the depths of my memory rose something else, a great animal grief clawing its way out of my chest; I could no longer keep it at bay. During the course of that night, as we cried and exhausted ourselves, I felt sure I was destroying all the trust and love she had ever felt for me, yet near dawn we reached a momentary truce; we knew it might be the only respite from the ragged months ahead. For a while we lay solicitous and comforting, our arms around each other.

"I couldn't tell you the truth," I said then. "I knew we would have to leave each other. I didn't want to lie to you, but I made myself not see it. It was like holding my hand right in front of my face and not seeing a hand."

"I think I knew also, all along," Rose said. "I knew, but I didn't know. But the truth is better. And I'm better off too, though it's going to take a long, long time to feel it. Now we're both free."

42

I stuffed my fraying winter coat into the trash and boarded a train for the West Coast. The hills of California were not so wondrous a sight at age twenty-eight as they'd appeared to me at eighteen, but their familiarity was welcome. I relied on familiar landmarks and known quantities, because in the months after I left Rose and returned to San Francisco, I fell to pieces. To admit my desire for men had unleashed a firestorm that engulfed not only my relationship with Rose but also the construction of my most fundamental, ancient understanding of myself. I would never have the future I'd nursed and held dear, of a family, a conventional home; and without that to guide me I no longer knew what I aimed for. I was forced to reimagine my very essence.

Doing so was an immensely solitary, internal experience. I was capable of daily activity—looking for a job, moving into an apartment, obeying traffic signals—but my mind was chaos, awkward and uncertain. I blurted my innermost secrets, and those of my friends, to strangers on different forms of public transportation. My fingernails were reduced to bleeding nubs. Violent emotion subsumed the desire for food and sleep, and late one night I found myself stomping through the streets of my neighborhood, waving my arms; a staccato hiss emitted from my mouth.

Fortunately, by then I had found work, and the job was too demanding of my time to allow for many episodes of psychosis. I found anchor in routine: the daily commute, a lunchtime swim, dinner with friends. On Thursday nights I went dancing at a club with my friend Kyra, and there I tried not to shy away from the friendly glances of other men; meeting their eyes sent through me a jolt, an electric, stunning shock. One night a swarthy fellow drunkenly kissed my cheek, and the contact—the warmth and softness of his lips—sent me into a swoon. I had returned to adolescence. On Sunday mornings, my one free day from work, I ran errands in the Castro, where men laughed together, communed, had coffee, their arms slung over one another's shoulders, their smiles a promise. Once, long ago, I had used errands as an opportunity to seek out men for my mother, and now I scouted for myself. I returned the smiles, met eyes, attempted to telegraph this information: I am one of you.

I felt raw, skeletal, unwieldy, and buoyant with terrific hope.

"I came out before AIDS. What a crazy time that was. Dancing all night long, taking all kinds of drugs, poppers that made you want to fuck like madmen, going to the baths, waking up in a different guy's bed every weekend. I've had a couple of lovers, but really most of my relationships were based on sex. I did a lot of wild things. I'm lucky to be alive, but I'm not sorry. Liberated desire was great."

The describer of this erotic carnival walked several paces ahead of me on a coastal cliffside trail high above the Pacific. His name was Octavio, a compact Cuban psychiatrist, whose looks—a serious mouth, round glasses, a goatee—bore a resemblance to those of a young Sigmund Freud. His hair was the color of rich coffee. I had met him through Kyra at the Thursday dance club, where for three months we waved hello, yelling a few pleasantries over the music, until at last I shouted a dinner invitation into his ear. That first dinner had led to another, and the second had led to this, a daylong hike along the corrugated coastline north of San Francisco.

"That's so different from me," I said. Such strange language to my ears: *lover, baths, coming out*; yet also familiar, as though I were hearing my native tongue after a lifetime of expatriation. "For me there was just Rose. Always. I met her when I was eighteen. She was my closest friend for five years, and then"—I tried out the word—"my lover for five more."

"But didn't you try to find sex with men? Didn't you *have* to?"

"A couple of times, and then I forced myself to forget."

"Once I tasted blood, I knew what I wanted. There was no going back." He too had lived with a lover for five years. He'd met Bob when he was twenty-two and had fallen deeply in love. Mixed with that love was the profound relief that he would not have to spent the rest of his life alone, as all the messages broadcast by society at large had taught him to believe he would. He and Bob had lived in Germany for three years, exchanged rings in Florence, but the relationship eventually faltered. Since then, Octavio said with a taint of bitterness, he had not been sure if he could ever love anyone again.

On a promontory overlooking the ocean we stopped for lunch. The December day had begun blustery and wet but had cleared over the course of our morning hike, warming enough for us to take off our jackets and feel the sun on our skin. Pulling the sandwiches from his backpack, Octavio dislodged a book, which I handed back to him: an anthology of American poets. "Is this in case you get bored?"

"There's a couple of poems I wanted to read to you."

"Oh." He pronounced the word as Texans did, and as I pronounced it: *poim.* I changed the subject. Did he know that this was the time of year for whale migrations?

Over lunch we reeled out more of our histories. His parents had immigrated to Texas from Cuba in a daring escape after the revolution; mine had come from Alabama with figurative banjoes on their knees. He'd grown up a devout Baptist and in college bitterly lost his faith; but my faith had been in my mother, and to finally understand her as human and imperfect, her life different from what I'd hoped it would be, was as catastrophic, I felt, as losing one's faith in God. His parents, Octavio admitted, still could not accept his homosexuality ten years after he'd come out to them, and I admitted that I felt myself to be my mother's worst nightmare—turned gay, she would believe, as the result of her divorces, and by the lack of a father. She'd blame herself. It would be impossible to tell her; the truth would break her heart and separate us forever.

"What kind of tree is that?" Octavio pointed to a stand of trees buffeted by the wind.

I was offended by this interruption of my heartfelt confession, but I followed the line of his arm. The trees shot up straight and tall, densely grouped, silvery leaves fluttering with the wind, drooping branches that touched one another so delicately as to seem like caresses, strips of ocher bark molting from the trunks. I knew that when we drew near them we'd inhale their powerful scent, one that was not found in Texas, that was bound up for me with my life in California. "Eucalyptus," I told him.

"No, it's not."

"Those trees there?" I said, offended a second time. "That's eucalyptus."

"No, it's not," he said flatly. "I've seen eucalyptus, and it doesn't look like that."

I thought: *what an asshole;* and I felt an inner despair. I did not want to be gay, I did not want to deal with the arrogance and combativeness of men. I'd watched my mother suffer from it all her life; men could never be trusted. I said, "Maybe what you saw wasn't eucalyptus. Those are eucalyptus."

He didn't contest me again but looked into my eyes with an unnerving directness, challenging but with a hint of playfulness. Then he placed his hand on my hiking boot and pushed up to his feet.

In the late afternoon we clambered down the cliff face to a beach littered with kelp and driftwood, and there conducted our own private investigations, Octavio of the shore, following the ebb of waves with the rapidly scissoring legs of a seabird, and I, surreptitiously, of him. How strange and coincidental, I thought, to have arrived here with this particular man. He was nothing like Rose, whom I knew so well; he was unfamiliar territory. Until a year ago my life had been rigidly planned and plotted, so deliberate as to have become a prison, and perhaps now it was opening up to chance, to surprise. I could no longer predict my future.

I perched on the rock where he'd tossed the backpack, and as Octavio continued to gambol back and forth with the tide, I drew out the book of poetry, its pages yellowed and soft. It fell open to the poem he'd marked, and I began to read carefully, as though it had been written for me as a gift.

Some Trees
by John Ashbery

These are amazing: each
Joining a neighbor, as though speech
Were a still performance.
Arranging by chance

To meet as far this morning
From the world as agreeing
With it, you and I
Are suddenly what the trees try

To tell us we are:
That their merely being there
Means something; that soon
We may touch, love, explain.

"Did you get bored?" Octavio stood close at my back.

"Oh, no." I jumped up, stuffing the book into the backpack. "I guess we better get going. Not much day left."

He smiled and tousled my hair. I set off at a clip back up the cliff and then along the trail until he called to me to slow down. Shouldn't we take a break, he suggested, to watch the sunset? With ineluctable steps we climbed to the peak of a hill and sat upon a gravelly patch, Octavio to the side of me, out of my sight. The ocean lay far below, distant enough to have fallen as silent as we had, whitecaps statically etched on its slate surface. I focused intently on the sun's descent, hardened to any romantic implications it presented.

"Pretty as a picture postcard," Octavio drawled.

"I thought we might see whales today," I said. "They're out there, right off the coast, migrating south to the Sea of Cortez. That's where they give birth, because it's so rich and warm. Have you been there? I went there once in college, scuba diving with friends. The land is all desert and barrenness, and then, when you slip below the surface of the water, it's explosive, so full of *life*."

I could feel the beam of Octavio's eyes upon me as I spoke, and a crunch of gravel warned me of his motion. In peripheral vision I watched him close in, his arms encircling me like a spider's. His touch would kill me, I knew, smite me with the very want that was forever forged to my being. But instead, as he held me against him and asked softly if it was alright, I saw a door creak open; a lamp was lit, an invitation offered. I went in.

43

Two years later. I sat in a circle with Octavio beside me, seven men and one woman who had gathered at this apartment to remember a friend recently dead of AIDS. The woman, Linda, read passages aloud from a book about the death of loved ones, New Age words that did not differ substantially from the words Christians offered one another, but I didn't understand how these husks could serve as the vessels of comfort. And so I held my uneasy place in this circle, made up mostly of strangers. I hadn't known the dead man, an ex-lover of Octavio's ex-lover, the kind of tenuous link, I was learning, that formed the web of gay community.

What I did know about the dead man made me angry; he'd broken from a devoted lover of many years and moved to San Francisco, where he'd fallen into a self-destructive spiral: heavy amphetamine use, a physically abusive relationship, and almost immediate infection with HIV. Perhaps my anger had its roots in the coincidence of names: I could not help but compare this John, who had tried so hard to annihilate himself, with my brother, who had tried so hard to live.

Linda finished reading and closed the book. Of course we all had ambivalent feelings about some of the choices John had made, she said, and maybe we'd never understand, but this memorial might allow us each to revisit him. To make that possible, Linda was now going to employ a technique used in neurolinguistic programming, a meditation that would bring our ambivalent feelings to the surface, where we could really grapple and make peace with them. *Ah, California,* I thought, and as though Octavio had sensed this mental eye rolling, he touched my hand. What had he taught me if not to be more open to the world? I had not come here to air my skepticism, but to respect these others as they honored the passing of a life.

Then Linda spoke my name. "You didn't know John well," she said, "but in these times I'd find it hard to believe that there hasn't been someone you've lost."

I said that there was.

She asked us to close our eyes. "I'd like you to find that part of yourself that is the keeper of your beliefs. It might be Christian, or secular, or mystical, or whatever, but try to go to that place now. When you get there, let John come to you."

Linda's voice was soft and even, full of feeling; I knew that I resisted words of comfort because I did not believe comfort possible. But I longed to believe it. Eyes closed, I tried to go to that place where I nurtured secret hopes. Alone, I descended slowly, as if through water, and as I sank deeper my skepticism came loose and fell from me like a mask.

"Let your memory speak," Linda said. "It doesn't have to be anything dramatic, just a time you spent with John. Don't force it. Just let him rest in your mind."

For years I'd been unable to picture John as he'd looked when healthy; the image of my brother in his hospital bed had burned over all other memories. But now, distilled from childhood, a scene: in winter, John and I built a fire in the woods beside our house, pretending to be mountain men. In the leisure of this memory I examined him closely. I saw the white blond crown of his head as he worked to light the kindling, his mouth drawn tight in a serious line. He wore a brown corduroy coat with sheepskin lining. Our bedrolls hugged the fire in a V, and when we lay down we spoke in excited whispers, our heads only inches apart.

"Let another memory come," Linda said.

John and I were at the bay house in summer, casting our fishing lines from the pier while a furious storm blew in. We stood into the wind at hilarious, impossible angles. Waterspouts formed over the bay. Sprinting for shelter, we were caught by torrential rain, and so we kept running past the house, our clothes sodden and heavy, and leapt into the pool: a plunge into water as warmly inviting as a bath, an explosion of bubbles, our laughter underwater loud enough for the other to hear.

"And another," Linda said.

At his wedding, John stood in the center of us, his sprawling family, for the photographer. Then, shockingly, I remembered him in Oklahoma, nearly bald from the chemotherapy, lifting his daughter into the air with delight.

"Now," Linda said, "however you can, speak to him."

What I saw then was not memory. John and I stood on the opposite sides of a river. But the river was not wide; we were nearly close enough to touch. He appeared young and vital, and I felt my own physicality as well; I inhabited my body. I seemed to exist in two places at once, here with John, and in this apartment with the others, with Octavio and with the guiding presence of Linda's voice. Behind my brother stretched a plain, and beyond that a high sierran ridge. The look he gave me was amused and loving, with an impatience I remembered from childhood, when in spite of all obstacles I had tracked him down to a private enclave, so desirous was I of his company.

I heard Linda ask me to tell John I loved him, that I forgave him, and I did so. All the while he looked at me playfully, as though he were the one bestowing forgiveness. I told him that I was a different person now, since he'd died.

"Now," Linda said. "Tell him good-bye."

I erected a hurricane resistance. I would never say good-bye, now that I'd found him again.

"Tell him good-bye, and let him go." Her voice calling me back to the land of the living.

John began to back away from the riverbank. I won't let you go, I shouted, but he was already too far to hear.

"Let him go."

John waved to me, and then he turned, walking off into the mountain plain. Octavio's hand clasped mine. I felt in that contact the spark of truce, surprising, unexpected, a coexistence of peace and loss. I watched John recede until he was just a speck.

44

"Mom, there's something I have to tell you, something really difficult." On a spring day, she and I walked along the lake in Austin, wildflowers lining our path, Indian paintbrush and blue bonnets. "I'm in love with a man. We're moving in together. I know this is hard for you to understand, but for the first time in my life I'm really happy."

Tears shone in her eyes. She kissed my forehead. "Honey, of course I've lived with prejudices. We all do. But they're nothing compared to my happiness for you."

Scenes danced in my head for months, some of them sugarcoated with absurd hope, others the bitter opposite. I finally went to Austin for a week in summer, bent on my task; I had to tell my mother who I was, as she, over my lifetime, had shown me who she was. Each night I steeled myself to make my announcement, and each night I chickened out. Near the end of my visit, my mother and I found ourselves beside the lake at sunset as an immense colony of bats emerged from their roost beneath the Congress Avenue bridge, thousands of them, like smoke billowing into the night. It was the first time all week we'd been alone, and we stood nearly touching, silently scanning the sky. On the drive home I privately rehearsed my speech, sick with nervousness, postponing and postponing until I pulled up to the house and stomped on the brake, continuing to press the pedal with such force my leg began to tremble. At last I spoke.

"There's something I have to tell you." My voice quaked so terribly I wanted to laugh and let her in on the joke. "Something really difficult."

Then my mouth closed. I couldn't say another word. My mother lay her hand on my arm, and I felt sure she knew. "What is it, honey?"

"I tried so hard to be happy with Rose. I really did. But I couldn't, and the reason was staring me in the face the whole time. I finally had to deal with the fact that I was gay."

The word surprised me: *gay*—until this moment I'd never used it to describe myself—and I was almost distracted enough not to hear the noise my mother made, a sharp exhalation as though from a kick to her stomach. The car was so dark I could see only the shape of her head turned toward the window away from me. I waited, but she said nothing, so I began to tell her what I had all my life kept secret, the early knowledge of my attraction to men, the immediate suppression of that knowledge, and the painful decision to live truthfully with myself and now to be truthful with her. I spoke frankly, with an openness that frightened and exhilarated me. My mother sniffed quietly so that I wouldn't know she was crying. But as her silence continued, I grew bolder. How could she be surprised, I joked, she who had watched me grow and knew my eccentricities better than anyone? I told her of Octavio, that we were nearing three years together, that we'd both tested negative for HIV. My entire life I'd been living like the boy in the antiseptic bubble, I said, and now I could feel the air on my skin.

My mother's hand had lain warmly on my forearm throughout my monologue, but I felt as though I were walking along a wobbly plank over a void; if she were to withdraw her hand, if she rejected me, called me an abomination against God, I did not think I could survive that kind of loneliness. When I ran out of words we sat in silence for some time. The inside of the car was sweltering. Finally, without turning her head to face me, she responded. "I love you more than anything in the world," my mother whispered, "and I'm glad you're happy"—then came the words I knew I'd have to bear—"but I can't be happy for you right now."

In the following days we were clumsy and embarrassed, silently angry at each other, both too willing to feel guilt for what we saw as our separate failures, hers as a mother, mine as a man. She didn't really want to talk about it, not directly, and neither did I. We simply wanted assurance of one thing, and it was the same thing, that I was still her son.

This encouraged me to get out in the yard and dig some holes. At the side of my mother's house, I noticed that cinder blocks and rocks, planks with rusted nails sticking out of them, and other vegetable and mineral collections lay strewn about, just waiting for me to get my hands on them, and not twenty-four hours had passed before I'd imposed a semblance of order on that parcel of the world. I set to work on the unfinished garden in the backyard, digging deep with a shovel to overturn the earth, mixing in mulch and manure, creating a curved limestone border. Around the patio I spotted various relics from my mother's Mexico trips, which she had finally given up; the business never turned a profit. The Great White Hunter had gone by the wayside as well. On their African safari he shot an ostrich, because, he explained, he'd never killed one before, and that was more than she needed to serve him his walking papers.

As I worked, I caught my mother watching me through her office window, and though she was nearly obscured by the reflection on the glass of this bright July afternoon, there was no mistaking her expression. One day, I hope, she will be able to accept my life without sorrow and to understand that at last she can truly know me, but that is something I will never be able to give her, as much as I would like to; she will have to find it on her own. Of all the people I am bound to by love and history, my mother most shares with me the understanding that the expectations we build for our lives can become a kind of prison, a structure of such artful and inspired design we might never dream of escaping. She states that she will never marry again, and yet I know she still yearns to find companionship with a man, to rest the burdens of her life in a man's arms, and I still want to marry her off as fiercely as I did when I was a child. As for myself, I feel lucky that Rose and I have, over time, painstakingly been able to reforge our friendship, though it is not without an ache; the loss of that existence I might have shared with her in the house on an Oregon riverbank, raising our four children, will always seem to me one of my life's great misfortunes. I could choose to believe that I have been sculpted by the chiseling blows of loss, as could we all—who of us escapes heartbreak?—and perhaps I almost did just that, but I've come to know that there is a better way for me to live.

Eventually my mother joined me out in the garden, and we worked together until evening shadows lengthened over us. Her knowledgeable hands sought the roots of weeds as she talked. She was worried about Celeste, of course, who was still plagued by the bitter residue of my father's abandonment and, perhaps as a result, was having serious troubles in her marriage to a nine-fingered chef. And Scotty, what was to become of him? He wanted to learn an actor's craft but hardly seemed interested in learning how to support himself. Henry would never have that problem—he'd held a job since he was thirteen—but he was eaten alive by his own anxiety, had twice seen a doctor to check for an ulcer, and he was crushed by his father's recent refusal to help him financially with college, after years of promises.

At my prompting, my mother spoke about herself. She'd finally completed the rigorous training program to become a counselor at her church and had since begun helping others confront life's tragedies and flux. "Lord knows I've had enough experience for the job," she said. The previous summer she'd traveled to Guatemala City with members of the same church to build houses for families actually living on top of the city dump, where they picked through trash to find enough objects to sell, or even to eat, somehow managing to survive. They had nothing, she told me, not even shelter, and the children! To forget their hunger, many of them had become addicted to sniffing glue; they faced hopeless lives. The houses at least gave them a chance. The church had built a training center also, where the children might learn skills that could earn them jobs, that might allow them to leave the dump forever.

That night my mother showed me a videotape of her trip. I witnessed her arrival in the Guatemala City airport with the rest of the members of this mission, most of them in their twenties, swathed in the same style of loose, hippie-ish clothes my mother had worn when I was a boy. In the next scene she was at church, singing hymns in Spanish, and then I saw her at the dump, a limitless landscape of trash, in a sweatshirt and visor. Speaking to the camera, she held her arm over the shoulders of a tiny woman, hunchbacked and grizzled, whose mouth lay claim to no more than a couple of teeth.

"That's Doña Eduarda," my mother said excitedly. "She's *my* age. Can you believe it? Her house was made of plastic bags and pieces of tin she'd picked up in the dump, and she burned plastic for the fire she cooked with." On the television, a young man carried beams, dug holes in the ground, filled them with cement. I watched a structure emerge. "She didn't trust us at all," my mother continued. "Our plan at first was to build her a new roof, but one of her walls collapsed right as we started. She burst into tears. So we ended up building her a whole new house. I've already decided to go back this summer." Then, as though the idea had just this moment sprung entire into her mind, she said, "Why don't you come with me? We could take Spanish classes in Antigua."

"Maybe," I told her.

I turned back to the video, where my mother was at work with hammer and saw under the watchful, anxious eyes of Doña Eduarda. *Don't worry,* I could tell Doña Eduarda when we met, speaking to her in the Spanish my mother and I had learned together. *You will be safe here. My mother builds a strong house, a fine and lasting house. I should know. I've lived in it all my life.*